Karen Armstrong spent seven years as a Roman Catholic nun, an experience she recollected in her bestselling autobiography, *Through the Narrow Gate*. She is the author of the worldwide bestseller, *A History of God* (which has now appeared in more than thirty languages), the highly acclaimed *A History of Jerusalem*, *The Battle for God* and, most recently, *Buddha*. She is a teacher at the Leo Baeck College for the Study of Judaism and, in 1999, she received the Muslim Public Affairs Council Media Award.

By Karen Armstrong

Buddha

Islam: A Short History

The Battle for God

In the Beginning: A New Interpretation of Genesis

A History of Jerusalem: One City, Three Faiths

Through the Narrow Gate

A History of God: The 4,000-Year Quest of
Judaism, Christianity and Islam

Muhammad: A Biography of the Prophet

ISLAM

A Short History

Karen Armstrong

PHOENIX

A PHOENIX PAPERBACK

First published in Great Britain
by Weidenfeld & Nicolson in 2000
This paperback edition published in 2001
by Phoenix Press,
a division of The Orion Publishing Group Ltd,
Orion House, 5 Upper St Martin's Lane,
London WC2H 9EA

17 19 20 18 16

A CIP catalogue record for this book
is available from the British Library.

ISBN-13 978-1-8421-2583-0

Printed and bound in Great Britain by
Clays Ltd, St Ives plc

The Orion Publishing Group's policy is to use papers that
are natural, renewable and recyclable products and
made from wood grown in sustainable forests. The logging
and manufacturing processes are expected to conform to
the environmental regulations of the country of origin.

www.orionbooks.co.uk

Contents

5 ISLAM AGONISTES

Maps

Preface

The external history of a religious tradition often seems divorced from the *raison d'être* of faith. The spiritual quest is an interior journey; it is a psychic rather than a political drama. It is preoccupied with liturgy, doctrine, contemplative disciplines and an exploration of the heart, not with the clash of current events. Religions certainly have a life outside the soul. Their leaders have to contend with the state and affairs of the world, and often relish doing so. They fight with members of other faiths, who seem to challenge their claim to a monopoly of absolute truth; they also persecute their co-religionists for interpreting a tradition differently or for holding heterodox beliefs. Very often priests, rabbis, imams and shamans are just as consumed by worldly ambition as regular politicans. But all this is generally seen as an abuse of a sacred ideal. These power struggles are not what religion is really about, but an unworthy distraction from the life of the spirit, which is conducted far from the madding crowd, unseen, silent and unobtrusive. Indeed, in many faiths, monks and mystics lock themselves away from the world, since the clamour and strife of history is regarded as incompatible with a truly religious life.

In the Hindu tradition, history is dismissed as evanescent, unimportant and insubstantial. The philosophers of ancient Greece were concerned with the eternal laws underlying the flux of external events, which could be of no real interest to a serious thinker. In the gospels, Jesus often went out of his way to explain to his followers that his Kingdom was not of this world, but could only be found within the believer. The Kingdom would not arrive with a great political fanfare, but would develop as quietly and imperceptibly as a germinating mustard-seed. In the modern West, we have made a point of separating religion from politics; this secularization was originally seen by the *philosophes* of the Enlightenment as a means of liberating religion from the corruption of state affairs, and allowing it to become more truly itself.

But however spiritual their aspirations, religious people have to seek God or the sacred in this world. They often feel that they have a duty to bring their ideals to bear upon society. Even if they lock themselves away, they are inescapably men and women of their time and are affected by what goes on outside the monastery, although they do not fully realize this. Wars, plagues, famines, economic recession and the internal politics of their nation will intrude upon their cloistered existence and qualify their religious vision. Indeed, the tragedies of history often goad people into the spiritual quest, in order to find some ultimate meaning in what often seems to be a succession of random, arbitrary and dispiriting incidents. There is a symbiotic relationship between history and religion, therefore. It is, as the Buddha remarked, our perception that existence is awry that forces us to find an alternative which will prevent us from falling into despair.

Perhaps the central paradox of the religious life is that it seeks transcendence, a dimension of existence that goes beyond our mundane lives, but that human beings can only experience this transcendent reality in earthly, physical phenomena. People have sensed the divine in rocks, mountains, temple buildings, law codes, written texts, or in other men and women. We never experience transcendence directly: our ecstasy is always 'earthed', enshrined in something or someone here below. Religious people are trained to look beneath the unpromising surface to find the sacred within it. They have to use their creative imaginations. Jean-Paul Sartre defined the imagination as the ability to think of what is not present. Human beings are religious creatures because they are imaginative; they are so constituted that they are compelled to search for hidden meaning and to achieve an ecstasy that makes them feel fully alive. Each tradition encourages the faithful to focus their attention on an earthly symbol that is peculiarly its own, and to teach themselves to see the divine in it.

In Islam, Muslims have looked for God in history. Their sacred scripture, the Quran, gave them a historical mission. Their chief duty was to create a just community in which all members, even the most weak and vulnerable, were treated with absolute respect. The experience of building such a society and living in it would give them intimations of the divine, because they would be living in accordance with God's will. A Muslim had to redeem history, and that meant that state affairs were not a distraction from spirituality but the stuff of religion itself. The political wellbeing of the Muslim community was a matter of supreme importance. Like any religious ideal, it was almost impossibly difficult to implement in the flawed and tragic conditions of history, but after each failure Muslims had to get up and begin again.

Muslims developed their own rituals, mysticism, philosophy, doctrines, sacred texts, laws and shrines like everybody else. But all these religious pursuits sprang directly from the Muslims' frequently anguished contemplation of the political current affairs of Islamic society. If state institutions did not measure up to the Quranic ideal, if their political leaders were cruel or exploitative, or if their community was humiliated by apparently irreligious enemies, a Muslim could feel that his or her faith in life's ultimate purpose and value was in jeopardy. Every effort had to be expended to put Islamic history back on track, or the whole religious enterprise would fail, and life would be drained of meaning. Politics was, therefore, what Christians would call a sacrament: it was the arena in which Muslims experienced God and which enabled the divine to function effectively in the world. Consequently, the historical trials and tribulations of the Muslim community – political assassinations, civil wars, invasions, and the rise and fall of the ruling dynasties – were not divorced from the interior religious quest, but were of the essence of the Islamic vision. A Muslim would meditate upon the current events of their time and upon past history as a Christian would contemplate an icon, using the creative imagination to discover the hidden divine kernel. An account of the external history of the Muslim people cannot, therefore, be of mere secondary interest, since one of the chief characteristics of Islam has been its sacralization of history.

610 The Prophet Muhammad receives the first revelations of the Quran in Mecca and, two years later,
begins to preach.

616 Relations between the Meccan establishment and
Muhammad's converts deteriorate; there is persecution and Muhammad's position becomes
increasingly untenable in Mecca.

620 Arabs from the settlement of Yathrib (later called
Medina) make contact with Muhammad and invite
him to lead their community.

622 The Prophet together with some seventy Muslim
families make the *hijrah*, or migration, from Mecca
to Medina and the Meccan establishment vows
revenge. The *hijrah* marks the beginning of the
Muslim era.

624 Muslims inflict a dramatic defeat on Mecca at the
Battle of Badr.

625 Muslims suffer a severe defeat at the hands of
the Meccan army at the Battle of Uhud, outside
Medina.
The Jewish tribes of Qaynuqah and Nadir are
expelled from Medina for collaborating with Mecca.

627 Muslims soundly defeat the Meccan army at the
Battle of the Trench. This is followed by the massacre of the men of the Jewish tribe of Qurayzah,
which had supported the Meccans against the
Muslims.

628 Muhammad's daring peace initiative results in the
Treaty of Hudaybiyyah between Mecca and Medina.
He is now seen as the most powerful man in Arabia
and attracts many of the Arabian tribes into his
confederacy.

630 The Meccans violate the Treaty of Hudaybiyyah. Muhammad marches on Mecca with a large army of Muslims and their tribal allies. Mecca recognizes its defeat and voluntarily opens the gates to Muhammad, who takes the city without bloodshed and without forcing anybody to convert to Islam.

632 Death of the Prophet Muhammad.
Abu Bakr is elected his *khalifah* (representative).

632–4 The caliphate of Abu Bakr and the wars of *riddah* against tribes who secede from the confederacy. Abu Bakr manages to subdue the revolt and unite all the tribes of Arabia.

634–44 The caliphate of Umar ibn al-Khattab.
The Muslim armies invade Iraq, Syria and Egypt.

638 The Muslims conquer Jerusalem, which becomes the third holiest city in the Islamic world after Mecca and Medina.

641 The Muslims control Syria, Palestine and Egypt; they have defeated the Persian Empire and, when manpower is available, will occupy its territories.
The garrison towns of Kufah, Basrah and Fustat are built to house the Muslim troops, who live separately from the subject population.

644 Caliph Umar is assassinated by a Persian prisoner of war.
Uthman ibn Affan is elected the third caliph.

644–50 Muslims conquer Cyprus, Tripoli in North Africa and establish Muslim rule in Iran, Afghanistan and Sind.

656 Caliph Uthman is asassinated by malcontent Muslim soldiers, who acclaim Ali ibn Abi Talib as the new caliph, but not all accept Ali's rule.

656–60 The first *fitnah*. Civil war ensues.

656 The Battle of the Camel. Aisha, the Prophet's wife, Talhah and Zubayr lead a rebellion against Ali for not avenging Uthman's murder. They are defeated by Ali's partisans.

In Syria the opposition is led by Uthman's kinsman, Muawiyyah ibn Abi Sufyan.

657   An attempt is made to arbitrate between the two sides at Siffin; when the arbitration goes against Ali, Muawiyyah deposes him and is proclaimed caliph in Jerusalem.

The Kharajites secede from Ali's camp.

661   Ali is murdered by a Kharajite extremist.

Ali's supporters acclaim his son Hasan as the next caliph, but Hasan comes to an agreement with Muawiyyah and retires to Medina.

661–80   The caliphate of Muawiyyah I. He founds the Umayyad dynasty, and moves his capital from Medina to Damascus.

669   The death of Hasan ibn Ali in Medina.

680   Yazid I becomes the second Umayyad caliph on the death of his father Muawiyyah.

680–92   The second *fitnah*. Another civil war ensues.

680   The Muslims of Kufah, who call themselves the Shiah i-Ali (the Partisans of Ali) acclaim Husain, the second son of Ali ibn Abi Talib, as caliph. Husain sets out from Medina to Kufah with a tiny army and is killed on the plain of Kerbala by Yazid's troops.

Abdallah ibn al-Zubayr revolts against Yazid in Arabia.

683   Death of Yazid I.

Death of his infant son, Muawiyyah II.

Accession of Marwan I, the Umayyad claimant to the caliphate, who is supported by the Syrians.

684   Kharijite rebels against the Umayyads set up an independent state in central Arabia.

Kharajite uprisings in Iraq and Iran.

Shii uprising in Kufah.

685–705   Caliphate of Abd al-Malik, who manages to restore Umayyad rule.

691   Umayyad forces defeat the Kharijite and Shii rebels.

The Dome of the Rock is completed in Jerusalem.

692   Umayyad forces defeat and kill Ibn al-Zubayr.

As a result of the *fitnah* wars, a religious movement develops in Basrah, Medina and Kufah; various schools campaign for a more stringent application of the Quran in public and private life.

705–15 Caliphate of al-Walid.
Muslim armies continue the conquest of North Africa and establish a kingdom in Spain.

717–20 Caliphate of Umar II. The first caliph to encourage conversion to Islam. He tries to implement some of the ideals of the religious movement.

720–24 Caliphate of Yazid II, a dissolute ruler. There is widespread Shii and Kharijite discontent with Umayyad government.

724–43 Caliphate of Hisham I, a devout but more autocratic ruler, who also antagonizes the more pious Muslims.

728 Death of Hasan al-Basri, *hadith* scholar, religious reformer and ascetic.

732 The Battle of Poitiers. Charles Martel defeats a small raiding party of Spanish Muslims.
Abu Hanifah pioneers the study of *fiqh*.
Muhammad ibn Ishaq writes the first major biography of the Prophet Muhammad.

743–4 The Abbasid faction begin to muster support against the Umayyads in Iran, fighting under the banner of the Shiah.

743 Caliphate of Walid II.

744–9 Marwan II seizes the caliphate and tries to restore Umayyad supremacy against the insurgents. His Syrian forces suppress some of the Shii revolts, but:

749 The Abbasids conquer Kufah and overthrow the Umayyads.

750–54 Caliph Abu al-Abbas al-Saffah, the first Abbasid caliph, massacres all the members of the Umayyad family. A sign of an absolute monarchy that is new to Islam.

755–75 Caliphate of Abu Jafar al-Mansur. He murders prominent Shiis.

756 Spain secedes from the Abbasid caliphate, setting

up an independent kingdom under the leadership of one of the Umayyad refugees.

762 The foundation of Baghdad, which becomes the new Abbasid capital.

765 The death of Jafar as-Sadiq, the Sixth Imam of the Shiah, who urges his Shii disciples to withdraw on principle from politics.

769 Death of Abu Hanifah, the founder of the first of the great schools of Islamic law.

775–85 Caliphate of al-Mahdi. He encourages the development of *fiqh*, acknowledges the piety of the religious movement, which gradually learns to coexist with the absolutism of the Abbasid dynasty.

786–809 Caliphate of Harun al-Rashid. The zenith of Abbasid power. A great cultural renaissance in Baghdad and other cities of the empire. Besides patronizing scholarship, science and the arts, the caliph also encourages the study of *fiqh* and the anthologization of *ahadith* which will enable the formation of a coherent body of Islamic law (Shariah).

795 Death of Malik ibn Anas, founder of the Maliki school of jurisprudence.

801 Death of Rabiah, the first great woman mystic.

809–13 Civil war between al-Mamun and al-Amin, the two sons of Harun al-Rashid. Al-Mamun defeats his brother.

813–33 Caliphate of al-Mamun.

814–15 A Shii rebellion in Basrah.

A Kharijite revolt in Khurasan.

An intellectual, a patron of arts and learning, the caliph inclines towards the rationalistic theology of the Mutazilah, who had hitherto been out of favour. The caliph tries to reduce tension by wooing some of the rival religious groups.

817 Al-Mamun appoints al-Rida, the Eighth Shii Imam, as his successor.

818 Al-Rida dies, possibly murdered.

A state-sponsored inquisition (*mihnah*) tries to enforce Mutazilah views over those of the more popular *ahl al-hadith*, who are imprisoned for their doctrines.

833–42 Caliphate of al-Mutasim. The caliph creates his own personal corps of Turkish slave soldiers and moves his capital to Samarra.

842–7 Caliphate of al-Wathiq.

847–61 Caliphate of al-Mutawakkil.

848 Ali al-Hadi, the Tenth Shii Imam, is imprisoned in the Askari fortress in Samarra.

855 Death of Ahmad ibn Hanbal, a hero of the *ahl al-hadith*, and the founder of the Hanbali school of jurisprudence.

861–2 Caliphate of al-Muntasir.

862–6 Caliphate of al-Mustain.

866–9 Caliphate of al-Mutazz.

868 Death of the Tenth Shii Imam. His son Hasan al-Askari continues to live as a prisoner in Samarra.

869–70 Caliphate of al-Muhtadi.

870 Death of Yaqub ibn Ishaq al-Kindi, the first of the Muslim Faylasufs.

870–92 Caliphate of al-Mutamid.

874 Hasan al-Askari, the Eleventh Shii Imam, dies in prison in Samarra. His son Abu al-Qasim Muhammad is said to have gone into hiding to save his life. He is known as the Hidden Imam.

Death of Abu Yazid al-Bistami, one of the earliest of the 'drunken Sufi' mystics.

892–902 Caliphate of al-Mutadid.

902–8 Caliphate of al-Muktafi.

908–32 Caliphate of al-Muqtadir.

909 Shii Fatimids seize power in Ifriqiyyah, Tunisia.

910 Death of Junayd of Baghdad, the first of the 'sober Sufis'.

922 The execution for blasphemy of the 'drunken Sufi' Husain al-Mansur, known as al-Hallaj, the Wool-Carder.

923 Death in Baghdad of the historian Abu Jafar al-Tabari.

932–4 Caliphate of al-Qahir.

934–40 Caliphate of al-Radi.
934 The 'Occultation' of the Hidden Imam in a transcendent realm is announced.
935 Death of the philosopher Hasan al-Ashari.

From this point, the caliphs no longer wield temporal power but retain merely a symbolic authority. Real power now resides with the local rulers, who establish dynasties in various parts of the empire. Most of them acknowledge the suzerainty of the Abbasid caliphs. Many of these local rulers of the tenth century have Shii leanings.

874–999 **The Samanids**, a Sunni Iranian dynasty, rule in Khurasan, Rayy, Kirman, and Transoxania, with a capital at Bukhara. Samarkand is also an important cultural centre of a Persian literary renaissance. In the 990s the Samanids begin to lose power east of the Oxus to the Kharakhanid Turks, and in the west to the Ghaznavids.

The Spanish kingdom of al-Andalus
912–61 Rule of Caliph Abd al-Rahman III, an absolute ruler.
969–1027 Cordova a centre of learning.
1010 Central power weakens and petty emirates establish local rule.
1064 Death of Ibn Hazm, poet, vizier and theologian.
1085 Toledo falls to the Christian armies of the Reconquista.

929–1003 **The Hamdanids**, Arab tribesmen, rule Aleppo and Mosul. Court patronage of scholars, historians, poets and Faylasufs.
950 Death of Abu Nasr al-Farabi, Faylasuf and court musician at Aleppo.

c.930–1030 **The Buyids**. Twelver Shiis and mountain dwellers from Daylam in Iran, begin to seize power in western Iran during the 930s.
945 The Buyids seize power in Baghdad, south Iraq and Oman.

Baghdad begins to lose its prominence to Shiraz, which becomes a centre of learning.

983 Buyid unity begins to disintegrate. They eventually succumb to Mahmud of Ghaznah in Rayy (1030) and the Ghaznavids in the plateau areas of western Iran.

935–69 The Ikhshids, founded by the Turk Muhammad ibn Tugh, rule Egypt, Syria and the Hijaz.

969–1171 The Shii Fatimids (originally established in Tunisia in 909) rule North Africa, Egypt and parts of Syria, establishing a rival caliphate.

972 The Fatimids move their capital to Cairo, which becomes a centre of Shii learning, and build the *madrasah* of al-Azhar there.

976–1118 The Ghaznavids

999–1030 Mahmud of Ghaznah establishes a permanent Muslim power in north India, and seizes power from the Samanids in Iran. A brilliant court.

1037 Death in Hamadan of the great Faylasuf Ibn Sina (Avicenna in the West).

990–1118 The Seljuk Empire

990s The Seljuk Turkish family from Central Asia convert to Islam. In the early eleventh century they enter Transoxania and Khwarazm with their cavalry of nomadic troops.

1030s The Seljuks in Khurasan.

1040 They take western Iran from the Ghaznavids, and enter Azerbaijan.

1055 Sultan Togril-beg rules the Seljuk Empire from Baghdad as the lieutenant of the Abbasid caliphs.

1063–73 The rule of Sultan Arp Arslan.

1065–7 The Nizamiyyah *madrasah* built in Baghdad.

1073–92 Malikshah rules the empire, with Nizalmulmulk as vizier.

The Turkish troops enter Syria and Anatolia.

1071 Seljuk troops defeat the Byzantines at the Battle of Manzikurt, establish themselves in Anatolia, reaching the Aegean Sea (1080).

Seljuks war with the Fatimids and local rulers in Syria.

1094 Byzantine emperor Alexius Comnenus I asks Western Christendom for help against the Seljuk infiltration of his territory.

1095 Pope Urban II preaches the First Crusade.

1099 The Crusaders conquer Jerusalem.

The Crusaders establish four Crusader states in Palestine, Anatolia and Syria.

1090s The Ismailis begin their revolt against Seljuk and Sunni hegemony. Local Turkish dynasties start to arise in various parts of the empire.

1111 Death in Baghdad of the theologian and legist Abu Hamid al-Ghazzali.

1118 Seljuk domains break up into independent principalities.

1118–1258 Small dynasties now function independently, acknowledging the suzerainty of the Abbasid caliphate, but in practice bowing only to the superior power of a neighbouring dynasty. Notable examples are:

1127–73 The Zanghid dynasty, founded by a Seljuk commander, begins to unite Syria in a riposte against the Crusaders.

1130–1269 The Almohads, a Sunni dynasty, attempt to reform North Africa and Spain according to the principles of al-Ghazzali.

1150–1220 The Khwarazmshahs from north-west Transoxania defeat the remaining small Seljuk dynasties in Iran.

1171–1250 The Ayyubid dynasty, founded by the Kurdish general Saladin, continues the Zanghid campaign against the Crusaders, defeats the Fatimid caliphate in Egypt, and converts it to Sunni Islam.

1180–1225 Al-Nasir, Abbasid caliph in Baghdad, attempts to use the Islamic *futuwwah* guilds as a basis for more effective rule.

1187 Saladin defeats the Crusaders at the battle of Hattin and restores Jerusalem to Islam.

1191 The Sufi mystic and philosopher Yahya Suhrawardi dies, possibly executed by the Ayyubids for heresy, in Aleppo.

1193 The Iranian Ghurid dynasty takes Delhi and establishes rule in India.

1198 Death in Cordova of the Faylasuf Ibn Rushd (known in the West as Averroes).

1199–1220 Ala al-Din Mahmoud, Khwarazmshah, determines to create a great Iranian monarchy.

1205–87 A Turkish slave dynasty defeats the Ghurids in India and establishes the Sultanate of Delhi, ruling the whole of the Ganges Valley. But soon these smaller dynasties have to face the Mongol threat.

1220–31 The first great Mongol raids, with immense destruction of cities.

1224–1391 The Golden Horde Mongols rule the lands north of the Caspian and Black Seas and convert to Islam.

1225 The Almohads abandon Spain, where Muslim power is eventually reduced to the small Kingdom of Granada.

1227 Death of the Mongol leader Genghis Khan.

1227–1358 The Chaghaytay Mongol Khans rule Transoxania and convert to Islam.

1228–1551 The Hafsid dynasty replace the Almohads in Tunisia.

1240 Death of the Sufi philosopher Muid ad-Din Ibn al-Arabi.

1250 The Mamluks, a slave corps, overthrow the Ayyubids, and establish a ruling dynasty in Egypt and Syria.

1256–1335 The Mongol Il-Khans rule Iraq and Iran and convert to Islam.

1258 They destroy Baghdad.

1260 The Mamluk sultan Baybars defeats the Mongol Il-Khans at the Battle of Ain Jalut, and goes on to destroy many of the remaining strongholds on the Syrian coast.

1273 Death of Jalal al-Din Rumi in Anatolia, founder of the Whirling Dervishes.

1288 Uthman, a *ghazi*, on the Byzantine frontier, founds the Ottoman dynasty in Anatolia.

1326–59 Orkhan, Uthman's son, establishes an independent Ottoman state, with its capital at Bursa, and dominates the declining Byzantine Empire.

1328 Death of the reformer Ahmad ibn Taymiyyah in Damascus.

1334–53 Yusuf, king of Granada, builds the Alhambra, which is completed by his son.

1369–1405 Timur Lane revives Chaghaytay Mongol power in Samarkand, conquers much of the Middle East and Anatolia, and sacks Delhi. But his empire disintegrates after his death.

1389 The Ottomans subdue the Balkans by defeating the Serbians at Kossovo Field. They go on to extend their power in Anatolia, but are overthrown by Timur Lane in 1402.

1403–21 After the death of Timur, Mehmed I revives the Ottoman state.

1406 Death of the Faylasuf and historian Ibn Khaldun.

1421–51 Murad I asserts Ottoman power against Hungary and the West.

1453 Memed II 'the Conqueror' conquers Constantinople, henceforth known as Istanbul, and makes it the capital of the Ottoman Empire.

1492 The Muslim Kingdom of Granada is conquered by the Catholic monarchs Ferdinand and Isabella.

1502–24 Ismail, head of the Safavid Sufi Order, conquers Iran, where he establishes the Safavid Empire. Twelver Shiism is now the official religion of Iran and Ismail's brutal attempts to suppress Sunni Islam in his domains inspire a persecution of Shiis in the Ottoman Empire.

1510 Ismail pushes the Sunni Uzbeks out of Khurasan and establishes Shii rule there.

1513 Portuguese traders reach south China.

1514 Sultan Selim I defeats Shah Ismail's Safavid army at the Battle of Chaldiran, halting the Safavid westward advance into Ottoman territory.

1517 The Ottomans conquer Egypt and Syria from the Mamluks.

1520–66 Suleiman, known in the West as the Magnificent, expands the Ottoman Empire and develops its distinctive institutions.

1522 The Ottomans take Rhodes.

1524–76 Tahmasp I, the second Safavid shah of Iran, strengthens Shii dominance there. His court becomes a centre of art, especially known for its painting.

1526 Babur establishes the Moghul Empire in India.

1529 The Ottomans besiege Vienna.

1542 The Portuguese establish the first European commercial empire.

1543 The Ottomans subjugate Hungary.

1552–6 The Russians conquer the old Mongol khanates of Kazan and Astrakhan on the River Volga.

1560–1605 Akbar is the emperor of Moghul India, which reaches the zenith of its power. Akbar fosters Hindu–Muslim cooperation, and conquers territory in south India. He presides over a cultural renaissance.

The Ottomans and Portuguese conduct a naval war in the Indian Ocean.

1570 The Ottomans take Cyprus.

1578 Death of the Ottoman court architect Sinan Pasha.

1580s Portuguese weakened in India.

1588–1629 Shah Abbas I rules the Safavid Empire in Iran, building a magnificent court in Isfahan. Drives the Ottomans out of Azerbaijan and Iraq.

1590s The Dutch begin to trade in India.

1601 The Dutch begin to seize Portuguese holdings.

1602 Death of the Sufi historian Abdulfazl Allami.

1625 Death of the reformer, Ahmad Sirhindi.

1627–58 Shah Jihan rules the Moghul Empire, which reaches

the height of its refinement. Builds the Taj Mahal.

1631 Death of the Shii philosopher Mir Dimad in Isfahan.

1640 Death of the Iranian philosopher and mystic Mulla Sadra.

1656 Ottoman viziers halt the decline of the Ottoman Empire.

1658–1707 Aurengzebe, the last of the major Moghul emperors, tries to Islamize all India, but inspires lasting Hindu and Sikh hostility.

1669 Ottomans take Crete from Venice.

1681 The Ottomans cede Kiev to Russia.

1683 The Ottomans fail in their second siege of Vienna, but they recover Iraq from the Safavids.

1699 Treaty of Carlowicz cedes Ottoman Hungary to Austria, the first major Ottoman reversal.

1700 Death of Muhammad Baqir Majlisi, the influential Shii *alim* of Iran.

1707–12 The Moghul Empire loses its southern and eastern provinces.

1715 Rise of the Austrian and Prussian kingdoms.

1718–30 Sultan Ahmad III attempts the first Westernizing reform in the Ottoman Empire, but the reforms end with the revolt of the Janissaries.

1722 Afghan rebels attack Isfahan and massacre the nobility.

1726 Nadir Shah temporarily restores the military power of the Iranian Shii Empire.

1739 Nadir Shah sacks Delhi and puts an end to effective Moghul rule in India. The Hindus, Sikhs and Afghans compete for power.
Nadir Shah tries to return Iran to Sunni Islam. As a result, the leading Iranian *mujtahids* leave Iran and take refuge in Ottoman Iraq, where they establish a power base independent of the shahs.

1748 Nadir Shah is assassinated. A period of anarchy ensues, during which the Iranians who adhere to the Usuli position achieve predominance, thus providing the people with a source of legality and order.

1762 Death of Shah Vali-ullah, the Sufi reformer, in India.

1763 The British expand their control over the dismembered Indian states.

1774 Ottomans totally defeated by the Russians. They lose the Crimea and the tsar becomes the 'protector' of Orthodox Christians in Ottoman lands.

1779 Aqa Muhammad Khan begins to found the Qajar dynasty in Iran, which by the end of the century is able to restore strong government.

1789 The French Revolution.

1789–1807 Selim III lays the groundwork for new Westernizing reforms in the Ottoman Empire, and establishes the first formal Ottoman embassies in European capitals.

1792 Death of the militant Arabian reformer Muhammad ibn Abd al-Wahhab.

1793 The first Protestant missionaries arrive in India.

1797–1818 Fath Ali Shah rules Iran. Rise of British and Russian influence there.

1798–1801 Napoleon occupies Egypt.

1803–13 The Wahhabis occupy the Arabian Hijaz, wresting it from Ottoman control.

1805–48 Muhammad Ali attempts to modernize Egypt.

1808–39 Sultan Mahmud II introduces the modernizing 'Tanzimat' reforms in the Ottoman Empire.

1814 Treaty of Gulistan: Caucasian territory is ceded to Russia.

1815 Serbian revolt against Ottoman control.

1821 Greek war of independence against the Ottomans.

1830 France occupies Algeria.

1831 Muhammad Ali occupies Ottoman Syria and penetrates deeply into Anatolia, creating within the Ottoman Empire a virtually independent *imperium in imperio*. The European powers intervene to save the Ottoman Empire and force Muhammad Ali to withdraw from Syria (1841).

1836 Death of the Neo-Sufi reformer Ahmad ibn Idris.

1839 The British occupy Aden.

1839–61 Sultan Abdulhamid inaugurates more modernizing reforms to halt the decline of the Ottoman Empire.

1843–9   The British occupy the Indus Basin.

1854–6   The Crimean War, which arises from European rivalry over the protection of Christian minorities in the Ottoman Empire.
Said Pasha, governor of Egypt, grants the Suez Canal concession to the French. Egypt contracts its first foreign loans.

1857–8   Indian Mutiny against British rule. The British formally depose the last Moghul emperor. Sir Sayyid Ahmad Khan argues for the reform of Islam on Western lines and the adoption of British culture.

1860–61   After a massacre of Christians by Druze rebels in Lebanon, the French demand that it become an autonomous province with a French governor.

1861–76   Sultan Abdulaziz continues the reform of the Ottoman Empire, but contracts huge foreign loans which result in the bankruptcy of the empire and the control of Ottoman finances by European governments.

1863–79   Ismail Pasha, governor of Egypt, undertakes extensive modernization, but contracts foreign loans, which result in bankruptcy, the sale of the Suez Canal to the British (1875), and the establishment of European control of Egyptian finances.

1871–9   Al-Afghani, the Iranian reformer, resides in Egypt and founds a circle of Egyptian reformers, including Muhammad Abdu. Their aim is to halt the cultural hegemony of Europe by a revitalization and modernization of Islam.

1872   Intensification of British–Russian rivalry in Iran.

1876   The Ottoman sultan Abdulaziz is deposed by a palace coup. Abdulhamid II is persuaded to promulgate the first Ottoman constitution, which, however, the sultan later suspends. Major Ottoman reforms in education, transportation and communications.

1879   Ismail Pasha is deposed.

1881   France occupies Tunisia.

1881–2   A mutiny of native Egyptian officers join forces with

Constitutionalists and reformers, who manage to impose their government on Khedive Tewfiq. But a popular uprising leads to the British military occupation of Egypt with Lord Cromer as governor (1882–1907)

Secret societies campaign for Syrian independence.

1889 Britain occupies the Sudan.

1892 The Tobacco Crisis in Iran. A *Fatwah* by a leading *mujtahid* forces the shah to rescind the tobacco concession he had given to the British.

1894 Between 10,000 and 20,000 Armenian revolutionaries against Ottoman rule are brutally massacred.

1896 Nasiruddin shah of Iran assassinated by one of al-Afghani's disciples.

1897 The first Zionist conference is held in Basel. Its ultimate aim is to create a Jewish state in the Ottoman province of Palestine.

Death of al-Afghani.

1901 Oil is discovered in Iran and the concession given to the British.

1903–11 Fears that the British intend to divide Hindus and Muslims in India, following the British partition of Bengal, leads to communalist anxiety and the formation of the Muslim League (1906).

1905 Death of the Egyptian reformer Muhammad Abdu.

1906 Constitutional Revolution in Iran forces the shah to proclaim a constitution and establish a Majlis, but an Anglo–Russian agreement (1907) and a Russian-supported counter-coup by the shah revokes the constitution.

1908 The Young Turk revolution forces the sultan to restore the constitution.

1914–18 The First World War.

Egypt is declared a protectorate by Britain; Iran is occupied by British and Russian troops.

1916–21 The Arab revolt against the Ottoman Empire in alliance with the British.

1917 The Balfour Declaration formally gives British

support to the creation of a Jewish homeland in Palestine.

1919–21 The Turkish War of independence. Atatürk is able to keep the European powers at bay and set up an independent Turkish state. He adopts radical secularizing and modernizing policies (1924–8).

1920 The publication of the Sykes-Picot agreement: in the wake of the Ottoman defeat in the First World War, its provinces are divided between the British and the French, who establish mandates and protectorates, even though the Arabs had been promised independence after the war.

1920–22 Gandhi mobilizes the Indian masses in two civil disobedience campaigns against British rule.

1921 Reza Khan leads a successful *coup d'état* in Iran and founds the Pahlavi dynasty. He introduces a brutal modernizing and secularizing policy in Iran.

1922 Egypt granted formal independence, but Britain retains control of defence, foreign policy and the Sudan. Between 1923 and 1930, the popular Wafd Party win three large electoral victories, but each time it is forced to resign by either the British or the king.

1932 Kingdom of Saudi Arabia founded.

1935 Death of the Muslim reformer and journalist Rashid Rida, founder of the Salafiyyah movement in Egypt.

1938 Death of the Indian poet and philosopher Muhammad Iqbal.

1939–45 The Second World War. The British depose Reza Shah, who is succeeded by his son, Muhammad Reza (1944).

1940s The Muslim Brotherhood become the most powerful political force in Egypt.

1945 Turkey joins the United Nations and becomes a multiparty state (1947). Formation of the Arab League.

1946 Communal rioting in India, following the Muslim League's campaign for a separate state.

1947 The creation of Pakistan from areas with a large

Muslim majority. The partition of India leads to massacres and killings of both Muslims and Hindus.

1948   The end of the British Mandate in Palestine and the creation of the Jewish state of Israel, as a result of a United Nations declaration. Israeli forces submit a devastating defeat on the five Arab armies who invade the new Jewish state. Some 750,000 Palestinians leave the country during the hostilities and are not permitted to return to their homes afterwards.

1951–3 Muhammad Musaddiq and the National Front party nationalise Iranian oil. After anti-royalist demonstrations, the shah flees Iran but is returned to power in a *coup* organized by the CIA and British intelligence and new agreements are made with European oil companies.

1952   In Egypt, the revolution of the Free Officers led by Jamal Abd al-Nasser deposes King Faruk. Al-Nasser suppresses the Muslim Brotherhood and imprisons thousands of Brothers in concentration camps.

1954   The secularist National Liberation Front (FLN) lead a revolution against French colonial rule in Algeria.

1956   The first constitution of Pakistan is ratified.
        Jamal Abd al-Nasser nationalizes the Suez Canal.

1957   Shah Muhammad Reza Pahlavi of Iran founds the secret police force SAVAK with the held of the American CIA and the Israeli MOSSAD.

1958–69 The secularist government of General Muhammad Ayub Khan in Pakistan.

1961   Muhammad Reza Phalavi, Shah of Iran, announces the White Revolution of modernization, which further marginalizes religion and exacerbates the divisions within Iranian society.

1963   The NLF establish a socialist government in Algeria. Ayatollah Ruhollah Khomeini attacks the Pahlavi regime, inspires street demonstrations throughout Iran, is imprisoned and eventually exiled to Iraq.

1966 Al-Nasser orders the execution of the leading Egyptian fundamentalist ideologue Sayyid Qutb.

1967 The Six-Day War between Israel and its Arab neighbours. The Israeli victory and the humiliating Arab defeat lead to a religious revival throughout the Middle East, since the old secularist policies seem discredited.

1970 Death of al-Nasser; he is succeeded by Anwar al-Sadat, who courts the Egyptian Islamists to gain their support.

1971 Sheikh Ahmad Yasin founds Mujamah (Congress), a welfare organization, and campaigns against the secular nationalism of the PLO, seeking an Islamic identity for Palestine; Mujamah is supported by Israel.

1971–7 Prime Minister Ali Bhutto of Pakistan leads a leftist and secularist government, which makes concessions to the Islamists, but these measures are not sufficient.

1973 Egypt and Syria attack Israel on Yom Kippur, and make such an impressive showing on the battlefield that al-Sadat is in a position to make a daring peace initiative with Israel, signing the Camp David Accords in 1978.

1977–88 The devout Muslim Zia al-Haqq leads a successful *coup* in Pakistan, and creates a more overtly Islamic government, which still, however, separates religion from *realpolitik*.

1978–9 The Iranian Revolution. Ayatollah Khomeini becomes the Supreme Faqih of the Islamic Republic (1979–89).

1979 Death of the Pakistani fundamentalist ideologue Abu Ala Mawdudi.
Several hundred Sunni fundamentalists in Saudi Arabia occupy the Kabah in Mecca and proclaim their leader as Mahdi; the state suppresses the uprising.

1979–81 American hostages are held prisoner in the United States embassy in Tehran.

1981   President Anwar al-Sadat is murdered by Muslim extemists, who condemn his unjust and coercive treatment of the Egyptian people and his peace treaty with Israel.

1987   The *intifadah*, a popular Palestinian uprising in protest against the Israeli occupation of the West Bank and the Gaza Strip. HAMAS, an offshoot of Mujamah, now enters the fray against Israel as well as against the PLO.

1989   Ayatollah Khomeini issues a *fatwah* against the British author Salman Rushdie for his allegedly blasphemous portrayal of the Prophet Muhammad in his novel *The Satanic Verses*. A month later, the *fatwah* is condemned as un-Islamic by forty-eight out of the forty-nine member states of the Islamic conference.

After the death of Ayatollah Khomeini, Ayatollah Khameini becomes the Supreme Faqih of Iran and the pragmatic Hojjat ol-Islam Rafsanjani becomes President.

1990   The Islamic Salvation Front (FIS) score major victories in the Algerian local elections against the secularist FLN. They look set for victory in the 1992 national elections.

President Saddam Hussein, a secularist ruler, invades Kuwait; in response the United States and its Western and Middle Eastern allies launch Operation Desert Storm against Iraq (1991).

1992   The military stage a *coup* to prevent the FIS from coming to power in Algeria, and suppress the movement. As a result, the more radical members launch a horrific terror campaign.

Members of the Hindu BJP party dismantle the Mosque of Babur at Ayodhya.

1992–9 Serbian and Croatian nationalists systematically kill and force the Muslim inhabitants of Bosnia and Kosovo to leave their homes.

1993   Israel and the Palestinians sign the Oslo Accords.

1994   Following   the   assassination   of   twenty-nine

Muslims in the Hebron mosque by a Jewish extremist, HAMAS suicide bombers attack Jewish civilians in Israel.

President Yitzak Rabin is assassinated by a Jewish extremist for signing the Oslo accords.

The Taliban fundamentalists come to power in Afghanistan.

1997   The liberal cleric Hojjat ol-Islam Sayyid Khatemi is elected President of Iran in a landslide victory.

1998   President Khatemi dissociates his government from Khomeini's *fatwah* against Salman Rushdie.

2001   September 11th Nineteen Muslim extremists, apparently members of Osama Bin Laden's group of Al-Qaeda, hijack American passenger planes and drive them into the World Trade Center and the Pentagon.

October 7th   In retaliation, the United States initiates a military campaign against the Taliban and Al-Qaeda in Afghanistan.

I   BEGINNINGS

The Prophet (570–632)

During the holy month of Ramadan in 610 CE, an Arab businessman had an experience that changed the history of the world. Every year at this time, Muhammad ibn Abdallah used to retire to a cave on the summit of Mount Hira, just outside Mecca in the Arabian Hijaz, where he prayed, fasted and gave alms to the poor. He had long been worried by what he perceived to be a crisis in Arab society. In recent decades his tribe, the Quraysh, had become rich by trading in the surrounding countries. Mecca had become a thriving mercantile city, but in the aggressive stampede for wealth some of the old tribal values had been lost. Instead of looking after the weaker members of the tribe, as the nomadic code prescribed, the Quraysh were now intent on making money at the expense of some of the tribe's poorer family groupings, or clans. There was also spiritual restlessness in Mecca and throughout the peninsula. Arabs knew that Judaism and Christianity, which were practised in the Byzantine and Persian empires, were more sophisticated than their own pagan traditions. Some had come to believe that the High God of their pantheon, Al-Lah (whose name simply meant 'God') was the deity worshipped by the Jews and the Christians, but he had sent the Arabs no prophet and no scripture in their own language. Indeed, the Jews and Christians whom they met often taunted the Arabs for being left out of the divine plan. Throughout Arabia one tribe fought another, in a murderous cycle of vendetta and counter-vendetta. It seemed to many of the more thoughtful people in Arabia that the Arabs were a lost race, exiled for ever from the civilized world and ignored by God himself. But that changed on the night of the 17 Ramadan, when Muhammad woke to find himself overpowered by a devastating presence, which squeezed him tightly until he heard the first words of a new Arabic scripture pouring from his lips.

For the first two years, Muhammad kept quiet about his experience. He had new revelations, but confided only in his wife Khadija and her cousin Waraqa ibn Nawfal, a Christian. Both were convinced that these revelations came from God, but it was only in 612 that Muhammad felt empowered to preach, and gradually gained converts: his young cousin, Ali ibn Abi Talib, his friend Abu Bakr, and the young merchant Uthman ibn Affan from the powerful Umayyad family. Many of the converts, including a significant number of women, were from the poorer clans; others were unhappy about the new inequity in Mecca, which they felt was alien to the Arab spirit. Muhammad's message was simple: He taught the Arabs no new doctrines about God: most of the Quraysh were already convinced that Allah had created the world and would judge humanity in the Last Days, as Jews and Christians believed. Muhammad did not think that he was founding a new religion, but that he was merely bringing the old faith in the One God to the Arabs, who had never had a prophet before. It was wrong, he insisted, to build a private fortune, but good to share wealth and create a society where the weak and vulnerable were treated with respect. If the Quraysh did not mend their ways, their society would collapse (as had other unjust societies in the past) because they were violating the fundamental laws of existence.

This was the core teaching of the new scripture, called the *quran* (recitation), because believers, most of whom, including Muhammad himself, were illiterate, imbibed its teachings by listening to public readings of its chapters (*surahs*). The Quran was revealed to Muhammad verse by verse, *surah* by *surah* during the next twenty-one years, often in response to a crisis or a question that had arisen in the little community of the faithful. The revelations were painful to Muhammad, who used to say: 'Never once did I receive a revelation, without thinking that my soul had been torn away from me.'[1] In the early days, the impact was so frightening that his whole body was convulsed; he would often sweat profusely, even on a cool day, experience a great heaviness, or hear strange sounds and voices. In purely secular terms, we could say that Muhammad had perceived the great problems confronting his people at a deeper level than most of his contemporaries, and that as he 'listened' to events, he had to delve deeply and painfully into his inner being to find a solution that was not only politically viable but spiritually illuminating. He was also creating a new literary form and a masterpiece of Arab prose and poetry. Many of the first believers were converted by the sheer beauty of the Quran, which resonated with their deepest aspirations, cutting through their intellectual preconceptions in the manner of great art, and inspiring them, at a level more profound than the cerebral, to alter their whole way of life. One of the most dramatic of these conversions was that of Umar ibn al-Khattab, who was devoted to the old paganism, passionately opposed to Muhammad's message, and was determined to wipe out the new sect. But he was also an expert in Arabian poetry, and the first time he heard the words of the Quran he was overcome by their extraordinary eloquence. As he said, the language broke through all his reservations about its message: 'When I heard the Quran my heart was softened and I wept, and Islam entered into me.'²

The new sect would eventually be called *islam* (surrender); a *muslim* was a man or a woman who had made this submission of their entire being to Allah and his demand that human beings behave to one another with justice, equity and compassion. It was an attitude expressed in the prostrations of the ritual prayer (*salat*) which Muslims were required to make three times a day. (Later this prayer would be increased to five times daily.) The old tribal ethic had been egalitarian; Arabs did not approve of the idea of monarchy, and it was abhorrent to them to grovel on the ground like a slave. But the prostrations were designed to counter the hard arrogance and self-sufficiency that was growing apace in Mecca. The postures of their bodies would re-educate the Muslims, teaching them to lay aside their pride and selfishness, and recall that before God they were nothing. In order to comply with the stern teaching of the Quran, Muslims were also required to give a regular proportion of their income to the poor in alms (*zakat*). They would also fast during Ramadan to remind themselves of the privations of the poor, who could not eat or drink whenever they chose.

Social justice was, therefore, the crucial virtue of Islam. Muslims were commanded as their first duty to build a community (*ummah*) characterized by practical compassion, in which there was a fair distribution of wealth. This was far more important than any doctrinal teaching about God. In fact the Quran has a negative view of theological speculation, which it calls *zannah*, self-indulgent whimsy about ineffable matters that nobody can ascertain one way or the other. It seemed pointless to argue about such abstruse dogmas; far more crucial was the effort (*jihad*) to live in the way that God had intended for human beings. The political and social welfare of the *ummah* would have sacramental value for Muslims. If the *ummah* prospered, it was a sign that Muslims were living according to God's will, and the experience of living in a truly *islamic* community, which made this existential surrender to the divine, would give Muslims intimations of sacred transcendence. Consequently, they would be affected as profoundly by any misfortune or humiliation suffered by the *ummah*, as Christians by the spectacle of somebody blasphemously trampling on the Bible or ripping the Eucharistic host apart.

This social concern had always been an essential part of the visions of the great world religions, which had developed during what historians have called the Axial Age (*c.*700 BCE to 200 BCE), when civilization, as we know it, developed, together with the confessional faiths which have continued to nourish humanity: Taoism and Confucianism in China; Hinduism and Buddhism in the Indian subcontinent; monotheism in the Middle East; and rationalism in Europe. These faiths all reformed the old paganism, which was no longer adequate in the larger and more complex societies that evolved once people had created a mercantile economy capable of supporting this cultural effort. In the larger states, people acquired broader horizons, and the old local cults ceased to be appropriate; increasingly, the Axial Age faiths focused on a single deity or supreme symbol of transcendence. Some were concerned about the fundamental injustice of their society. All pre-modern civilizations were based economically upon a surplus of agricultural produce; they therefore depended upon the labour of peasants who could not enjoy their high culture, which was only for an elite. To counter this, the new faiths stressed the importance of compassion. Arabia had remained outside the civilized world. Its intractable climate meant that the Arabs lived on the brink of starvation; there seemed no way that they could acquire an agrarian surplus that would put them on a footing with Sassanid Persia or Byzantium. But when the Quraysh began to develop a market economy their perspective began to change. Many were still happy with the old paganism, but there was a growing tendency to worship only one God; and there was, as we have seen, a creeping unease about the inequity of the new civilization that was developing in Mecca. The Arabs were now ready for an Axial Age faith of their own.

But that did not mean a wholesale rejection of tradition. The Axial Age prophets and reformers all built on the old pagan rites of their region, and Muhammad would do the same. He did demand that they ignore the cult of such popular Arabian goddesses as Manat, al-Lat and al-Uzzah, however, and worship Allah alone. The pagan deities are said in the Quran to be like weak tribal chiefs, who were a liability for their people, because they could not give them adequate protection. The Quran did not put forward any philosophical arguments for monotheism; its approach was practical, and, as such, it appealed to the pragmatic Arabs. The old religion, the Quran claimed, was simply not working.[3] There was spiritual malaise, chronic and destructive warfare, and an injustice that violated the best Arab traditions and tribal codes. The way forward lay in a single God and a unified ummah, which was governed by justice and equity.

Radical as this sounded, the Quran insisted that its message was simply a 'reminder' of truths that everybody knew.[4] This was the primordial faith that had been preached to the whole of humanity by the prophets of the past. God had not left human beings in ignorance about the way they should live: he had sent messengers to every people on the face of the earth. Islamic tradition would later assert that there had been 124,000 such prophets, a symbolic number suggesting infinity. All had brought their people a divinely inspired scripture; they might express the truths of God's religion differently, but essentially the message was always the same. Now at last God had sent the Quraysh a prophet and a scripture. Constantly the Quran points out that Muhammad had not come to cancel the older religions, to contradict their prophets or to start a new faith. His message is the same as that of Abraham, Moses, David, Solomon, or Jesus.[5] The Quran mentions only those prophets who were known to the

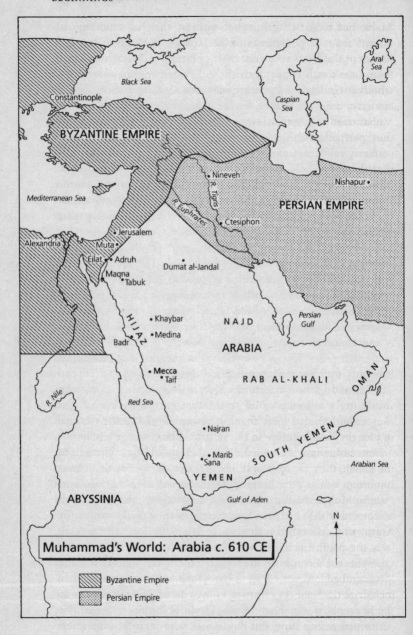

Muhammad's World: Arabia c. 610 CE

Byzantine Empire

Persian Empire

Arabs, but today Muslim scholars argue that had Muhammad known about the Buddhists or the Hindus, the Australian Aborigines or the Native Americans, the Quran would have endorsed their sages too, because all rightly guided religion that submitted wholly to God, refused to worship man-made deities, and preached justice and equality came from the same divine source. Hence Muhammad never asked Jews or Christians to accept Islam, unless they particularly wished to do so, because they had received perfectly valid revelations of their own. The Quran insists strongly that 'there shall be no coercion in matters of faith,'[6] and commands Muslims to respect the beliefs of Jews and Christians, whom the Quran calls *ahl al-kitab*, a phrase usually translated 'People of the Book' but which is more accurately rendered: 'people of an earlier revelation':

> Do not argue with the followers of earlier revelation otherwise than in a most kindly manner – unless it be such of them as are bent on evil-doing – and say: 'We believe in that which has been bestowed from on high upon us, as well as that which has been bestowed upon you; for our God and your God is one and the same, and it is unto Him that we [all] surrender ourselves.[7]

It is only our more modern culture that can afford to prize originality and jettison tradition wholesale. In pre-modern society, continuity was crucial. Muhammad did not envisage a violent rupture with the past or with other faith communities. He wanted to root the new scripture in the spiritual landscape of Arabia.

Hence Muslims continued to perform the customary rituals at the Kabah, the cube-shaped shrine in the heart of Mecca, the most important centre of worship in Arabia. It was extremely ancient even in Muhammad's time, and the original meaning of the cult associated with it had been forgotten, but it was still loved by the Arabs, who assembled each year for the *hajj* pilgrimage from all over the peninsula. They would circle the shrine seven times, following the direction of the sun around the earth; kiss the Black Stone embedded in the wall of the Kabah, which was probably a meteorite that had once hurtled to the ground, linking the site to the heavenly world. These rites (known as the *umrah*) could be performed at any time, but during the *hajj* pilgrims would also run between the steps of al-Safa beside the Kabah across the valley to al-Marwah, where they prayed. They then moved to the environs of Mecca: on the plain of Arafat, they stood all night in vigil; they rushed in a body to the hollow of Muzdalifah; hurled pebbles at a rock in Mina, shaved their heads, and on the Id al-Adha, the final day of the pilgrimage, they performed an animal sacrifice.

The ideal of community was central to the cult of the Kabah. All violence was forbidden in Mecca and the surrounding countryside at all times. This had been a key factor in the commercial success of the Quraysh, since it enabled Arabs to trade there without fearing the reprisals of vendetta warfare. During the *hajj* pilgrims were forbidden to carry arms, to argue, to kill game, or even to kill an insect or speak a cross word. All this was clearly congenial to Muhammad's ideal for the *ummah*, and he was himself devoted to the shrine, often made the *umrah*, and liked to recite the Quran beside the Kabah. Officially, the shrine was dedicated to Hubal, a Nabatean deity, and there were 360 idols arranged around the Kabah, probably representing the days of the year. But by Muhammad's time, it seems that the Kabah was venerated as the shrine of Allah, the High God, and it is a mark of the widespread conviction that Allah was the same as the deity worshipped by monotheists that those Arabs in the northern tribes on the borders of the Byzantine Empire who had converted to Christianity used to make the *hajj* alongside the pagans. Yet for all this, in the early days of his mission, Muhammad still made the Muslims perform the *salat* prayer facing Jerusalem, the holy city of the *ahl al-kitab*, turning their backs on the pagan associations of the Kabah. This expressed his longing to bring the Arabs into the monotheistic family.

Muhammad acquired a small following and eventually some seventy families had converted to Islam. At first, the most powerful men in Mecca ignored the Muslims, but by 616 they had become extremely angry with Muhammad who, they said, reviled the faith of their fathers, and was obviously a charlatan, who only pretended to be a prophet. They were particularly incensed by the Quran's description of the Last Judgement, which they dismissed as primitive and irrational. Arabs did not believe in the afterlife and should give no credence to such 'fairy tales'.[8] But they were especially concerned that in the Quran this Judaeo-Christian belief struck at the heart of their cut-throat capitalism. On the Last Day, Arabs were warned that the wealth and power of their tribe would not help them; each individual would be tried on his or her own merits: why had they not taken care of the poor? Why had they accumulated fortunes instead of sharing their money? Those Quraysh who were doing very well in the new Mecca were not likely to look kindly on this kind of talk, and the opposition grew, led by Abu al-Hakam (who is called Abu Jahl, 'Father of Lies', in the Quran), Abu Sufyan, an extremely intelligent man, who had once been a personal friend of Muhammad, and Suhayl ibn Amr, a devout pagan. They were all disturbed by the idea of abandoning the faith of their ancestors; all had relatives who had converted to Islam; and all feared that Muhammad was plotting to take over the leadership of Mecca. The Quran insisted that Muhammad had no political function but that he was simply a *nadhir*, a 'warner',[9] but how long would a man who claimed to receive instructions from Allah accept the rulings of more ordinary mortals like themselves?

Relations deteriorated sharply. Abu Jahl imposed a boycott on Muhammad's clan, forbidding the Quraysh to marry or trade with the Muslims. This meant that nobody could sell them any food. The ban lasted for two years, and the food shortages may well have been responsible for the death of Muhammad's beloved wife Khadija, and it certainly ruined some of the Muslims financially. Slaves who had converted to Islam were particularly badly treated, tied up, and left to burn in the blazing sun. Most seriously, in 619, after the ban had been lifted, Muhammad's uncle and protector (*wali*) Abu Talib died. Muhammad was an orphan; his parents had died in his infancy. Without a protector who would avenge his death, according to the harsh vendetta lore of Arabia, a man could be killed with impunity, and Muhammad had great difficulty finding a Meccan chieftain who would become his patron. The position of the *ummah* was becoming untenable in Mecca, and a new solution clearly had to be found.

Muhammad was, therefore, ready to listen to a delegation of chiefs from Yathrib, an agricultural settlement some 250 miles north of Mecca. A number of tribes had abandoned the nomadic way of life and settled there, but after centuries of warfare on the steppes found it impossible to live together peacefully. The whole settlement was caught up in one deadly feud after another. Some of these tribes had either converted to Judaism or were of Jewish descent, and so the people of Yathrib were accustomed to monotheistic ideas, were not in thrall to the old paganism, and were desperate to find a new solution that would enable their people to live together in a single community. The envoys from Yathrib, who approached Muhammad during the *hajj* in 620, converted to Islam and made a pledge with the Muslims: each vowed that they would not fight each other, and would defend each other from common enemies. Eventually, in 622, the Muslim families slipped away, one by one, and made the migration (*hijrah*) to Yathrib. Muhammad, whose new protector had recently died, was almost assassinated before he and Abu Bakr were able to escape.

The *hijrah* marks the start of the Muslim era, because it was at this point that Muhammad was able to implement the Quranic ideal fully and that Islam became a factor in history. It was a revolutionary step. The *hijrah* was no mere change of address. In pre-Islamic Arabia the tribe was a sacred value. To turn your back on your blood-group and join another was unheard of; it was essentially blasphemous, and the Quraysh could not condone this defection. They vowed to exterminate the *ummah* in Yathrib. Muhammad had become the head of a collection of tribal groups that were not bound together by blood but by a shared ideology, an astonishing innovation in Arabian society. Nobody was forced to convert to the religion of the Quran, but Muslims, pagans and Jews all belonged to one *ummah*, could not attack one another, and vowed to give each other protection. News of this extraordinary new 'supertribe' spread, and though at the outset nobody thought that it had a chance of survival, it proved to be an inspiration that would bring peace to Arabia before the death of the Prophet in 632, just ten years after the *hijrah*.

Yathrib would become known as al-Medinah (*the* City), because it became the pattern of the perfect Muslim society. When Muhammad arrived in Medina, one of his first actions was to build a simple mosque (*masjid*: literally place of prostration). It was a rough building, which expressed the austerity of the early Islamic ideal. Tree trunks supported the roof, a stone marked the *qiblah* (the direction of prayer), and the Prophet stood on a tree trunk to preach. All future mosques would, as far as possible, be built according to this model. There was also a courtyard, where Muslims met to discuss all the concerns of the *ummah* – social, political and military as well as religious. Muhammad and his wives lived in small huts around the edge of the courtyard. Unlike a Christian church, which is separated from mundane activities and devoted only to worship, no activity was excluded from the mosque. In the Quranic vision there is no dichotomy between the sacred and the profane, the religious and the political, sexuality and worship. The whole of life was potentially holy and had to be brought into the ambit of the divine. The aim was *tawhid* (making one), the integration of the whole of life in a unified community, which would give Muslims intimations of the Unity which is God.

Muhammad's numerous wives have occasioned a good deal of prurient interest in the West, but it would be a mistake to imagine the Prophet basking decadently in sensual delight, like some of the later Islamic rulers. In Mecca, Muhammad had remained monogamous, married only to Khadija, even though polygamy was common in Arabia. Khadija was a good deal older than he, but bore him at least six children, of whom only four daughters survived. In Medina, Muhammad became a great *sayyid* (chief), and was expected to have a large harem, but most of these marriages were politically motivated. As he formed his new supertribe, he was anxious to forge marriage ties with some of his closest companions, to bind them firmly together. His favourite new wife was Aisha, the daughter of Abu Bakr, and he also married Hafsah, the daughter of Umar ibn al-Khattab. He married two of his daughters to Uthman ibn Affan and Ali ibn Abi Talib. Many of his other wives were older women, who were without protectors or were related to the chiefs of those tribes who became the allies of the *ummah*. None of them bore the Prophet any children.[10] His wives were sometimes more of a hindrance than a pleasure. On one occasion, when they were squabbling about the division of booty after a raid, the Prophet threatened to divorce them all unless they lived more strictly in accordance with Islamic values.[11] But it is still true that Muhammad was one of those rare men who truly enjoy the company of women. Some of his male companions were astonished by his leniency towards his wives and the way they stood up to him and answered him back. Muhammad scrupulously helped with the chores, mended his own clothes, and sought out the companionship of his wives. He often liked to take one of them on expeditions, and would consult them and take their advice seriously. On one occasion his most intelligent wife, Umm Salamah, helped to prevent a mutiny.

The emancipation of women was a project dear to the Prophet's heart. The Quran gave women rights of inheritance and divorce centuries before Western women were accorded such status. The Quran prescribes some degree of segregation and veiling for the Prophet's wives, but there is nothing in the Quran that requires the veiling of *all* women or their seclusion in a separate part of the house. These customs were adopted some three or four generations after the Prophet's death. Muslims at that time were copying the Greek Christians of Byzantium, who had long veiled and segregated their women in this manner; they also appropriated some of their Christian misogyny. The Quran makes men and women partners before God, with identical duties and responsibilities.[12] The Quran also came to permit polygamy; at a time when Muslims were being killed in the wars against Mecca, and women were left without protectors, men were permitted to have up to four wives provided that they treat them all with absolute equality and show no signs of favouring one rather than the others.[13] The women of the first *ummah* in Medina took full part in its public life, and some, according to Arab custom, fought alongside the men in battle. They did not seem to have experienced Islam as an oppressive religion, though later, as happened in Christianity, men would hijack the faith and bring it into line with the prevailing patriarchy.

In the early years at Medina there were two important developments. Muhammad had been greatly excited by the prospect of working closely with the Jewish tribes, and had even, shortly before the *hijrah*, introduced some practices (such as communal prayer on Friday afternoons, when Jews would be preparing for the Sabbath, and a fast on the Jewish Day of Atonement) to align Islam more closely with Judaism. His disappointment, when the Jews of Medina refused to accept him as an authentic prophet, was one of the greatest of his life. For Jews, the era of prophecy was over, so it was not surprising that they could not accept

Muhammad, but the polemic with the Jews of Medina occupies a significant proportion of the Quran and shows that it troubled Muhammad. Some of the Quranic stories about such prophets as Noah or Moses were different from those of the Bible. Many of the Jews used to scoff when these were recited in the mosque. The three main Jewish tribes also resented Muhammad's ascendancy; they had formed a powerful bloc before his arrival in the settlement, and now felt demoted and determined to get rid of him.

But some of the Jews in the smaller clans were friendly and enhanced Muhammad's knowledge of Jewish scripture. He was especially delighted to hear that in the Book of Genesis Abraham had two sons: Isaac and Ishmael (who became Ismail in Arabic), the child of his concubine Hagar. Abraham had been forced to cast Hagar and Ismail out into the wilderness, but God had saved them and promised that Ismail too would be the father of a great nation, the Arabs.[14] Local tradition had it that Hagar and Ismail had settled in Mecca, that Abraham had visited them there, and that together Abraham and Ismail had rebuilt the Kabah (which had originally been erected by Adam but had fallen into disrepair).[15] This was music to Muhammad's ears. It seemed that the Arabs had not been left out of the divine plan after all, and that the Kabah had venerable monotheistic credentials.

By 624 it was clear that most of the Jews of Medina would never be reconciled with the Prophet. Muhammad had also been shocked to learn that the Jews and Christians (whom he had assumed to belong to a single faith) actually had serious theological differences, even though he appears to have thought that not all the *ahl al-kitab* condoned this disgraceful sectarianism. In January 624 he made what must be one of his most creative gestures. During the *salat* prayer, he told the congregation to turn around, so that they prayed in the direction of Mecca rather than Jerusalem. This change of *qiblah* was a declaration of independence. By turning away from Jerusalem towards the Kabah, which had no connection with Judaism or Christianity, Muslims tacitly demonstrated that they were reverting to the original pure monotheism of Abraham, who had lived before the revelation of either the Torah or the Gospel and, therefore, before the religion of the one God had been split into warring sects.[16] Muslims would direct themselves to God alone: it was idolatrous to bow before a human system or an established religion rather than before God himself:

> Verily, as for those who have broken the unity of their faith and become sects – thou hast nothing to do with them ... Say: 'Behold, my Sustainer has guided me to a straight way through an ever-true faith – in the way of Abraham, who turned away from all that is false, and was not of those who ascribe divinity to aught beside Him.' Say: 'Behold, my prayer, and [all] my acts of worship, and my living and dying are for God alone.'[17]

The change of *qiblah* appealed to all Arab Muslims, especially to the emigrants who had made the *hijrah* from Mecca. Muslims would no longer tag lamely behind those Jews and Christians who ridiculed their aspirations, but would take their own direct route to God.

The second major development occurred shortly after the change of the *qiblah*. Muhammad and the emigrants from Mecca had no means of earning a living in Medina; there was not enough land for them to farm, and, in any case, they were merchants and businessmen not agriculturalists. The Medinese, who were known as the *ansar* (the helpers), could not afford to keep them *gratis*, so the emigrants resorted to the *ghazu*, the 'raid', which was a sort of national sport in Arabia, as well as being a rough-and-ready means of redistributing resources in a land where there was simply not enough to go round. Raiding parties would attack a caravan or contingent from a rival tribe and carry off booty and livestock, taking care to avoid killing people since this would mean a vendetta. It was forbidden to conduct a raid against a tribe that had become an ally or 'client' (a weaker tribal group who had sought protection from one of the more powerful tribes). The emigrants, who had been persecuted by the Quraysh and forced to leave their homes, began to conduct *ghazu* against the rich Meccan caravans, which brought them an income, but to conduct a *ghazu* against one's *own* tribe was a serious breach in precedent. The raiding parties enjoyed some initial success, but in March 624 Muhammad led a large band of emigrants to the coast to intercept the largest Meccan caravan of the year. When they heard of this outrage, the Quraysh dispatched an army to defend the caravan, but, against the odds, the Muslims inflicted a stunning defeat on the Meccans at the well of Badr. Even though the Meccans were superior in terms of numbers, they fought in the old Arab style with careless bravado, each chief leading his own men. Muhammad's troops, however, were carefully drilled and fought under his unified command. It was a rout that impressed the Bedouin tribes, some of whom enjoyed the spectacle of seeing the mighty Quraysh brought low.

There then ensued desperate days for the *ummah*. Muhammad had to contend with the hostility of some of the pagans in Medina, who resented the power of the Muslim newcomers and were determined to expel them from the settlement. He also had to deal with Mecca, where Abu Sufyan now directed the campaign against him, and had launched two major offensives against the Muslims in Medina. His object was not simply to defeat the *ummah* in battle, but to annihilate all the Muslims. The harsh ethic of the desert meant that there were no half-measures in warfare: if possible, a victorious chief was expected to exterminate the enemy, so the *ummah* faced the threat of total extinction. In 625 Mecca inflicted a severe defeat on the *ummah* at the Battle of Uhud, but two years later the Muslims trounced the Meccans at the Battle of the Trench, so called because Muhammad protected the settlement by digging a ditch around Medina, which threw the Quraysh, who still regarded war rather as a chivalric game and had never heard of such an unsporting trick, into confusion, and rendered their cavalry useless. Muhammad's second victory over the numerically superior Quraysh (there had been ten thousand Meccans to three thousand Muslims) was a turning point. It convinced the nomadic tribes that Muhammad was the coming man, and made the Quraysh look decidedly *passé*. The gods in whose name they fought were clearly not working on their behalf. Many of the tribes wanted to become the allies of the *ummah*, and Muhammad began to build a powerful tribal confederacy, whose members swore not to attack one another and to fight each other's enemies. Some of the Meccans also began to defect and made the *hijrah* to Medina; at last, after five years of deadly peril, Muhammad could be confident that the *ummah* would survive.

In Medina, the chief casualties of this Muslim success were the three Jewish tribes of Qaynuqah, Nadir and Qurayzah, who were determined to destroy Muhammad and who all independently formed alliances with Mecca. They had powerful armies, and obviously posed a threat to the Muslims, since their territory was so situated that they could easily join a besieging Meccan army or attack the *ummah* from the rear. When Qaynuqah staged an unsuccessful rebellion against Muhammad in 625, they were expelled from Medina, in accordance with Arab custom. Muhammad tried to reassure Nadir, and made a special treaty with them, but when he discovered that they had been plotting to assassinate him they too were sent into exile, where they joined the nearby Jewish settlement of Khaybar, and drummed up support for Abu Sufyan among the northern Arab tribes. Nadir proved to be even more of a danger outside Medina, so when the Jewish tribe of Qurayzah sided with Mecca during the Battle of the Trench, when for a time it seemed that the Muslims faced certain defeat, Muhammad showed no mercy. The seven hundred men of Qurayzah were killed, and their women and children sold as slaves.

The massacre of Qurayzah was a horrible incident, but it would be a mistake to judge it by the standards of our own time. This was a very primitive society: the Muslims themselves had just narrowly escaped extermination, and had Muhammad simply exiled Qurayzah they would have swelled the Jewish opposition in Khaybar and brought another war upon the *ummah*. In seventh-century Arabia an Arab chief was not expected to show mercy to traitors like Qurayzah. The executions sent a grim message to Khaybar and helped to quell the pagan opposition in Medina, since the pagan leaders had been the allies of the rebellious Jews. This was a fight to the death, and everybody had always known that the stakes were high. The struggle did not indicate any hostility towards Jews in general, but only towards the three rebel tribes. The Quran continued to revere Jewish prophets and to urge Muslims to respect the People of the Book. Smaller Jewish groups continued to live in Medina, and later Jews, like Christians, enjoyed full religious liberty in the Islamic empires. Anti-semitism is a Christian vice. Hatred of the Jews became marked in the Muslim world only after the creation of the state of Israel in 1948 and the subsequent loss of Arab Palestine. It is significant that Muslims were compelled to import anti-Jewish myths from

Europe, and translate into Arabic such virulently anti-semitic texts as the *Protocols of the Elders of Zion*, because they had no such traditions of their own. Because of this new hostility towards the Jewish people, some Muslims now quote the passages in the Quran that refer to Muhammad's struggle with the three rebellious Jewish tribes to justify their prejudice. By taking these verses out of context, they have distorted both the message of the Quran and the attitude of the Prophet, who himself felt no such hatred of Judaism.

Muhammad's intransigence towards Qurayzah had been designed to bring hostilities to an end as soon as possible. The Quran teaches that war is such a catastrophe that Muslims must use every method in their power to restore peace and normality in the shortest possible time.[18] Arabia was a chronically violent society, and the *ummah* had to fight its way to peace. Major social change of the type that Muhammad was attempting in the peninsula is rarely achieved without bloodshed. But after the Battle of the Trench, when Muhammad had humiliated Mecca and quashed the opposition in Medina, he felt that it was time to abandon the *jihad* and begin a peace offensive. In March 628 he set in train a daring and imaginative initiative that brought the conflict to a close. He announced that he was going to make the *hajj* to Mecca, and asked for volunteers to accompany him. Since pilgrims were forbidden to carry arms, the Muslims would be walking directly into the lions' den and putting themselves at the mercy of the hostile and resentful Quraysh. Nevertheless, about a thousand Muslims agreed to join the Prophet and set out for Mecca, dressed in the traditional white robes of the *hajji*. If the Quraysh forbade Arabs to approach the Kabah or attacked *bona fide* pilgrims they would betray their sacred duty as the guardians of the shrine. The Quraysh did, however, dispatch troops to attack the pilgrims before they reached the area outside the city where violence was forbidden, but the Prophet evaded them and, with the help of some of his Bedouin allies, managed to reach the edge of the sanctuary, camped at Hudaybiyyah, and awaited developments. Eventually the Quraysh were pressured by this peaceful demonstration to sign a treaty with the *ummah*. It was an unpopular move on both sides. Many of the Muslims were eager for action, and felt that the treaty was shameful, but Muhammad was determined to achieve victory by peaceful means.

Hudaybiyyah was another turning point. It impressed still more of the Bedouin, and conversion to Islam became even more of an irreversible trend. Eventually in 630, when the Quraysh violated the treaty by attacking one of the Prophet's tribal allies Muhammad marched upon Mecca with an army of ten thousand men. Faced with this overwhelming force and, as pragmatists, realizing what it signified, the Quraysh conceded defeat, opened the city gates, and Muhammad took Mecca without shedding a drop of blood. He destroyed the idols around the Kabah, rededicated it to Allah, the one God, and gave the old pagan rites of the *hajj* an Islamic significance by linking them to the story of Abraham, Hagar and Ismail. None of the Quraysh was forced to become Muslim, but Muhammad's victory convinced some of his most principled opponents, such as Abu Sufyan, that the old religion had failed. When Muhammad died in 632, in the arms of his beloved wife Aisha, almost all the tribes of Arabia had joined the *ummah* as Confederates or as converted Muslims. Since members of the *ummah* could not, of course, attack one another, the ghastly cycle of tribal warfare, of vendetta and counter-vendetta, had ended. Single-handedly, Muhammad had brought peace to war-torn Arabia.

The Rashidun (632–661)

The life and achievements of Muhammad would affect the spiritual, political and ethical vision of Muslims for ever. They expressed the Islamic experience of 'salvation', which does not consist of the redemption of an 'original sin' committed by Adam and the admittance to eternal life, but in the achievement of a society which puts into practice God's desires for the human race. This not only redeemed Muslims from the sort of political and social hell that existed in pre-Islamic Arabia, but also provided them with a context within which they could more easily make that wholehearted surrender to God which alone can fulfil them. Muhammad became the archetypal example of that perfect submission to the divine, and Muslims, as we shall see, would attempt to conform to this standard in their spiritual and social lives.

Muhammad was never venerated as a divine figure, but he was held to be the Perfect Man. His surrender to God had been so complete that he had transformed society and enabled the Arabs to live together in harmony. The word *islam* is etymologically related to *salam* (peace), and in these early years Islam did promote cohesion and concord.

But Muhammad had achieved this success by being the recipient of a divine revelation. Throughout his career, God had sent down the oracles that formed the Quran. When faced with a crisis or dilemma, Muhammad had entered deeply into himself and heard a divinely inspired solution. His life had thus represented a constant dialogue between transcendent reality and the violent, puzzling and disturbing happenings of the mundane world. The Quran had, therefore, followed public and current events, bringing divine guidance and illumination to politics. Muhammad's successors, however, were not prophets, but would have to rely on their own human insights. How would they ensure that Muslims continued to respond creatively and directly to this sacred imperative? The *ummah* that they ruled would be much larger and increasingly more complex than the little community of Medina, where everybody knew everybody else and there had been no need for officialdom and a bureaucracy. How would the new deputy (*khalifah*) of Muhammad preserve the essence of the first *ummah* in very different circumstances?

The first four caliphs to succeed Muhammad grappled with these difficult questions. They were all men who had been among the Prophet's closest companions, and had played a leading role in Mecca and Medina. They are known as the *rashidun*, the 'rightly guided' caliphs, and their period of rule would be just as formative as that of the Prophet himself. Muslims would define themselves and their theology according to the way they assessed the turbulent, glorious and tragic events of these years.

After the Prophet's death, the leading Muslims had to decide what form the *ummah* should take. Some may not have believed that there ought to be a 'state', a polity which had no precedent in Arabia. Some seemed to think that each tribal group should elect its own *imam* (leader). But the Prophet's companions Abu Bakr and Umar ibn al-Khattab argued that the *ummah* must be a united community, and should have a single ruler, as it had under the Prophet. Some believed that Muhammad would have wanted to be succeeded by Ali ibn Abi Talib, his closest male relative. In Arabia, where the blood-tie was sacred, it was thought that a chief's special qualities were passed down the line of his descendants, and some Muslims believed that Ali had inherited something of Muhammad's special charisma. But although Ali's piety was beyond question, he was still young and inexperienced, and therefore Abu Bakr was elected the first *khalifah* of the Prophet by a majority of votes.

Abu Bakr's reign (632–4) was short but crucial. He was chiefly preoccupied by the so-called wars of *riddah* (apostasy) when various tribes tried to break away from the *ummah* and reassert their former independence. It would, however, be a mistake to regard this as a widespread religious defection. The revolts were entirely political and economic. Most of the Bedouin tribes who had entered the Islamic Confederacy had little interest in the details of Muhammad's religion. The Prophet, a realist, had recognized that many of the alliances he had formed were purely political, a matter of one chief joining forces with another, as was customary in the Arabian steppes. Some chiefs may have believed that their pact had been only with Muhammad and not with his successor, and that after his death they were free to raid tribes in the *ummah*, thus calling upon themselves a Muslim riposte.

It was, however, significant that many of the rebels felt impelled to give their revolts a religious justification; the leaders often claimed to be prophets, and produced Quranic-style 'revelations'. The Arabs had been through a profound experience. It was not 'religious' in our modern sense of the word, since for many it was not a private faith, following an interior conversion. The Prophet had broken the old mould, and suddenly – if momentarily – the Arabs had found themselves for the first time members of a united community, free from the burden of constant, debilitating warfare. For the brief years of Muhammad's career they had glimpsed the possibility of an entirely different way of life, bound up with a religious change. What had happened had been so astounding that even those who wanted to break away from the *ummah* could only think in prophetic terms. It was probably during the *riddah* wars that Muslims began to assert that Muhammad had been the last and greatest of the prophets, a claim that is not made explicitly in the Quran, as Muslims countered the challenge of these *riddah* prophets.

Abu Bakr quelled the uprisings with wisdom and clemency, and thus completed the unification of Arabia. He dealt creatively with the complaints of the rebels, and there were no reprisals taken against those who returned to the fold. Some were enticed back by the prospect of taking part in the lucrative *ghazu* raids in the neighbouring lands, which gained dramatic momentum under the rule of the second caliph, Umar ibn al-Khattab (634–44). These raids were a response to a problem that had arisen from the new Islamic peace in the peninsula. For centuries, the Arabs had eked out their inadequate resources by means of the *ghazu*, but Islam had put a stop to this because the tribes of the *ummah* were not permitted to attack one another. What would replace the *ghazu*, which had enabled Muslims to scratch out a meagre livelihood? Umar realized that the *ummah* needed order. Lawless elements had to be brought under control, and energies which had previously been expended in raiding and feuding now had to be channelled into a common activity. The obvious answer was a series of *ghazu* raids against the non-Muslim communities in the neighbouring countries. The unity of the *ummah* would be preserved by an outwardly directed offensive. This would also enhance the caliph's authority. The Arabs traditionally disliked kingship and would be leery of any ruler who assumed the style of a monarch. But they would accept the authority of a chief during a military campaign or while they were journeying to new pastures. Umar therefore called himself *amir al-muminim* (the commander of the faithful), and Muslims accepted his rulings in matters that concerned the *ummah* as a whole, but not on matters that individuals could decide for themselves.

Under Umar's leadership, therefore, the Arabs burst into Iraq, Syria and Egypt, achieving a series of astonishing victories. They overcame the Persian army at the Battle of Qadisiyyah (637), which led to the fall of the capital of the Persian Sassanids at Ctesiphon. As soon as they had the manpower, Muslims would thus be able to occupy the whole of the Persian Empire. They encountered stiffer resistance in the Byzantine Empire, and conquered no territory in the Byzantine heartlands in Anatolia. Nevertheless, the Muslims were victorious at the Battle of

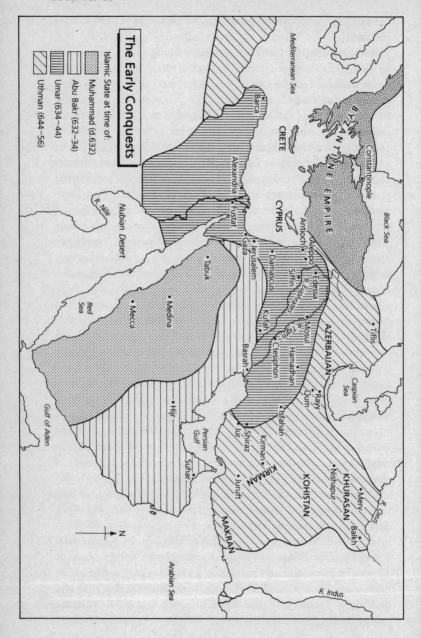

The Early Conquests

Islamic State at time of:

Muhammad (d.632)

Abu Bakr (632–34)

Umar (634–44)

Uthman (644–56)

Mediterranean Sea

Barca

CRETE

CYPRUS

BYZANTINE EMPIRE

Constantinople

Black Sea

R. Nile

Nubian Desert

Alexandria

Fustat

Gaza

Jerusalem

Damascus

Aleppo

Antioch

Edessa

R. Euphrates

Siffin

Kufah

Mosul

R. Tigris

Ctesiphon

Hamadhan

AZERBAIJAN

Tiflis

Basrah

Rayy

Qum

Caspian Sea

Tabuk

Red Sea

Mecca

Medina

Hijr

Persian Gulf

Jur

Isfahan

Shiraz

Kirman

KIRMAN

KOHISTAN

KHURASAN

Nishapur

Merv

Balkh

R. Oxus

Suhar

Juruft

MAKRAN

Gulf of Aden

N

Arabian Sea

R. Indus

24

Yarmuk (636) in northern Palestine, conquered Jerusalem in 638, and controlled the whole of Syria, Palestine and Egypt by 641. The Muslim armies went on to seize the North African coast as far as Cyrenaica. Just twenty years after the Battle of Badr, the Arabs found themselves in possession of a sizeable empire. This expansion continued. A century after the Prophet's death, the Islamic Empire extended from the Pyrenees to the Himalayas. It seemed yet another miracle and sign of God's favour. Before the coming of Islam, the Arabs had been a despised outgroup; but in a remarkably short space of time they had inflicted major defeats upon two world empires. The experience of conquest enhanced their sense that something tremendous had happened to them. Membership of the *ummah* was thus a transcendent experience, because it went beyond anything they had known or could have imagined in the old tribal days. Their success also endorsed the message of the Quran, which had asserted that a correctly guided society must prosper because it was in tune with God's laws. Look what had happened once they had surrendered to God's will! Where Christians discerned God's hand in apparent failure and defeat, when Jesus died on the cross, Muslims experienced political success as sacramental and as a revelation of the divine presence in their lives.

It is important, however, to be clear that when the Arabs burst out of Arabia they were not impelled by the ferocious power of 'Islam'. Western people often assume that Islam is a violent, militaristic faith which imposed itself on its subject peoples at sword-point. This is an inaccurate interpretation of the Muslim wars of expansion. There was nothing religious about these campaigns, and Umar did not believe that he had a divine mandate to conquer the world. The objective of Umar and his warriors was entirely pragmatic: they wanted plunder and a common activity that would preserve the unity of the *ummah*. For centuries the Arabs had tried to raid the richer settled lands beyond the peninsula; the difference was that this time they had encountered a power vacuum. Persia and Byzantium had both been engaged for decades in a long and debilitating series of wars with one another. Both were exhausted. In Persia, there was factional strife, and flooding had destroyed the country's agriculture. Most of the Sassanian troops were of Arab origin and went over to the invaders during the campaign. In the Syrian and North African provinces of Byzantium, the local population had been alienated by the religious intolerance of the Greek Orthodox establishment, and were not disposed to come to their aid when the Arabs attacked, though Muslims could make no headway in the Byzantine heart-lands of Anatolia.

Later, when the Muslims had established their great empire, Islamic law would give a religious interpretation of this conquest, dividing the world into the Dar al-Islam (the House of Islam), which was in perpetual conflict with the Dar al-Harb (the House of War). But in practice the Muslims accepted that they had reached the limits of their expansion by this date, and coexisted amicably with the non-Muslim world. The Quran does not sanc-tify warfare. It develops the notion of a just war of self-defence to protect decent values, but condemns killing and aggression.[19] Furthermore, once the Arabs had left the peninsula, they found that nearly everybody belonged to the *ahl al-kitab*, the People of the Book, who had received authentic scriptures from God. They were not, therefore, forced to convert to Islam; indeed, until the middle of the eighth century, conversion was not encouraged. The Muslims assumed that Islam was a religion for the descendants of Ismail, as Judaism was the faith of the sons of Isaac. Arab tribesmen had always extended protection to weaker clients (*mawali*). Once the Jews, Christians and Zoroastrians in their new empire had become *dhimmis* (protected subjects), they could not be raided or attacked in any way. It had always been a point of honour among Arabs to treat their clients well, to come to their aid, or to avenge an injury done to them. *Dhimmis* paid a poll tax in return for military protection, and were permitted to practise their own faith, as the Quran enjoined. Indeed some of the Chris-tians, who had been persecuted by the Greek Orthodox for their heretical opinions, greatly preferred Muslim to Byzantine rule.

Umar was determined to maintain good discipline. The Arab soldiers were not to enjoy the fruits of victory, the conquered lands were not to be divided among the generals, but left to the existing cultivators, who paid rent to the Muslim state. Muslims were not allowed to settle in the cities. Instead, new 'garrison towns' (*amsar*) were built for them at strategic locations: Kufah in Iraq, Basrah in Syria, Qum in Iran, and Fustat at the head of the

Nile. Damascus was the only old city to become a Muslim centre. A mosque was built in each of the *amsar*, where the Muslim troops attended Friday prayers. In these garrison towns, the soldiers were taught to live an Islamic life. Umar stressed the importance of family values, was hard on drunkenness, and promoted the ascetic virtues of the Prophet, who, like the caliph himself, had always lived frugally. But the garrison towns were also Arab enclaves, where those traditions that could be accommodated with the Quranic world-view were continued on foreign soil. At this point, Islam was an essentially Arab religion. Any *dhimmi* who did convert had to become a 'client' of one of the tribes and be absorbed into the Arab system.

But this period of triumph came to an abrupt end in November 644, when Umar was stabbed in the mosque of Medina by a Persian prisoner-of-war who had a personal grievance against him. The last years of the *rashidun* were characterized by violence. Uthman ibn Affan was elected as the third caliph by six of the Prophet's companions. He was a weaker character than his predecessors, but for the first six years of his reign the *ummah* continued to prosper. Uthman governed well and the Muslims conquered new territory. They seized Cyprus from the Byzantines, thus finally ejecting them from the western Mediterranean, and in North Africa the armies reached Tripoli in what is now Libya. In the East, the Muslim troops took much of Armenia, penetrated the Caucasus, and established Muslim rule as far as the River Oxus in Iran, Herat in Afghanistan, and Sind in the Indian subcontinent.

But, despite these victories, the soldiers were becoming discontented. They had undergone a massive change. In just over a decade they had exchanged a harsh nomadic existence for the very different lifestyle of the professional army. They spent the summer fighting and winter far from home in the garrison towns. The distances were now so vast that the campaigns were more exhausting, and they were taking less plunder than before. Uthman still refused to allow the commanders and the richest Meccan families to establish private estates in such countries as Iraq, and this made him unpopular, especially in Kufah and Fustat. Uthman also alienated the Muslims of Medina by giving the most prestigious posts to members of his own Umayyad family. They accused him of nepotism, even though many of the Umayyad officials were men of great ability. Uthman had, for example, appointed Muawiyyah, the son of Muhammad's old enemy Abu Sufyan, governor of Syria. He was a good Muslim, and a skilled administrator, known for his steadiness of character and his measured assessment of circumstances. But it seemed wrong to the Muslims of Medina, who still boasted of being the *ansar* (helpers) of the Prophet, that they should be passed over in favour of Abu Sufyan's offspring. The Quran-reciters, who knew the scripture by heart and had become the chief religious authorities, were also incensed when Uthman insisted that only one version of the sacred text be used in the garrison towns, and suppressed variants, which many of them preferred, but which differed in minor details. Increasingly, the malcontents looked to Ali ibn Abi Talib, the Prophet's cousin, who, it seems, had opposed the policies of both Umar and Uthman, standing for 'soldiers' rights' against the power of the central authority.

In 656 the discontent culminated in outright mutiny. A group of Arab soldiers from Fustat returned to Medina to claim their due, and when fobbed off they besieged Uthman's simple house, broke in, and assassinated him. The mutineers acclaimed Ali as the new caliph.

The First Fitnah

Ali seemed an obvious choice. He had grown up in the Prophet's household and was imbued with the ideals promoted by Muhammad. He was a good soldier and wrote inspiring letters to his officers, which are still classic Muslim texts, preaching the necessity of justice and the importance of dealing compassionately with the subject peoples. But despite his intimacy with the Prophet, his rule was not universally accepted. Ali was supported by the *ansar* of Medina and those Meccans who resented the rise of the Umayyads. He also enjoyed the support of Muslims who still lived the traditional nomadic life, especially in Iraq, whose garrison town Kufah was an Alid stronghold. But the assassination of Uthman, who, like Ali himself, had been Muhammad's son-in-law, and had been one of the earliest converts to Islam, was a shocking event which inspired a five-year civil war within the *ummah*, which is known as the *fitnah*, the time of temptation.

After a brief delay, Muhammad's favourite wife Aisha, together with her kinsman Talhah, and Zubayr, one of the Prophet's Meccan companions, attacked Ali for not punishing Uthman's assassins. Since the army was in the provinces, the rebels marched from Medina to Basrah. Ali was in a difficult position. He must himself have been shocked by Uthman's murder, which, as a devout man, he could not condone. But his supporters insisted that Uthman deserved death, since he had not ruled justly, according to the Quranic ideal. Ali could not disown his partisans, and took refuge in Kufah, which he made his capital. He then advanced on Basrah with his army, which easily defeated the rebels there in the Battle of the Camel, so called because Aisha, who rode with the troops, had watched the fighting on the back of her camel. After his victory, Ali gave his supporters the top jobs, divided his treasury among them, but he still did not accord them full 'soldiers' rights' by allowing them to annex the Sawad, the rich agricultural land around Kufah, which had provided the old Persian Empire with most of its revenue. He was failing to satisfy his own party but also, in not condemning Uthman's murder, casting himself in a highly dubious light.

Ali's rule had not been accepted in Syria, where the opposition was led by Muawiyyah from his capital in Damascus. Uthman had been his kinsman, and, as the new head of the Umayyad family, it was his duty as an Arab chieftain to avenge his death. He was supported by the wealthy Meccan clans and the Arabs of Syria, who had appreciated his strong and wise government. Ali probably felt some sympathy for Muawiyyah's position, and initially took no steps against him. But the spectacle of the Prophet's relatives and companions poised to attack one another was profoundly disturbing. Muhammad's mission had been to promote unity among Muslims and to integrate the *ummah* so that it reflected the unity of God. To prevent the appalling possibility of further conflict, the two sides tried to negotiate a settlement at Siffin on the upper Euphrates in 657, but the discussions were inconclusive. Muawiyyah's supporters put copies of the Quran on the tip of their lances and called for neutral Muslims to arbitrate between the contestants in accordance with God's word. It appeared that the arbitration went against Ali, and many of his followers tried to persuade him to accept it. Feeling thus empowered, Muawiyyah deposed Ali, sent troops into Iraq, and had himself proclaimed caliph in Jerusalem.

But some of Ali's more radical supporters refused to accept the arbitration and were shocked by Ali's submission. In their view, Uthman had failed to live up to the standard of the Quran. Ali had compromised with the supporters of injustice by failing to right the wrongs committed by Uthman and was, therefore, no true Muslim. They withdrew from the *ummah*, which they claimed had betrayed the spirit of the Quran, and set up their own camp with an independent commander. Ali suppressed these extremists, who became known as the *kharajis* (seceders), wiping out the original rebels, but the movement gained adherents throughout the empire. Many had been perturbed by the nepotism of Uthman's reign, and wanted to implement the egalitarian spirit of the Quran. The Kharijites were always a minority group, but their position was important, since it was the first instance of an important Muslim trend, whereby the politics that affected the morality of the *ummah* led to a new theological development. The Kharajites insisted that the ruler of the Islamic community should not be the most powerful but the most committed Muslim; caliphs should not be power-seekers like Muawiyyah. God had given human beings free will and, since he was just, he would punish such evil-doers as Muawiyyah, Uthman and Ali, who by betraying Islam had become apostates. The Kharajites were extremists but they forced Muslims to consider the question of who was and who was not a Muslim. So important was the political leadership as a religious idea that it led to discussions about the nature of God, predestination and human freedom.

Ali's harsh treatment of the Kharajites cost him much support, even in Kufah. Muawiyyah made steady gains and many of the Arabs remained neutral. A second attempt at arbitration, which tried to find another candidate for the caliphate, failed; Muawiyyah's army defeated the resistance to his rule in Arabia, and in 661 Ali was murdered by a Kharajite. Those who remained loyal to Ali's cause in Kufah acclaimed his son Hasan, but Hasan came to an agreement with Muawiyyah, and, for a financial consideration, retired to Medina, where he lived without further political involvement until his death in 669.

The *ummah* had thus entered a new phase. Muawiyyah made Damascus his capital and set about restoring the unity of the Muslim community. But a pattern had been set. The Muslims of Iraq and Syria now felt antagonistic towards one another. With hindsight, Ali was regarded as a decent, pious man who had been defeated by the logic of practical politics. The murder of the man who had been the first male convert to Islam and was the Prophet's closest male relative was rightly seen as a disgraceful event, which posed grave questions about the moral integrity of the *ummah*. According to common Arab belief, Ali was thought to have inherited some of the Prophet's exceptional qualities, and his male descendants were revered as leading religious authorities. The fate of Ali, a man betrayed by his friends as well as his enemies, became a symbol of the inherent injustice of life. From time to time, Muslims who protested against the behaviour of the reigning caliph would retreat from the *ummah*, like the Kharajites, and summon all true Muslims to join them in a struggle (*jihad*) for higher Islamic standards. Often they would claim that they belonged to the Shiah-i Ali, the Party of Ali.

Others, however, took a more neutral stance. They had been appalled by the murderous divisions that had torn the *ummah* apart, and henceforth unity became a more crucial value in Islam than ever. Many had been dissatisfied with Ali, but could see that Muawiyyah was far from ideal. They began to look back on the period of the four *rashidun* as a time when Muslims had been ruled by devout men, who had been close to the Prophet but had been brought low by evil-doers. The events of the first *fitnah* had become symbolic, and rival parties now drew upon these tragic incidents as they struggled to make sense of their Islamic vocation. All agreed, however, that the shift from Medina, the capital of the Prophet and the *rashidun*, to Umayyad Damascus was more than a political expedient. The *ummah* seemed to be moving away from the world of the Prophet, and was in danger of losing its *raison d'être*. The more pious and concerned Muslims were resolved to find new ways of putting it back on track.

2   DEVELOPMENT

The Umayyads and the Second Fitnah

Caliph Muawiyyah (661–80) managed to restore the unity of the empire. Muslims had been horrified by the *fitnah*, and had realized how vulnerable they were in their garrison towns, isolated from their fellow-Arabs and surrounded by potentially hostile subjects. They simply could not afford such lethal civil war. They wanted strong government, and Muawiyyah, an able ruler, was able to give it to them. He revived Umar's system of segregating the Arab Muslims from the population, and even though some Muslims in Arabia were still agitating for the right to build estates in the occupied territories, Muawiyyah continued to forbid this. He also discouraged conversion, and built an efficient administration. Islam thus remained the religion of the conquering Arab elite. At first the Arabs, who had no experience of imperial government, relied on the expertise of non-Muslims, who had served the previous Byzantine and Persian regimes, but gradually the Arabs began to oust the *dhimmis* from the top posts. In the course of the next century, the Umayyad caliphs would gradually transform the disparate regions conquered by the Muslim armies into a unified empire, with a common ideology. This was a great achievement; but the court naturally began to develop a rich culture and luxurious lifestyle, and became indistinguishable in many respects from any other ruling class.

Therein lay a dilemma. It had been found, after centuries of experience, that an absolute monarchy was the only effective way of governing a pre-modern empire with an agrarian-based economy, and that it was far more satisfactory than a military oligarchy, where commanders usually competed with one another for power. The idea of making one man so privileged that rich and poor alike are vulnerable before him is abhorrent to us in our democratic era, but we must realize that democracy is made

35

possible by an industrialized society which has the technology to replicate its resources indefinitely: this was not an option before the advent of Western modernity. In the pre-modern world, a monarch who was so powerful that he had no rivals, did not need to fight his own battles, could settle the quarrels of the great, and had no reason to ignore the entreaties of those who pleaded for the poor. So strong was this preference for monarchy that, as we shall see, even when real power was wielded by local rulers in a large empire, they still paid lip service to the king and claimed to be acting as his vassals. The Umayyad caliphs governed a vast empire, which continued to expand under their rule. They would find that in order to preserve the peace they would have to become absolute monarchs too, but how would this cohere with Arab traditions, on the one hand, and with the radical egalitarianism of the Quran on the other?

The first Umayyad caliphs were not absolute monarchs. Muawiyyah still ruled like an Arab chief, as *primus inter pares*. The Arabs had always distrusted kingship, which was not feasible in a region where numerous small groups had to compete for the same inadequate resources. They had no system of dynastic rule, since they always needed the best man available as their chief. But the *fitnah* had shown the dangers of a disputed succession. It would be wrong to think of the Umayyads as 'secular' rulers. Muawiyyah was a religious man and a devout Muslim, according to the prevailing notion of Islam. He was devoted to the sanctity of Jerusalem, the first Muslim *qiblah* and the home of so many of the great prophets of the past. He worked hard to maintain the unity of the *ummah*. His rule was based on the Quranic insistence that all Muslims were brothers and must not fight one another. He accorded the *dhimmis* religious freedom and personal rights on the basis of Quranic teaching. But the experience of the *fitnah* had convinced some Muslims, such as the Kharajites, that Islam should mean more than this, in both the public and the private domain.

There was, therefore, a potential conflict between the needs of the agrarian state and Islam, and this became tragically clear after Muawiyyah's death. He had already realized that he must depart from Arab traditions in order to secure the succession, and before he died he arranged the accession of his son, Yazid I (680–83). But there was an immediate outcry. In Kufah, loyal Alids called for the rule of Ali's second son Husain, who set out from Medina to Iraq with a small band of followers, together with their wives and children. In the meantime, the Kufans had been intimidated by the local Umayyad governor and withdrew their support. Husain refused to surrender, however, convinced that the sight of the Prophet's family on the march in quest for true Islamic values would remind the *ummah* of its prime duty. On the plain of Kerbala, just outside Kufah, he and his followers were surrounded by the Umayyad troops and massacred. Husain was the last to die, holding his infant son in his arms. All Muslims lament this tragic death of the Prophet's grandson, but Husain's fate focused the attention of those who regarded themselves as the Shiah-i Ali even more intensely on the Prophet's descendants. Like the murder of Ali, the Kerbala tragedy became a symbol for Shii Muslims of the chronic injustice that seems to pervade human life; it also seemed to show the impossibility of integrating the religious imperative in the harsh world of politics, which seemed murderously antagonistic to it.

Even more serious was the revolt in the Hijaz led by Abdallah ibn al-Zubayr, the son of one of the rebels against Ali at the Battle of the Camel; this was also an attempt to return to the pristine values of the first *ummah*, by wresting power away from the Umayyads and restoring it to Mecca and Medina. In 683 Umayyad troops took Medina, but lifted their siege of Mecca in the confusion that followed the premature death of Yazid I and his infant son Muawiyyah II that year. Yet again the *ummah* was ripped apart by civil war. Ibn Zubayr achieved widespread recognition as caliph, but he was isolated in the Hijaz when Kharajite rebels established an independent state in central Arabia in 684; there were other Kharajite uprisings in Iraq and Iran; Shiis rose up in Kufah to avenge the death of Husain, and to promote the candidature of another of Ali's sons. The rebels all asserted the egalitarian ideals of the Quran, but it was the Syrian forces who carried the day in the name of Marwan, an Umayyad cousin of Muawiyyah I, and his son Abd al-Malik. By 691 they had disposed of all their rivals, and the following year had defeated and killed Ibn al-Zubayr himself.

Abd al-Malik (685–705) was able to reassert Umayyad rule, and the last twelve years of his reign were peaceful and prosperous. He was not yet an absolute monarch, but after the second *fitnah* he was clearly tending that way. He upheld the solidarity of the *ummah* against the local Arab chieftains, brought rebels to heel, and pursued a determined policy of centralization. Arabic replaced Persian as the official language of the empire; for the first time there was an Islamic coinage, decorated with Quranic phrases. In Jerusalem, the Dome of the Rock was completed in 691, the first major Islamic monument, which proudly asserted the supremacy of Islam in this holy city which had a large Christian majority. It announced that Islam had come to stay. The Dome also laid the foundations of the unique architectural and artistic style of Islam. There was to be no figurative art, which might distract worshippers from the transcendence that cannot adequately be expressed in human imagery. Instead, the inside of the dome was decorated with Quranic verses, the Word of God. The dome itself, which would become so characteristic of Muslim architecture, is a towering symbol of the spiritual ascent to heaven to which all believers aspire, but it also reflects the perfect balance of *tawhid*. Its exterior, which reaches towards the infinity of the sky, is a perfect replica of its internal dimension. It illustrates the way in which the human and the divine, the inner and the outer worlds complement one another as two halves of a single whole. Muslims were becoming more confident, and were beginning to express their own unique spiritual vision.

In this changed climate, the strict rules that had isolated Muslims from the subject peoples slowly relaxed. Non-Muslims began to settle in the garrison towns; peasants got work in Muslim areas and learned to speak Arabic. Merchants began to trade with the Muslims and, even though conversion was still not encouraged, some imperial officials did embrace Islam. But as the old segregation broke down, the population began to resent the privileges of the Arab Muslims. The suppression of the Kharajites and Shiis had left a bad taste, and Abd al-Malik was aware of a new Islamic movement in Arabia and the garrison towns which pressed for a more stringent application of Islamic ideals. Abd al-Malik was interested in these new ideas, but claimed that the Quran supported *his* policies. Some of these new pietists, however, wanted the Quran to take a more active role, and to lead the way instead of being used as a mere support or prop.

The Religious Movement

The civil wars raised many crucial questions. How could a society that killed its devout leaders (*imams*) claim to be guided by God? What kind of man should lead the *ummah*? Should the caliph be the most pious Muslim (as the Kharajites believed), a direct descendant of the Prophet (as the Shiis contended), or should the faithful accept the Umayyads, with all their failings, in the interests of peace and unity? Had Ali or Muawiyyah been right during the first *fitnah*? And how Islamic was the Umayyad state? Could rulers who lived in such luxury and condoned the poverty of the vast majority of the people be true Muslims? And what about the position of non-Arab converts to Islam, who had to become 'clients' (*mawali*) of one of the Arab tribes? Did this not suggest a chauvinism and inequity that was quite incompatible with the Quran?

It was from these political discussions that the religion and piety of Islam, as we know it, began to emerge. Quran-reciters and other concerned people asked what it really meant to be a Muslim. They wanted their society to be Islamic first and Arab second. The Quran spoke of the unification (*tawhid*) of the whole of human life, which meant that all the actions of the individual and all the institutions of the state should express a fundamental submission to God's will. At an equally formative stage of their history, Christians had held frequently vituperative discussions about the nature and person of Jesus, which helped them to evolve their distinctive view of God, salvation and the human condition. These intense Muslim debates about the political leadership of the *ummah* after the civil wars played a role in Islam that was similar to the great Christological debates of the fourth and fifth centuries in Christianity.

The prototype and supreme exemplar of this new Muslim piety was Hasan al-Basri (d. 728), who had been brought up in Medina in circles close to the Prophet's family, and lived through the death of Uthman. Later he moved to Basrah, where he developed a spirituality based on contempt for worldly goods, which harked back to the Prophet's ascetic lifestyle. But Hasan became the most famous preacher in Basrah, and his frugal way of life became an eloquent and potentially subversive criticism of the luxury of the court. Hasan initiated a religious reform in Basrah, teaching his followers to meditate deeply on the Quran, and that reflection, self-examination and a total surrender to God's will were the source of true happiness, since they resolved the tensions between human desires and what God desired for men and women. Hasan supported the Umayyads, but made it clear that he reserved the right to criticize them if they deserved it. He had opted for a theology known as the Qadariyyah, because it studied the decrees (*qadar*) of God. Human beings had free will and were responsible for their actions; they were not predestined to act in a certain way, since God was just and would not command them to live virtuously if it was not in their power. Therefore, the caliphs must be accountable for their deeds, and must be taken to task if they disobeyed God's clear teaching. When Caliph Abd al-Malik heard that Hasan had been spreading this potentially rebellious doctrine, he summoned him to court, but Hasan was so popular that the caliph dared not punish him. Hasan had begun the strong Muslim tradition of combining a disciplined interior life with political opposition to the government.

Qadarites accepted Umayyad rule, because it alone seemed able to preserve the unity of the *ummah*; they therefore opposed the Kharajites, who held that the Umayyads were apostates and deserving of death. Hasan's pupil, Wasan ibn Ata (d. 748), founded a moderate school which 'withdrew' (*itazahu*) from these two extreme positions. The Mutazilah agreed with the Qadarites in stressing the freedom of the human will, in condemning the luxurious lifestyle of the court, and in their insistence on the equality of all Muslims. But the Mutazilites' emphasis on the justice of God made them highly critical of Muslims who behaved exploitatively towards others. On the political question, they 'withdrew' from making a judgement between Ali and Mua-wiyyah, since they claimed that only God could know what was in men's hearts. This obviously countered the extremism of the Kharajites, but the Mutazilites were often political activists, nevertheless. The Quran exhorts Muslims to 'command what is good and forbid what is evil',[1] and, like the Kharajites, some of the Mutazilah took this very seriously. Some supported Shii rebellions; others, like Hasan al-Basri, castigated the rulers who did not live up to the Quranic ideal. The Mutazilah would dominate the intellectual scene in Iraq for over a century. Mutazilites developed a rationalistic theology (kalam), which emphasized the strict unity and simplicity of God, which the integrity of the ummah was supposed to reflect.

The Murjites, another school, also refused to judge between Ali and Muawiyyah, since it was a man's interior disposition that counted. Muslims must 'postpone' (arja) judgement, in accordance with the Quran.[2] The Umayyads should not be prejudged or dismissed as illegitimate rulers before they had done anything to deserve it, therefore, but should be severely rebuked if they contravened the standards of scripture. The most famous adherent of this school was Abu Hanifah (699–767), a merchant from Kufah. He had converted to Islam and pioneered the new discipline of jurisprudence (fiqh), which would have an immense impact on Islamic piety, and become the main discipline of higher education in the Muslim world. Fiqh also had its origins in the widespread discontent after the civil wars. Men would gather in each other's houses or in the mosques to discuss the inadequacies of Umayyad government. How could society be run according to Islamic principles? The jurists wanted to establish precise legal norms that would make the Quranic command to build a just society that surrendered wholly and in every detail to God's will a real possibility rather than a pious dream. In Basrah, Kufah, Medina and Damascus these early jurists (faqihs) worked out a legal system for their particular locality. Their problem was that the Quran contains very little legislation, and what laws there were had been designed for a much simpler society. So some of the jurists began to collect 'news' or 'reports' (ahadith; singular: hadith) about the Prophet and his companions to find out how they had behaved in a given situation. Others took the customary practice (sunnah) of Muslims in their city as a starting point, and tried to trace it back to one of the companions who had settled there in the early days. Thus, they believed, they would gain true ilm, a knowledge of what was right and how to behave. Abu Hanifah became the greatest legal expert of the Umayyad period, and founded a school (*madhhab*) of jurisprudence which Muslims still follow today. He wrote little himself, but his disciples preserved his teachings for posterity, while later jurists, who developed slightly different theories, founded new *madhhabs*.

Islamic historiography emerged from the same kind of discussion circles. In order to evolve a solution to their current difficulties, Muslims were finding that they had to look back to the period of the Prophet and the *rashidun*. Should the caliph be a member of the tribe of Quraysh, or was a descendant of one of the *ansar* acceptable? Had Muhammad expressed any view about this? What arrangements had Muhammad made about the succession? What had actually happened after the murder of Uthman? Historians such as Muhammad ibn Ishaq (d. 767) started to collect *ahadith* which explained some of the passages of the Quran by relating them to the historical circumstances in which the Prophet had received a particular revelation. Ibn Ishaq wrote a detailed biography (*sirah*) of the Prophet Muhammad, which stressed the virtue of the *ansar* and the iniquity of the Meccans who had opposed Muhammad. He clearly inclined to the Shii position that it was not fitting that Muslims should be ruled by the descendants of Abu Sufyan. History had thus become a religious activity that justified a principled opposition to the regime.

The political health of the *ummah* was, therefore, central to the emerging piety of Islam. While the caliph and his administration struggled with the problems that beset any agrarian empire, and tried to develop a powerful monarchy, the devout were utterly opposed to any such solution. From a very early stage, therefore, the behaviour and policies of a ruler had acquired a religious significance that had profound reverberations with the asceticism, mysticism, sacred jurisprudence and early theological speculation of the Muslim world.

The Last Years of the Umayyads (705–750)

Despite the disapproval of the more devout, Abd al-Malik was able to ensure that his son al-Walid I succeeded him: for the first time, the dynastic principle was accepted in the Islamic world without demur. The Umayyad dynasty had reached its zenith.

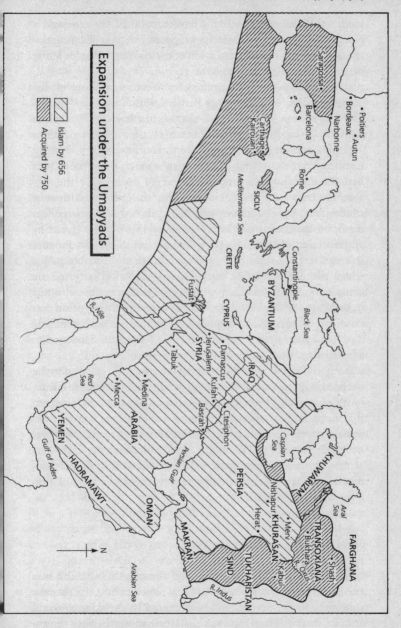

Expansion under the Umayyads

Islam by 656
Acquired by 750

Poitiers
Autun
Bordeaux
Saragossa
Narbonne
Barcelona
Carthage
Kairouan
Rome
SICILY
Mediterranean Sea
CRETE
Constantinople
BYZANTIUM
Black Sea
CYPRUS
Fustat
R. Nile
Damascus
Jerusalem
Kufah
SYRIA
Tabuk
IRAQ
Basrah
Ctesiphon
Caspian Sea
Mecca
Medina
ARABIA
Red Sea
Persian Gulf
PERSIA
KHUWARIZM
Aral Sea
YEMEN
HADRAMAWT
Gulf of Aden
OMAN
MAKRAN
Nishapur
Herat
Merv
KHURASAN
TRANSOXIANA
Bukhara
Oxus R.
Kabul
FARGHANA
Shash
SIND
TUKHARISTAN
R. Indus
Arabian Sea
N

Under al-Walid, the Muslim armies continued the conquest of North Africa, and established a kingdom in Spain. This marked the limit of the western expansion of Islam. When Charles Martel defeated the Muslim troops at Poitiers in 732, this was not regarded by Muslims as a great disaster. Western people have often exaggerated the importance of Poitiers, which was no Waterloo. The Arabs felt no compulsion – religious or otherwise – to conquer western Christendom in the name of Islam. Indeed, Europe seemed remarkably unattractive to them: there were few opportunities for trade in that primitive backwater, little booty to be had, and the climate was terrible.

By the end of the reign of Umar II (717–20), the empire was in trouble. Any pre-modern empire had a limited lifespan; based as it was on an agrarian surplus, there would inevitably come a time when a large, expanding state would outrun its resources. Umar had to pay for a disastrous attempt to conquer Constantinople, which had not only failed but led to heavy loss of manpower and equipment. Umar was the first caliph to encourage the *dhimmis* to convert to Islam, and they were eager to join this dynamic new faith, but since they no longer had to pay the poll tax (*jizyah*), the new policy resulted in a drastic loss of revenue. Umar was a devout man, who had been brought up in Medina and had been influenced by the religious movement there. He tried to model his behaviour on that of the *rashidun*, stressed the ideal of Islamic unity, treated all the provinces on an equal basis (instead of favouring Syria), and was humane towards the *dhimmis*. He was very popular, but his Islamic policies, which endeared him to the pious, were not good for the economy of the ailing empire. The reigns of his successors were punctuated with revolts and rumbling discontent. It made little difference whether the caliphs were dissolute, like Yazid II (720–24), or devout, like Hisham I (724–43). Hisham was a strong and effective caliph, who was able to put the empire back on a more sound economic basis, but he achieved this by making the state more rigidly centralized and his own rule more autocratic. He was becoming more like a conventional absolute monarch, and the empire benefited from this politically. The problem was that this type of autocracy was abhorrent to the devout, and fundamentally un-Islamic. Was it, after all, impossible to run a state on Quranic norms? Shiis became increasingly active. Their leaders claimed descent from Ali, believing that the *ilm* that would enable Muslims to inaugurate a just society had been preserved most fully in Muhammad's family and that they alone should rule. The more radical Shiis blamed all the present problems of the *ummah* on the first three *rashidun* (Abu Bakr, Umar and Uthman), who should have allowed Ali to take the leadership in the first place. Many of the more extreme Shiis (known as the *ghulat*: exaggerators) were converts and brought some of their old beliefs into Islam with them. They saw Ali as an incarnation of the divine (like Jesus), believed that Shii leaders who had been killed in an insurrection were in temporary 'occultation', and would return to inaugurate a utopian realm of justice and peace in the Last Days.

But the religious were not the only people who felt alienated from Umayyad rule. The converts to Islam (*mawalis*: clients) objected to their second-class status. There were tribal divisions among the Arab Muslims, some of whom wanted to settle down and integrate with the subject peoples, and others who wanted to continue the old expansionist wars. But the Islamic sentiment had become so widespread that the various revolts and uprisings nearly all adopted a religious ideology. This was certainly true of the revolt that finally toppled the Umayyad dynasty. The Abbasid faction capitalized on the widespread desire to see a member of Muhammad's family on the throne, and emphasized the descent of their leader from the Prophet's uncle Abbas and his son Abdallah, one of the most eminent of the early Quran-reciters. They began to muster support in the Iranian provinces in 743, occupied Kufah in August 749, and defeated the last Umayyad caliph, Mansur II, in Iraq the following year. When they had finally subdued the empire, the Abbasid caliphs would inaugurate a very different kind of society.

The Abbasids: The High Caliphal Period (750–935)

The Abbasids had won support by carefully presenting themselves in a Shii light, but once in power they shed this religious camouflage and showed that they were determined to make the caliphate an absolute monarchy in the traditional agrarian way. Abu al-

Abbas al-Saffah (750–54), the first Abbasid caliph, massacred all the Umayyads he could lay his hands upon. Hitherto the indiscriminate slaughter of a noble Arab family would have been unthinkable. Caliph Abu Jafar al-Mansur (754–75) murdered all the Shii leaders whom he considered a danger to his rule. These caliphs gave themselves titles expressive of the divine right of kings. Al-Mansur indicated that God would give him 'special help' to achieve victory; his son styled himself al-Mahdi (775–85) (the Guided One), the term used by Shiis to describe a leader who would establish the age of justice and peace.

Caliph al-Mahdi might have been trying to woo the Shiis after the bloodshed committed by his father when he chose this title. The Abbasids were acutely aware of the discontent that had helped to bring the Umayyads down and realized that they must make concessions to the disaffected groups. Even though they were Arabs themselves, their victory ended the old practice of giving Arabs privileged status in the empire. They moved their capital from Damascus to Iraq, settling first in Kufah and then in Baghdad. They promised to treat all the provinces equally and not to allow any ethnic group special status, which satisfied the *mawalis*. Their empire was egalitarian in that it was possible for any man of ability to make his way in the court and administration. But the move from Kufah to Baghdad was significant. The caliphs had left behind the ambience of the garrison towns, which had been built on the old tribal model and made each quarter equal and independent. The centre of Baghdad was the famous 'round city', which housed the administration, the court and the royal family. The bazaars and homes of the artisans and servants were relegated to the periphery. Baghdad was built in a convenient location, beside the Tigris and close to the Sawad, the agricultural base of Iraq. But it was also close to Ctesiphon, the capital of the Persian Sassanids, and the new caliphate was modelled on the old pre-Islamic autocracy.

By the time of Caliph Harun al-Rashid (786–809), the transformation was complete. Al-Rashid ruled like an old-style absolute monarch, not like the *rashidun*. He was isolated from his subjects; the old informality that had characterized life under the first caliphs was replaced by elaborate pomp. Courtiers kissed the ground when they came into his presence, in a way that would

have been unimaginable in the days when Arabs prostrated themselves only before God. Where the Prophet had always been
addressed informally by his given name, like any other mortal,
the caliph was styled the 'Shadow of God on earth'. The exe-
cutioner stood behind him, to show that the caliph had the power
of life and death. The caliph no longer supervised the affairs of
the *ummah* himself, but left government to his vizier. His role
was to be a court of ultimate appeal, beyond the reach of factions
and politicking. He led the prayers on Friday afternoons and led
his army into major battles. The army itself had changed, however.
It was no longer a people's army, open to any Muslim, but a corps
of Persians, who had helped the Abbasids into power, who were
seen as the caliph's personal troops.

This was, of course, abhorrent to the religious movement,
whose members had had high hopes of the Abbasids when they
first came to power. But however un-Islamic it was, the new
caliphate was a political and economic success in these early days.
The caliph's role was to provide his subjects with security, and
under Harun al-Rashid, when the caliphate was at its peak, the
empire enjoyed an unprecedented peace. Uprisings had been ruth-
lessly quashed, and the populace could see that opposition to this
regime was pointless, but the upside was that people were able to
live more normal, undisturbed lives. Harun al-Rashid was a patron
of the arts and scholarship, and inspired a great cultural renaissance. Literary criticism, philosophy, poetry, medicine, mathematics and astronomy flourished not only in Baghdad but in
Kufah, Basrah, Jundayvebar and Harran. *Dhimmis* participated in
the floresence by translating the philosophical and medical texts
of classical Hellenism from Greek and Syriac into Arabic. Building
on the learning of the past, which had thus become available to
them, Muslim scholars made more scientific discoveries during
this time than in the whole of previously recorded history. Industry and commerce also flourished, and the elite lived in refinement
and luxury. But it was difficult to see how this regime was in
any way Islamic. The caliph and his entourage lived in splendid
isolation, which could not have been in more marked contrast to
the asceticism of the Prophet and the *rashidun*. Far from confining
themselves to the four wives prescribed in the Quran, they had
vast harems like Sassanian monarchs. Nevertheless, the religious

reformers had no choice but to accept the Abbasids. Islam is a realistic and practical faith, which does not normally encourage the spirit of martyrdom or the taking of pointless risks.

This realism was especially evident among the Shiis. After the tragic death of Husain in Kerbala, his immediate descendants had lived secluded and devout lives in Medina, even though many regarded them as the rightful *imams* of the *ummah*. Husain's oldest son Ali Zayn al-Abidin (d. 714), who was known by Shiis as the Fourth Imam, since he had followed Ali, Hasan and Husain, was a mystic and left behind a beautiful collection of prayers.[3] Muhammad al-Baqir, the Fifth Imam (d. 735), had developed an esoteric method of reading the Quran: each word, each verse had a hidden (*batin*) meaning, which could only be discerned by means of mystical techniques of concentration, similar to those developed in all the world faiths to give the contemplative access to the inner regions of their being. This *batin* meaning probably expounded al-Baqir's new doctrine of the *Imamate*. His brother Zayd ibn Ali was a political activist and was eventually killed in an uprising against the Umayyads in 740. To counter Zayd's claim to be the Imam of his time, al-Baqir argued that the unique *ilm* of the Prophet was passed down the line of Ali's immediate descendants. Each one of the Imams chose his successor and passed on the esoteric lore that enabled him to discover the sacred meaning of scripture. Only the Imam who had received this special designation (*nass*) from his predecessor was the legitimate leader of the Muslims. He – al-Baqir – had received this *nass* from his father; Zayd had not. In 740, however, al-Baqir had few followers; most Shiis preferred Zayd's revolutionary politics to al-Baqir's mystical quietism, but after the Abbasids' ruthless suppression of all Shii dissent, they were ready to listen to Jafar al-Sadiq (d. 765), the Sixth Imam, who had himself been imprisoned by Caliph al-Mansur. Al-Sadiq reaffirmed and developed the doctrine of *nass*, declaring that even though he, as the designated Imam, was the true leader of the *ummah*, he would not press his claim to the caliphate. Henceforth the Imam would be a spiritual teacher; he would impart the divine *ilm* to his generation and guide them in the *batin* reading of the Quran, but Shiis must keep their doctrines and political beliefs to themselves in this dangerous political climate.

But this appealed only to a mystically inclined elite. Most Muslims needed a more accessible piety, and they found it in a new type of devotion, which had first emerged at the end of the Umayyad period but only achieved prominence during the reign of Harun al-Rashid. It was similar to the Christian devotion to Jesus, since it saw the Quran as God's uncreated Word, which had existed with him from all eternity, and which had, as it were, taken flesh and human form in the scripture revealed to Muhammad. Muslims could not see God, but they could hear him each time they listened to a recitation of the Quran, and felt that they had entered the divine presence. When they uttered the inspired words, God's speech was on their tongues and in their mouths; they held him in their hands when they carried the sacred book. This appalled the Mutazilah, since it offended their rational piety and their strict sense of the unity and utter simplicity of God. This doctrine seemed to make the Quran a second divine being. But, like the esoteric Shiah, the Mutazilah was only for an intellectual minority, and this devotion to the Quran became extremely popular. Its adherents were known as the *ahl al-hadith*, the Hadith People, because they insisted that Muslim law must be based on the eyewitness 'reports' of the maxims and customary practice (*sunnah*) of the Prophet. They disagreed with the followers of Abu Hanifah, who had deemed it essential for jurists to use their powers of 'independent reasoning' (*ijtihad*), arguing that they must have the freedom to make new laws, even if they could not be based on a *hadith* or a Quranic utterance.

The *ahl al-hadith* were, therefore, conservatives; they were in love with an idealized past; they venerated all the *rashidun*, and even Muawiyyah, who had been one of the Prophet's companions. Unlike the Mutazilites, who had often been political activists, they insisted that the duty of 'commanding the right and forbidding the wrong' was only for the very few; the rank and file must obey the caliph, whatever his religious credentials. This was attractive to Harun al-Rashid, who was anxious to conciliate the more pious movements and approved of the anti-revolutionary tendency of the *ahl al-hadith*. The Mutazilites fell from favour in Baghdad, and the Hadith People felt encouraged to ostracize them socially. On occasion, at their request, the government even imprisoned leading Mutazilites.

The Abbasids were aware of the strength of the religious movement and, once they had established their dynasty, they had tried to give their regime Islamic legitimacy. They therefore encouraged the development of *fiqh* to regulate the life of the population. A split developed in the empire. The lives of the ordinary people would indeed be governed by the Shariah, as the body of Islamic law was called, but Muslim principles did not prevail in court circles nor among the higher officials of the government, who adhered to the more autocratic norms of the pre-Islamic period in order to make the Abbasid state a going concern.

Under the Umayyads, each town had developed its own *fiqh*, but the Abbasids pressed the jurists to evolve a more unified system of law. The nature of Muslim life had changed drastically since the time of the Quran. Since conversion to Islam had been encouraged, the *dhimmis* were becoming a minority. Muslims were no longer a small elite group, isolated from the non-Muslim majority in the garrison towns. They were now the majority. Some of the Muslims had come to the faith recently, and were still imbued with their old beliefs and practices. A more streamlined system and recognized religious institution was required to regulate Islamic life for the masses. A distinct class of *ulama* (religious scholars; singular: *alim*) began to emerge. Judges (*qadis*) received a more rigorous training, and both al-Mahdi and al-Rashid encouraged the study of law by becoming patrons of *fiqh*. Two outstanding scholars made a lasting contribution. In Medina, Malik ibn Anas (d. 795) compiled a compendium which he called *al-Mutawattah*, *The Beaten Path*. It was a comprehensive account of the customal law and religious practice of Medina, which, Malik believed, still preserved the original *sunnah* of the Prophet's community. Malik's disciples developed his theories into the Maliki School (*madhhab*), which became prevalent in Medina, Egypt and North Africa.

But others were not convinced that present-day Medina was really a reliable guide to pristine Islam. Muhammad Idris ibn al-Shafii (d. 820), who had been born in poverty in Gaza and had studied with Malik in Medina, argued that it was not safe to rely on any one Islamic city, however august its pedigree. Instead all jurisprudence should be based on *ahadith* about the Prophet, who should be seen as the inspired interpreter and not simply as the transmitter of the Quran. The commands and laws of scripture could be understood in the light of Muhammad's words and actions. But, Shafii insisted, each *hadith* had to be reliably supported by a chain (*isnad*) of devout Muslims leading directly back to the Prophet himself. The *isnad* must be stringently examined, and if the chain was broken or if any one of its 'links' could be shown to be a bad Muslim, the *hadith* must be rejected. Al-Shafii tried to mediate between the *ahl al-hadith* and those jurists, such as Abu Hanifah, who had insisted upon the necessity of *ijtihad*. Shafii agreed that some degree of *ijtihad* was necessary, but believed that it should be confined to a strict analogy (*qiyas*) between one of the Prophet's customs and contemporary practice. There were, al-Shafii taught, four 'roots' of sacred law (*usul al-fiqh*): the Quran, the *sunnah* of the Prophet, *qiyas* (analogy) and *ijmah*, the 'consensus' of the community. God would not allow the entire *ummah* to be in error, so if a custom was accepted by all Muslims, it must be recognized as authentic, even if no Quranic reference or *hadith* could be found in its support. Al-Shafii's method was not capable of ensuring the strict historicity of the Prophet's *sunnah*, according to modern standards of accuracy, but it did provide a blueprint for the creation of a way of life that certainly gave Muslims a profound and satisfying religious experience.

Al-Shafii's groundbreaking work led other scholars to the study of *ahadith*, according to his criteria. Two sound and authoritative anthologies were completed by al-Bukhari (d. 870) and Muslim (d. 878), which stimulated interest in *fiqh*, and led eventually to the creation of a homogeneous religious life, based on the sacred law of the Shariah, throughout the vast Islamic Empire. The inspiration of the law was the person of the Prophet, the Perfect Man. By imitating the smallest details of his external life and by reproducing the way he ate, washed, loved, spoke and prayed, Muslims hoped to be able to acquire his interior attitude of perfect surrender to God. Religious ideas and practices take root not because they are promoted by forceful theologians, nor because they can be shown to have a sound historical or rational basis, but because they are found in practice to give the faithful a sense of sacred transcendence. To this day, Muslims remain deeply attached to the Shariah, which has made them internalize the archetypal figure of Muhammad at a very deep level and, liberating him from the seventh century, has made him a living presence in their lives and a part of themselves.

But like all Islamic piety, the Shariah was also political. It constituted a protest against a society that was deemed by the religious to be corrupt. Both Malik ibn Anas and al-Shafii had taken part in Shii uprisings against the early Abbasids; both had been imprisoned for their politics, though they were released and patronized by al-Mahdi and Harun al-Rashid, who wanted to exploit their expertise and create a uniform legal system through-out the empire. The Shariah totally rejected the aristocratic, sophisticated ethos of the court. It restricted the power of the caliph, stressed that he did not have the same role as the Prophet or the *rashidun*, but that he was only permitted to administer the sacred law. Courtly culture was thus tacitly condemned as un-Islamic. The ethos of the Shariah, like that of the Quran, was egalitarian. There were special provisions to protect the weak, and no institution, such as the caliphate or the court, had any power to interfere with the personal decisions and beliefs of the individual. Each Muslim had a unique responsibility to obey God's commands, and no religious authority, no institution (such as 'the Church') and no specialized group of 'clergy' could come between God and the individual Muslim. All Muslims were on the same footing; there was to be no clerical elite or priesthood acting as an intermediary. The Shariah was thus an attempt to rebuild society on criteria that were entirely different from those of the court. It aimed to build a counter-culture and a protest movement that would, before long, bring it into conflict with the caliphate.

By the end of the reign of Harun al-Rashid, it was clear that the caliphate had passed its peak. No single government could control such vast territory indefinitely, before the advent of modern com-munications and modern means of coercion. Some of the per-ipheral provinces, such as Spain (where an escaping Umayyad had set up a rival dynasty in 756) were beginning to break away. The economy was in decline. Harun al-Rashid had tried to solve the problem by dividing the empire between his two sons, but this only resulted in a civil war between the brothers after his death (809–13). It was a mark of the secular spirit of the court at this date that unlike the *fitnah* wars of the past, there was no ideological or religious motivation in this struggle, which was simply a clash of personal ambition. When al-Mamun emerged as the victor and began his reign (813–33), it was clear that there were two main power blocs in the empire. One was the aristocratic circle of the court; the other, egalitarian and 'constitutionalist' bloc, was based on the Shariah.

Al-Mamun was aware of the fragility of his rule. His reign had started with a civil war, with a Shii rebellion in Kufah and Basrah (814–15), and a Kharajite revolt in Khurasan. He tried to woo these disparate groups and reduce the religious tension, but his policies only made matters worse. An intellectual himself, he felt naturally drawn to the rationalism of the Mutazilah and brought them back into favour. He could also see that the populist movement of the *ahl al-hadith*, which insisted that the divine law was directly accessible to every single Muslim, was not compatible with absolute monarchy. Once back in power, however, the Mutazilites turned upon the *ahl al-hadith*, who had persecuted them for so long. An 'inquisition' (*mihnah*) ensued, in which leading Hadith People, notably the popular Ahmad ibn Hanbal (d. 855), were imprisoned. Ibn Hanbal became a folk hero. Championing the Mutazilah had done al-Mamun no good; it had simply alienated the masses. At one point, the caliph tried to reach out towards the Shiis by naming Ali al-Rida, the Eighth Imam, as his heir, but the Shiis were, like the Mutazilah, simply another spiritual and intellectual elite and could not command the support of the ordinary people. A few months later, al-Rida conveniently died – possibly by foul play.

Later caliphs also tried to woo the Shiis and oscillated between one religious faction and another, to no avail. Caliph al-Mutasim (833–42) attempted to strengthen the monarchy by making the army into his own personal corps. These troops were Turkish slaves, who had been captured from beyond the River Oxus and converted to Islam. But this merely separated him still further from the populace, and there was tension between the Turkish soldiers and the people of Baghdad. To alleviate this, the caliph moved his capital to Samarra, some sixty miles to the south, but this simply isolated him still more, while the Turks, who had no natural links with the people, grew more powerful with every decade, until they would eventually be able to wrest effective control of the empire away from the caliphs. Increasingly, during the late ninth and early tenth centuries, there were armed revolts by those militant Shiis who were still committed to political activism and had not retreated into mystical quietism, and the economic crisis grew from bad to worse.

But these years of political disintegration also saw the consolidation of what would become known as Sunni Islam. Gradually, the various legists, the Mutazilah and the *ahl al-hadith* pooled their differences and drew closer together. An important figure in this process was Abu al-Hasan al-Ashari (d. 935), who attempted to reconcile the theology of the Mutazilah with that of the Hadith People. The Mutazilah had been so fearful of anthropomorphic notions of God that they denied that the divine had any 'human' attributes at all. How could we say that God 'spoke' or 'sat on a throne', as the Quran averred? How could we talk of Gods 'knowledge' or 'power'? The *ahl al-hadith* retorted that this wariness drained the experience of God of all content, and reduced the divine to a philosophical abstraction with no religious significance. Al-Ashari agreed, but appeased the Mutazilites by saying that God's attributes were not like human qualities. The Quran *was* God's uncreated speech, but the human words which expressed it and the ink and paper of the book itself were created. There was no point in searching for a mysterious essence underlying reality. All we could know for certain were the concrete facts of history. There were, in al-Ashari's view, no natural laws. The world was ordered at every moment by a direct intervention of God. There was no free will: men and women could not think unless the divine was thinking in and through them; fire burned not because it was its nature to do so, but because God wills it.

The Mutazilah had always been too abstruse for the vast majority of Muslims. Asharism became the predominant philosophy of Sunni Islam. It was obviously not a rationalist creed, but more of a mystical and contemplative discipline. It encouraged Muslims to see the divine presence everywhere, to look *through* external reality to the transcendent reality immanent within it, in the way that the Quran instructed. It satisfied the hunger, that was so evident in the ideas of the Hadith People, for an immediate experience of God in concrete reality. It was also a philosophy that was congenial to the spirit of the Shariah. By observing the *sunnah* of the Prophet in the smallest details of their lives, Muslims iden-tified themselves with Muhammad, whose life had been saturated with the divine. To imitate the Prophet, the Beloved (*habib*) of God – by being kind to orphans, to the poor, or to animals, or by behaving at meals with courtesy and refinement – was to be loved by God himself. By weaving the divine imperative into the interstices of their lives, Muslims were cultivating that constant remembrance (*dhikr*) of God enjoined by the Quran.[4] By the middle of the tenth century this Shariah piety had been established throughout the empire. There were four recognized law schools, each regarded with Muslim egalitarianism as equally valid: the Hanafi, Maliki, Shafii and Hanbali schools, the latter preserving the ideals of Ibn Hanbal and the Hadith People. In practice, these four *madhhab*s did not differ markedly from one another. Each Muslim could choose the one he or she would follow, though most tended towards the one that was prevalent locally.

But as one might expect, the chief factor that drew all Sunni Muslims together was political. The divine was experienced in the form taken by the community, and this affected a Muslim's personal piety. Sunni Muslims all revered Muhammad and all four *rashidun*. Despite the failures of Uthman or Ali, these rulers had been devout men who far surpassed contemporary rulers in the quality of their surrender to God. Sunnis refused to demote the first three *rashidun*, as the Shiis did, believing that Ali alone had been the legitimate *imam* of the *ummah*. Sunni piety was more optimistic than the tragic vision of the Shiah. It asserted that God could be with the *ummah* even in times of failure and conflict. The unity of the community was a sacred value, since it expressed the oneness of God. This was far more important than any sectarian division. It was crucial, therefore, for the sake of peace, to recognize the present caliphs, despite their obvious shortcomings. If Muslims lived according to the Shariah, they could create a counter-culture that would transform the corrupt political order of their day, and make it submit to God's will.

The Esoteric Movements

This piety did not satisfy all Muslims, however, though it became the faith of the majority. Those who were more intellectual or mystically inclined needed to interpret the religion differently. During the Abbasid period, four more complex forms of Islamic philosophy and spirituality emerged that appealed to an elite. These ideas were kept secret from the masses, because the adepts believed that they could easily be misunderstood by those of meaner intelligence, and that they only made sense in a context of prayer and contemplation. The secrecy was also a self-protective device. Jafar as-Sadiq, the Sixth Imam of the Shiah, told his disciples to practise *taqiyyah* (dissimulation) for their own safety. These were perilous times for Shiis, who were in danger from the political establishment. The *ulama*, the religious scholars, also doubted the orthodoxy of these esoteric groups. *Taqiyyah* kept conflict to a minimum. In Christendom, people who held beliefs that were different from the establishment were often persecuted as heretics. In Islam, these potential dissidents kept quiet about their ideas, and usually died in their beds. But the policy of secrecy also had a deeper significance. The myths and theological insights of the esoterics were part of a total way of life. Mystical doctrines in particular could be experienced as imaginatively and intuitively valid, but were not necessarily comprehensible to the ordinary rational understanding of an outsider. They were like a poem or a piece of music, whose effect cannot be explained rationally, and which often requires a degree of aesthetic training and expertise if it is to be appreciated fully.

The esoterics did not think that their ideas were heretical. They believed that they could see a more profound meaning in the revelation than the ordinary *ulama*. It must also be recalled that beliefs and doctrines are not as important in Islam as they are in Christianity. Like Judaism, Islam is a religion that requires people to live in a certain way, rather than to accept certain credal propositions. It stresses orthopraxy rather than orthodoxy. All the Muslims who were attracted to the esoteric disciplines observed the five 'Pillars' (*rukn*) or essential practices of Islam. They were all in full agreement with the *shahadah*, the brief Muslim confession of faith: 'There is no God but Allah, and Muhammad is his prophet.' They performed the *salat* prayer five times daily, paid the *zakat* alms, fasted during Ramadan, and, if their circumstances permitted, made the *hajj* to Mecca at least once in their lives. Anybody who remained faithful to the Pillars was a true Muslim, whatever his or her beliefs.

We have already discussed the quietist form of Shiism, expounded soon after the Abbasids came to power by Jafar as-Saddiq. Even though Shiis were as committed to Shariah piety as Sunnis and had their own *madhhab* (the Jafari School, named after as-Saddiq himself), they looked chiefly for guidance to the current Imam, the repository of divine *ilm* for his generation. The Imam was an infallible spiritual director and a perfect *qadi*. Like Sunnis, Shiis wanted to experience God as directly as the Muslims in the first community, who had witnessed the unfolding reve-lation of the Quran to the Prophet. The symbol of the divinely inspired Imam reflected the Shii sense of sacred presence, dis-cernible only to the true contemplative, but nevertheless imma-nent in a turbulent dangerous world. The doctrine of the Imamate also demonstrated the extreme difficulty of incarnating a divine imperative in the tragic conditions of ordinary political life. Shiis held that every single one of the Imams had been murdered by the caliph of his day. The martyrdom of Husain, the Third Imam, at Kerbala was a particularly eloquent example of the perils that could accrue from the attempt to do God's will in this world. By the tenth century Shiis publicly mourned Husain on the fast day of Ashura (10 Muharram), the anniversary of his death. They would process through the streets, weeping and beating their breasts, declaring their undying opposition to the corruption of Muslim political life, which continued to privilege the rich and oppress the weak, despite the clear commands of the Quran. Shiis who followed Jafar as-Saddiq may have abjured politics, but the passion for social justice was at the heart of their piety of protest.

During the ninth century the hostility between the Abbasid establishment and the Shiis came to the fore again as the caliphate declined. Caliph al-Mutawakkil (847–61) summoned the Tenth Imam, Ali al-Hadi, from Medina to Samarra and placed him under house arrest. He felt that he could not risk allowing this direct descendant of the Prophet to remain at large. Henceforth, the Imams were virtually inaccessible to the Shiah, and could only communicate with the faithful through 'agents'. When the Eleventh Imam died in 874, it was said that he left behind a young son, who had gone into hiding to save his life. Certainly there was no obvious trace of the Twelfth Imam, who may already have been dead. But still, the agents ruled the Shiah on his behalf, guiding their esoteric study of the Quran, collecting *zakat*, and issuing legal judgements. In 934, when the Hidden Imam would have reached the term of his natural life, the 'agent' brought the Shiis a special message from him. He had gone into 'occultation', and had been miraculously concealed by God; he could have no further contact with the Shiah. He would return one day to inaugurate an era of justice, but only after a long time had passed. The myth of the Occultation of the Hidden Imam was not intended to be taken literally, as a statement of mundane fact. It was a mystical doctrine, which expressed our sense of the divine as elusive, absent, or just out of reach, present in the world but not of it. It also symbolized the impossibility of implementing a truly religious policy in this world, since the caliphs had destroyed Ali's line and driven *ilm* from the earth. Henceforth the Shii *ulama* became the representatives of the Hidden Imam, and used their own mystical and rational insights to apprehend his will. Twelver Shiis (who believed in the twelve Imams) would take no further part in political life, since in the absence of the Hidden Imam, the true leader of the *ummah*, no government could be legitimate. Their messianic piety, which yearned for the Imam's return, was expressive of a divine discontent with the state of the community.

Not all Shiis were Twelvers, and not all abjured politics. Some (called Seveners or Ismailis) held that Ali's line had ended with Ismail, the son of Jafar as-Sadiq, who had been designated Imam but had died before his father. They did not, therefore, recognize the legitimacy of Jafar's second son Musa al-Kazim, whom Twelvers revered as the Seventh Imam.[5] They also developed an esoteric spirituality that looked for a hidden (*batin*) meaning in scripture, but instead of retiring from public life, they tried to devise a wholly different political system and were often activists. In 909 an Ismaili leader managed to seize control of the province of Tunisia, giving himself the messianic title of al-Mahdi (the Guided One). In 983 the Ismailis wrested Egypt from the Abbasids also, and set up their own rival caliphate in Cairo, which lasted nearly two hundred years. There were also secret Ismaili cells in Syria, Iraq, Iran and the Yemen. Members were initiated gradually into the sect by the local *dai* (agent). The religion practised in the lower grades was not unlike Sunnism, but as the initiate pro-gressed he was introduced to a more abstruse philosophy and spirituality, which made use of mathematics and science as a means of awakening a sense of transcendent wonder. Ismailis' meditations on the Quran gave them a cyclical view of history, which they believed to have been in decline ever since Satan had rebelled against God. There had been six great prophets (Adam, Noah, Abraham, Moses, Jesus and Muhammad) who had each reversed this downward trend. Each prophet had an 'executor' who taught the secret meaning of his message to those who were capable of understanding it. Aaron, for example, had been Moses's executor, and Ali had been Muhammad's. As the faithful struggled to put their teachings into practice, they would prepare the world for the final reign of justice, which would be inaugurated by the seventh prophet, the Mahdi.

It was an attractive movement. Where the Sunni protest against the court had made Sunnis suspicious of the arts and sciences, Ismailism offered the more intellectual Muslims a chance to study the new philosophy in a religious way. Their spiritual exegesis was a process of *tawil* (carrying back), which directed the attention of the worshipper beyond the literal meaning of scripture to the hidden, divine reality that was its original source. The Quran insists that God communicates with the faithful by means of 'symbols' (*ayat*), since the divine can never be expressed in wholly rational or logical discourse. Ismailis always alluded to God in the phrase, 'He Whom the boldness of thought cannot contain'. They also believed that no one revelation or theological system could ever be definitive, since God was always greater than human thought. Ismailis agreed that Muhammad had been the last and most important of the six major prophets, but also insisted that the full significance of the revelation that he had brought to the Arabs would only become clear when the Mahdi arrived. They were, therefore, open to the possibility of new truth, which was alarming to the more conservative of the *ulama*. But the Ismailis were not simply a contemplative sect. Like all true Muslims, they were concerned about the fate of the *ummah*, and believed that faith was worthless unless it was combined with political activism. By working for a just and decent society, they would pave the way for the arrival of the Mahdi. The Ismailis' success in establishing an enduring caliphate showed that their ideal had political potential, but it could never appeal to the majority. The Ismaili vision was too hierarchical and elitist to appeal to more than a small number of intellectual Muslims.

The Ismailis derived a good deal of their cosmic symbolism from Falsafah, the third of the esoteric movements that emerged at this time. It sprang from the cultural renaissance inaugurated by the Abbasids, in particular the discovery of Greek philosophy, science and medicine that were now available to Muslims in Arabic. The Faylasufs were enthralled by the Hellenistic cult of reason; they believed that rationalism was the highest form of religion, and wanted to relate its more elevated insights to the revelation of the Quran. They had a difficult task. The Supreme Deity of Aristotle and Plotinus was very different from Allah. It did not concern itself with earthly events, had not created the world, and would not judge it at the end of time. Where monotheists had experienced God in the historical events of this world, the Faylasufs agreed with the Greeks that history was an illusion; it had no beginning, middle or end, since the universe emanated eternally from its First Cause. The Faylasufs wanted to get beyond the transient flux of history, and learn to see the changeless, ideal world of the divine that lay beneath it. They regarded human reason as a reflection of the Absolute Reason which is God. By purifying our intellects of all that was not rational and learning to live in a wholly reasonable way, human beings could reverse the process of eternal emanation away from the divine, ascend from the multiplicity and complexity of life here below to the simplicity and singularity of the One. This process of catharsis, the Faylasufs believed, was the primordial religion of all humankind. All other cults were simply inadequate versions of the true faith of reason.

Yet the Faylasufs were usually devout men, who believed that they were good Muslims. Their rationalism was itself a kind of faith, because it takes courage and great trust to believe that the world is rationally ordered. A Faylasuf dedicated himself to living the whole of his life in a reasonable manner; he wanted to bring all his experiences and values together so that they formed a consistent, total and logical world-view. It was, perhaps, a philosophical version of *tawhid*. Faylasufs were good Muslims too in their social concern; they despised the luxurious society of the court and the despotism of the caliphs. Some of them wanted to transform society according to their ideal. They worked as astrologers and physicians in the court and other great households, and this had a marked though marginal effect on the culture. None of the Faylasufs attempted such a comprehensive reformation as the *ulama*, however, and produced nothing with the popular appeal of the Shariah.

Yaqub ibn Ishaq al-Kindi (d. 870) was the first major Faylasuf or 'Philosopher' of the Muslim world. Born in Kufah and educated in Basrah, he settled finally in Baghdad, where he enjoyed the patronage of al-Mamun. In the capital he worked closely with the Mutazilites in their attempt to rid theology (*kalam*) of anthropomorphism, but he did not confine himself, as they did, to Muslim sources, but sought wisdom also from the Greek sages. Thus he applied Aristotle's proof for the existence of the First Cause to the God of the Quran. Like all the later Faylasufs, he believed that Muslims should seek truth wherever it was found, even from foreign peoples whose religion was different from their own. The revealed teachings in the Quran about God and the soul were parables of abstract philosophical truths, which made them accessible to the masses, who were incapable of rational thought. Revealed religion, therefore, was a 'poor man's Falsafah', as it were. A Faylasuf like al-Kindi was not trying to subordinate revelation to reason, but to see the inner soul of scripture, in rather the same way as the Shiis sought the *batin* truth of the Quran.

It was, however, a musician of Turkish origin who fully established the Islamic tradition of rationalistic philosophy. Abu Nasr al-Farabi (d. 950) went further than al-Kindi in seeing philosophy as higher than revealed religion, which became, in his view, a mere expedient and a natural social necessity. Where al-Farabi differed from both the Greek rationalists and from Christian philosophers, however, was in the importance he gave to politics. He seems to have believed that the triumph of Islam had at last made it possible to build the rational society that Plato and Aristotle had only been able to dream about. Islam was a more reasonable religion than its predecessors. It had no illogical doctrines, such as the Trinity, and stressed the importance of law. Al-Farabi believed that Shii Islam, with its cult of the Imam as the guide of the community, could prepare ordinary Muslims to live in a society ruled by a philosopher-king on rational principles. Plato had argued that a well-ordered society needed doctrines which the masses believed to be divinely inspired. Muhammad had brought a law, backed by such divine sanctions as hell, which would persuade the ignorant in a way that more logical arguments could not. Religion was thus a branch of political science, and should be studied and observed by a good Faylasuf, even though he would see further to the kernel of the faith than the average Muslim.

It is significant, however, that al-Farabi was a practising Sufi. The different esoteric groups tended to overlap and to have more in common with one another than with the more conservative *ulama*. Mystically inclined Shiis and Faylasufs tended to gravitate together, as did Shiis and Sufis, who may have had different political views but shared a similar spiritual outlook. Sufism, the mysticism of Sunni Islam, is different from the other schools that we have considered, since it did not develop an overtly political philosophy. Instead, it seemed to have turned its back on history, and Sufis sought God in the depths of their being rather than in current events. But nearly all religious movements in Islam take off, at least, from a political perspective, and Sufism was no exception. It had its roots in the asceticism (*zuhd*) that developed during the Umayyad period as a reaction against the growing worldliness and luxury of Muslim society. It was an attempt to get back to the primitive simplicity of the *ummah* when all Muslims had lived as equals. The ascetics often wore the kind of coarse woollen garment (*tasawwuf*) that was standard among the poor, as the Prophet had done. By the early ninth century the term *tasawwuf* (which gives us our 'Sufi') had become synonymous with the mystical movement that was slowly developing in Abbasid society.

Sufism was also probably a reaction against the growth of jurisprudence, which seemed to some Muslims to be reducing Islam to a set of purely exterior rules. Sufis wanted to reproduce within themselves that state of mind that made it possible for Muhammad to receive the revelations of the Quran. It was his interior *islam* that was the true foundation of the law, rather than the *usul al-fiqh* of the jurists. Where establishment Islam was becoming less tolerant, seeing the Quran as the only valid scripture and Muhammad's religion as the one true faith, Sufis went back to the spirit of the Quran in their appreciation of other religious traditions. Some, for example, were especially devoted to Jesus, whom they saw as the ideal Sufi since he had preached a gospel of love. Others maintained that even a pagan who prostrated himself before a stone was worshipping the Truth (*al-haqq*) that existed at the heart of all things. Where the *ulama* and the jurists were increasingly coming to regard revelation as finished and complete, the Sufis, like the Shiis, were constantly open to the possibility of new truths, which could be found anywhere, even in other religious traditions. Where the Quran described a God of strict justice, Sufis, such as the great woman ascetic Rabiah (d. 801) spoke of a God of love.

All over the world and in every major faith tradition, men and women who have a talent for this type of interior journey have developed certain techniques that enable them to enter deeply into the unconscious mind and experience what seems like a presence in the depths of their being. Sufis learned to concentrate their mental powers while breathing deeply and rhythmically; they fasted, kept night vigils, and chanted the Divine Names attributed to God in the Quran as a mantra. Sometimes this induced a wild, unrestrained ecstasy, and such mystics became known as 'drunken Sufis'. One of the earliest of these was Abu Yazid al-Bistami (d. 874), who wooed Allah like a lover. But he also learned the discipline of *fanah* (annihilation): by gradually peeling away the layers of egotism (which, all spiritual writers agree, holds us back from the experience of the divine), Al-Bistami found an enhanced self in the ground of his own being that was nothing other than Allah himself, who told al-Bistami: 'I am through Thee; there is no god but Thou.' This potentially shocking rewording of the *shahadah* expresses a profound truth, which has been discovered by mystics in many different faith traditions. The *shahadah* proclaimed that there was no God, no reality but Allah, so it must be true that once self is finally cancelled out in a perfect act of *islam*, all human beings are potentially divine. Husain al-

Mansur (d. 922), also known as al-Hallaj, the Wool-Carder, is said to have made a similar claim, crying: '*Ana al-Haqq!*' ('I am the Truth!' or 'I am the Real!'), though some scholars have suggested that this should read: 'I *see* the Truth!'

Hallaj was executed by the *ulama* for claiming that it was possible to make a valid *hajj* in spirit, while staying at home. His death shows the hostility that was developing between the Sufis and the *ulama*. Junayd of Baghdad (d. 910), the first of the so-called 'sober Sufis', withdrew from this type of extremism. He thought that the intoxication experienced by al-Bistami was merely a phase which the mystic must transcend in order to achieve an enhanced sense of self and a more complete self-possession. When a Sufi first heard the divine call, he or she became aware of their painful separation from the source of all being. The mystical journey was simply a return to what is truly natural to humanity, a doctrine very similar to that held by Buddhists. Sufism remained a fringe movement during the first Abbasid period, but later Sufi masters would build on Junayd's system and create an esoteric movement which, unlike the others we have considered, would captivate the majority of Muslims.

Even though they all claimed to be devout, committed Muslims, the esoterics had all changed the religion of the Prophet. Muhammad would have been startled by the doctrines of the Faylasufs, and Ali would almost certainly not have recognized the ideas and myths of the Shiis, who declared themselves to be his partisans. But, despite the convictions of many of the faithful in any tradition, who are convinced that religion never changes and that their beliefs and practices are identical with those of the founders of their faith, religion must change in order to survive. Muslim reformers would find the esoteric forms of Islam inauthentic, and would try to get back to the purity of the first *ummah*, before it was corrupted by these later accretions. But it is never possible to go back in time. Any 'reformation', however conservative its intention, is always a new departure, and an adaptation of the faith to the particular challenges of the reformer's own time. Unless a tradition has within it the flexibility to develop and grow, it will die. Islam proved that it had this creative capacity. It could appeal at a profound level to men and women who lived in conditions that were quite different from the desperate, brutal era of the Prophet. They could see meaning in the Quran that went far beyond the literal sense of the words, and which transcended the circumstances of the original revelations. The Quran became a force in their lives that gave them intimations of the sacred, and which enabled them to build fresh spiritualities of great power and insight.

The Muslims of the ninth and tenth centuries had moved far from the first little beleaguered *ummah* in Medina. Their philosophy, *fiqh*, and mystical disciplines were rooted in the Quran and in the beloved figure of the Prophet, but because scripture was God's word, it was thought to be infinite and capable of multiple interpretation. They were thus able to make the revelation speak to Muslims who lived in a world that the Prophet and the *rashidun* could not have imagined. But one thing remained constant. Like the religion of the very first *ummah*, the philosophy, law and spirituality of Islam were profoundly political. Muslims were acutely aware – in a way that was admirable – that for all its glittering cultural attainments, the empire they had created did not live up to the standards of the Quran. The caliph was the leader of the *ummah*, but he lived and ruled in a way that would have horrified the Prophet. Whenever there was a marked discrepancy between the Quranic ideal and the current polity, Muslims would feel that their most sacred values had been violated; the political health of the *ummah* could touch the deepest core of their being. In the tenth century, the more perceptive Muslims could see that the caliphate was in trouble, but so alien was it to the spirit of Islam that Muslims would experience its decline as a liberation.

3 CULMINATION

A New Order (935–1258)

By the tenth century it was clear that Islamdom could no longer function effectively as a single political unit. The caliph would remain the nominal head of the *ummah* and retain a symbolic, religious function, but in practice the different regions of the empire were governed independently. From Egypt, the breakaway caliphate of the Ismaili Fatimids[1] ruled North Africa, Syria, much of Arabia, and Palestine; in Iraq, Iran and Central Asia, Turkish army officers (*amirs*) seized power and established what were really independent states, competing with one another militarily. The tenth century has been called the Shii century, because many of these dynasties had vague Shii leanings. But all the *amirs* continued to acknowledge the Abbasid caliph as the supreme leader of the *ummah*, so entrenched was the ideal of absolute monarchy. These dynasties achieved some political success. One even managed to found a permanent Muslim base in north-west India in the early eleventh century. But none managed to survive for very long, until the Seljuk Turks, from the lower Syr basin, seized power in Baghdad in 1055 and came to a special arrangement with the caliph, who recognized them as his lieutenants throughout the Dar al-Islam. During the years before the Seljuk victory, it had seemed as though the empire was doomed to perpetual disintegration. As one dynasty succeeded another and as frontiers shifted, an outside observer might have been justified in assuming that, after an initial period of success, Islamdom was in decline.

But he would have been wrong. In fact, almost by accident, a new order was emerging that would be much more congenial to the Muslim spirit. Despite the political turbulence, Islamic religion was going from strength to strength. Each region had its own capital, so that instead of one cultural centre in Baghdad, there

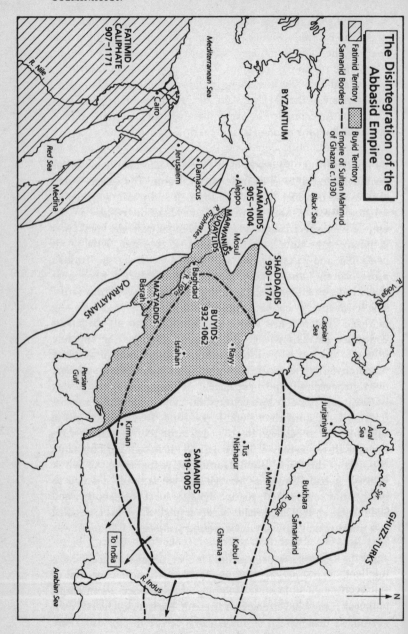

The Disintegration of the Abbasid Empire

Fatimid Territory
Samanid Borders
Buyid Territory
Empire of Sultan Mahmud of Ghazna c.1030

FATIMID CALIPHATE 909–1171

R. Nile
Cairo
Red Sea
Medina
Jerusalem
Damascus
Mediterranean Sea
BYZANTIUM
Aleppo
HAMANIDS 905–1004
Mosul
R. Euphrates
MARWANIDS
UQAYLIDS
Black Sea
SHADDADIS 950–1174
R. Volga
Caspian Sea
QARMATIANS
Basrah
MAZYADIDS
R. Tigris
Baghdad
BUYIDS 932–1062
Rayy
Isfahan
Persian Gulf
Kirman
To India
Arabian Sea
R. Indus
SAMANIDS 819–1005
Tus
Nishapur
Merv
R. Oxus
Bukhara
Samarkand
Kabul
Ghazna
Aral Sea
Jurjaniyah
R. Syr
GHUZZ-TURKS
N

were now several. Cairo became a vital city of art and learning under the Fatimids. Philosophy flourished there and in the tenth century the caliphs founded the college of al-Azhar, destined to become the most important Islamic university in the world. Samarkand also saw a Persian literary renaissance. One of its luminaries was the Faylasuf Abu Ali ibn Sina (980–1037), who is known as Avicenna in the West. Ibn-Sina had been a disciple of al-Farabi, but took religion far more seriously. In his view a prophet was the ideal philosopher, not merely a purveyor of abstract rational truth for the masses, because he had access to insights that did not depend upon discursive thought. Ibn Sina was interested in Sufism, and recognized that mystics attained an experience of the divine that could not be reached by logical processes, but which did cohere with Faylasuf notions. Both Falsafah and the faith of the mystics and the conventionally pious were therefore in harmony.

Cordova also experienced a cultural florescence, even though the Umayyad caliphate in Spain had eventually collapsed in 1010 and disintegrated into a number of rival, independent courts. The Spanish renaissance was particularly famous for its poetry, which resembled that of the French troubadour courtly tradition. The Muslim poet Ibn Hazam (994–1064) developed a simpler piety, which relied solely on *ahadith*, and jettisoned complex *fiqh* and metaphysical philosophy. Nevertheless, one of Spain's later intellectual stars was the Faylasuf Abu al-Walid Ahmad ibn Rushd (1126–98), who was less important in the Muslim world than the more mystically inclined Ibn-Sina, but whose rationalistic thought influenced such Jewish and Christian philosophers as Maimonides, Thomas Aquinas and Albert the Great. In the nineteenth century the philologist Ernest Renan hailed Ibn-Rushd (who is known in the West as Averroes) as a free spirit, an early champion of rationalism against blind faith. But in fact, Ibn-Rushd was a devout Muslim and a *qadi* judge of Shariah law. Like Ibn-Sina, he believed that there was no contradiction between religion and Falsafah, but that while religion was for everybody, only an intellectual elite should attempt philosophy.

It seems that once the caliphate had been – for all practical purposes – abandoned, Islam got a new lease of life. There had always been tension between the ideals of absolute monarchy and the Quran. The new polities that were emerging in the Islamic world by a process of trial and error were closer to the Islamic vision. Not that all the new rulers were pious Muslims – far from it – but the system of independent courts and rulers, all on a par with one another but contained within a loose notional unity, approximated more truly with the egalitarian spirit of the Quran. It was also in harmony with the art that was emerging in the Muslim world at this period. The arabesque does not give more emphasis to one letter than to another; each character has its place and makes its unique contribution to the whole. Muslim historians, such as Ibn Ishaq and Abu Jafar at-Tabari (d. 923) made little attempt to synchronize the sometimes conflicting traditions about the Prophet's life, but simply juxtaposed rival versions, giving each equal value. Muslims had accepted the caliphate because it guaranteed the unity of the *ummah*, but once the caliphs showed that they could not integrate the empire any longer, they were content to relegate them to symbolic status. There was a change in Islamic piety. Hitherto, theology and spirituality had nearly always been rooted in a political response to the historical circumstances of the Muslim community. But now that Muslims had more congenial political arrangements, Muslim thought and devotion were less driven by current events. Significantly, Islam became more political again during the modern period, when Muslims faced new perils which, they felt, put the moral, cultural and religious wellbeing of the *ummah* in jeopardy, and even threatened its very survival.

It was the Seljuk Turks who, more by accident than design, gave fullest expression to the new order in the Fertile Crescent, where this decentralization was more advanced. The Seljuks were Sunnis, with a strong tendency towards Sufism. Their empire was ruled from 1063 to 1092 by the brilliant Persian vizier Nizamulmulk, who wanted to use the Turks to restore unity to the empire and rebuild the old Abbasid bureaucracy. But it was too late to revive Baghdad, since the agricultural region of the Sawad, the basis of its economy, was in irreversible decline. Nor was Nizamulmulk able to control the Seljuk army, a cavalry force of nomadic tribesmen who were still a law unto themselves and moved with their herds wherever they wished. But, with the aid of a new slave corps, Nizamulmulk did build an empire which reached as far as the Yemen in the south, to the Syr-Oxus basin in the east, and into Syria in the west. This new Seljuk Empire had very few formal political institutions, and order was imposed at the local level by the *amirs* and the *ulama*, who set up an *ad hoc* partnership. The *amirs* who commanded the various districts pre-empted Nizamulmulk's centralizing plans by becoming virtually independent, administering their own regions, and taking the land revenues directly from the inhabitants instead of from Baghdad. This was not a feudal system, since, whatever the vizier may have intended, the *amirs* were not the vassals of the caliph nor of the Seljuk Sultan Malikshah. The *amirs* were nomads, who had no interest in farming their territory, so they did not form a feudal aristocracy, tied to the land. They were soldiers, and not much interested in the civil life of their subjects, which became in effect the province of the *ulama*.

The *ulama* held these scattered military regimes together. During the tenth century they had become dissatisfied with the standard of their education, and had established the first *madrasahs*, colleges for the study of Islamic sciences. This made their training more systematic, their learning more uniform, and enhanced the status of the clergy. Nizamulmulk encouraged the building of *madrasahs* throughout the Seljuk Empire, adding subjects to the curriculum that would enable the *ulama* to work in local government. In Baghdad, he founded the prestigious Nizamiyyah *madrasah* in 1067. Now that they had their own institutions, the *ulama* had a power base, which became distinct from but equivalent to the military courts of the *amirs*. The standardized *madrasahs* also promoted the homogeneous Muslim lifestyle fostered by the Shariah throughout the Seljuk domains. The *ulama* also monopolized the legal system in their Shariah courts. A *de facto* split had thus occurred between political power and the civil life of the community. None of the mini-states run by the *amirs* lasted long; they had no political ideology. The *amirs* were very temporary functionaries, and all the idealism of the empire was provided by the *ulama* and the Sufi masters (*pirs*), who had their own separate sphere. Learned *ulama* would travel from one *madrasah* to another; the Sufi *pirs* were notoriously mobile, journeying from one town and one centre to another.

The religious personnel began to provide the glue that held the disparate society together.

Thus after the demise of the effective caliphate the empire became more Islamic. Instead of feeling that they belonged to one of the ephemeral states of the *amirs*, Muslims began to see themselves as members of a more international society, represented by the *ulama*, which was coextensive with the whole Dar al-Islam. The *ulama* adapted the Shariah to these new circumstances. Instead of using Muslim law to build a counter-culture, the Shariah now saw the caliph as the symbolic guardian of the sacred law. As the *amirs* came and went, the *ulama*, with the backing of the Shariah, became the only stable authority, and as Sufism became more popular, the piety of the people deepened and acquired an interior dimension.

Sunni Islam now seemed in the ascendant almost everywhere. Some of the more radical Ismailis, who had become disillusioned with the Fatimid Empire, which had so signally failed to impose the true faith on the *ummah*, set up an underground network of guerrillas, dedicated to the overthrow of the Seljuks and the destruction of the Sunnah. From 1090 they conducted raids from their mountain fortress in Alamut, north of Qazvin, seizing Seljuk strongholds and murdering leading *amirs*. By 1092 this had become a full-scale revolt. The rebels became known by their enemies as the *hashishin* (which gives us our word 'assassin'), because they were said to use hashish to give them the courage to take part in attacks that often resulted in their own death. The Ismailis believed that they were the champions of the ordinary people, who were themselves often harassed by the *amirs*, but this campaign of terror turned most Muslims against the Ismailis. The *ulama* spread wild and inaccurate stories about them (the hashish legend being one of these myths); people who were suspected of being Ismailis were rounded up and killed, and these massacres led to fresh Ismaili attacks. But despite this opposition, the Ismailis managed to build a state around Alamut, which lasted 150 years and which only the Mongol invaders were able to destroy. The immediate effect of their *jihad* however, was not, as they had hoped, the advent of the Mahdi, but the discrediting of the whole of the Shiah. The Twelvers, who had taken no part in the Ismaili revolt, were careful to appease the Sunni authorities

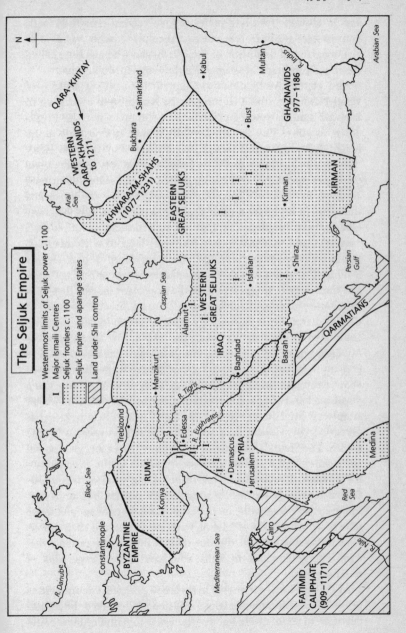

The Seljuk Empire

— Westernmost limits of Seljuk power c.1100
I Major Ismaili Centres
···· Seljuk frontiers c.1100
∴∴ Seljuk Empire and apanage states
▨ Land under Shii control

N

QARA-KHITAY

Arabian Sea

GHAZNAVIDS
977-1186

• Kabul
• Multan
R. Indus

• Bust

• Samarkand

WESTERN QARA-KHANIDS to 1211

• Bukhara

KIRMAN

Aral Sea

KHWARAZM-SHAHS
(1077-1231)

EASTERN
GREAT SELJUKS

• Kirman

I I I I I

I

I
I WESTERN
GREAT SELJUKS

• Isfahan

• Shiraz

Persian Gulf

Caspian Sea

Alamut I

I
IRAQ

I

QARMATIANS

Manzikurt

R. Tigris

• Baghdad

• Basrah

RUM

Trebizond

I • Edessa
R. Euphrates

• Damascus
SYRIA

Medina

Konya

• Jerusalem

Red Sea

Black Sea

Constantinople

• Cairo

R. Danube

BYZANTINE
EMPIRE

Mediterranean Sea

R. Nile

FATIMID
CALIPHATE
(909-1171)

and to abstain from any political involvement. For their part, Sunnis were ready to respond to a theologian, who was able to give magisterial definition of their faith, and who has been called the most important Muslim since the Prophet Muhammad.

Abu Hamid Muhammad al-Ghazzali (d. 1111), a protégé of vizier Nizamulmulk, a lecturer at the Nizamiyyah madrasah in Baghdad, and an expert in Islamic law, suffered a nervous breakdown in 1095. The Ismaili revolution was at this time at its height, but al-Ghazzali was chiefly distressed by the possibility that he was losing his faith. He found that he was paralyzed and could not speak; his doctors diagnosed a deep-seated emotional conflict, and later al-Ghazzali explained that he was concerned that though he knew a great deal *about* God, he did not know God himself. He therefore went off to Jerusalem, practised Sufi exercises, and returned to Iraq ten years later to write his masterpiece *Ihyah ulum al-Din* (*The Revival of the Religious Sciences*). It became the most-quoted Muslim text after the Quran and the *ahadith*. It was based on the important insight that only ritual and prayer could give human beings a direct knowledge of God; the arguments of theology (*kalam*) and Falsafah, however, could give us no certainty about the divine. The *Ihyah* provides Muslims with a daily spiritual and practical regimen, designed to prepare them for this religious experience. All the Shariah rules about eating, sleeping, washing, hygiene and prayer were given a devotional and ethical interpretation, so that they were no longer simply external directives, but enabled Muslims to cultivate that perpetual consciousness of the divine that is advocated by the Quran. The Shariah had thus become more than a means of social conformity, and a slavish exterior imitation of the Prophet and his *sunnah*: it became a way of achieving interior *islam*. Al-Ghazzali was not writing for the religious experts, but for devout individuals. There were, he believed, three sorts of people: those who accept the truths of religion without questioning them; those who try to find justification for their beliefs in the rational discipline of *kalam*; and the Sufis, who have a direct experience of religious truth.

Al-Ghazzali was aware that in their new political circumstances people needed different religious solutions. He disliked the Ismaili devotion to an infallible Imam: where was this Imam? How could ordinary people find him? This dependence upon an authority figure seemed to violate the egalitarianism of the Quran. Falsafah, he acknowledged, was indispensable for such disciplines as mathematics or medicine, but it could give no reliable guide to spiritual matters that lie beyond the use of reason. In al-Ghazzali's view, Sufism was the answer, because its disciplines could lead to a direct apprehension of the divine. In the early days, the *ulama* had been alarmed by Sufism, and regarded it as a dangerous fringe movement. Now al-Ghazzali urged the religious scholars to practise the contemplative rituals that the Sufi mystics had developed and to promote this interior spirituality at the same time as they propagated the external rules of the Shariah. Both were crucial to Islam. Al-Ghazzali had thus given mysticism a ringing endorsement, using his authority and prestige to assure its incorporation into mainstream Muslim life.

Al-Ghazzali was recognized as a supreme religious authority in his own time. During this period Sufism became a popular movement, and was no longer confined to an elite. Now that the people's piety was not preoccupied, as in the early days, with the politics of the *ummah*, they were ready for the a-historical, mythical inward journey of the mystic. Instead of being a solitary practice for esoteric Muslims, *dhikr* (the chanting of the Divine Names) became a group activity that propelled Muslims into an alternative state of consciousness, under the guidance of their *pir*. Sufis listened to music to heighten their awareness of transcendence. They clustered around their *pirs*, as Shiis had once gathered around their Imams, seeing them as their guide to God. When a *pir* died, he became, in effect, a 'saint', a focus of sacredness, and the people would pray and hold *dhikrs* at his tomb. Each town now had its *khanqah* (convent), as well as a mosque or a *madrasah*, where the local *pir* instructed his disciples. New Sufi orders (*tariqahs*) were formed, which were not bound to a particular region but which were international, with branches all over the Dar al-Islam. These *tariqahs* thus became another source of unity in the decentralized empire. So were the new brotherhoods and guilds (*futuwwahs*) for artisans and merchants in the towns, which were greatly influenced by Sufi ideals. Increasingly, it was the Islamic institutions that were pulling the empire together and, at the same time, the faith of even the most uneducated Muslims was acquiring an inner resonance that had once been the preserve of a sophisticated and esoteric elite.

Henceforth there would be no theological or philosophical discourse in Islam that was not deeply fused with spirituality. New 'theosophers' began to expound this new Muslim synthesis. In Aleppo, Yahya Suhrawardi (d. 1191) founded a school of illumination (al-ishraq) based on ancient pre-Islamic Iranian mysticism. He saw true philosophy as the result of a marriage between the disciplined training of the intellect through Falsafah, and the interior transformation of the heart effected by Sufism. Reason and mysticism must go hand in hand; both were essential to human beings, and both were needed in the pursuit of truth. The visions of the mystics and the symbols of the Quran (such as heaven, hell and the Last Judgement) could not be proved empirically, but could only be glimpsed by the trained intuitive faculty of the contemplative. Outside this mystical dimension, the myths of religion made no sense, because they were not 'real' in the same way as earthly phenomena which we experience with our normal waking consciousness. A mystic trained him- or herself to see the interior dimension of earthly existence by means of the Sufi disciplines. Muslims had to cultivate a sense of the *alam al-mithal*, 'the world of pure images', which exists between our ordinary world and God's. Even those who were not trained mystics became aware of this world in dreams or in the hypnogogic imagery that can surface as we fall asleep or into a tranced state. When a prophet or a mystic had a vision, Suhrawardi believed, he had become aware of this interior realm, which could correspond to what we call the unconscious mind today.

This type of Islam would have been unrecognizable to Hasan al-Basri or Shafii. Suhrawardi may have been executed for his views but he was a devout Muslim, who quoted the Quran more extensively than any previous Faylasuf. His works are still read as mystical classics. So are the books of the prolific and highly influential Spanish theosopher Muid ad-Din ibn al-Arabi (d. 1240), who also urged Muslims to discover the *alam al-mithal* within them, and taught that the way to God lay through the creative imagination. Ibn al-Arabi's books were not easy and appealed to the more intellectual Muslims, but he believed that anybody could be a Sufi, and that everybody should look for the symbolic, hidden meaning of scripture. Muslims had a duty to create their own theophanies, by training their imaginations to see below the surface to the sacred presence that resides in everything and everyone. Every single human being was a unique and unrepeatable revelation of one of God's hidden attributes, and the only God we will ever know was the Divine Name inscribed in our inmost self. This vision of a personal Lord was conditioned by the faith tradition into which a person was born. Thus the mystic must see all faiths as equally valid, and is at home in a synagogue, mosque, temple or church, for, as God says in the Quran: 'Wheresoever ye turn, there is the face of Allah.'[2]

Thus there had been a religious revolution after the demise of the caliphate. It affected the humble artisan as well as the sophisticated intellectual. A truly Muslim people had come into being, which had learned to endorse the faith at a profound level. Muslims had responded to what might have been a political disaster with a vast spiritual renewal, which reinterpreted the faith to meet the new conditions. Islam was now thriving without government support. Indeed, it was the only constant in a world of political flux.

The Crusades

The new order of politically autonomous *amirs*, which had come into being under the Seljuk Turks, continued after their empire had begun to fall apart at the end of the eleventh century. The system had obvious drawbacks. The *amirs* constantly fought one another, and found it very difficult to band together against an external foe. This became tragically apparent in July 1099, when the Christian Crusaders from western Europe attacked Jerusalem, the third holiest city in the Islamic world after Mecca and Medina, massacred its inhabitants, and established states in Palestine, the Lebanon and Anatolia. The *amirs* of the region, who were fighting each other as the Seljuk Empire declined, could make no united riposte, and seemed powerless against this aggressive Western intrusion. It was fifty years before Imad ad-Din Zangi, *amir* of Mosul and Aleppo, was able to drive the Crusaders from Armenia in 1144, and almost another half-century before Yusuf ibn Ayyub

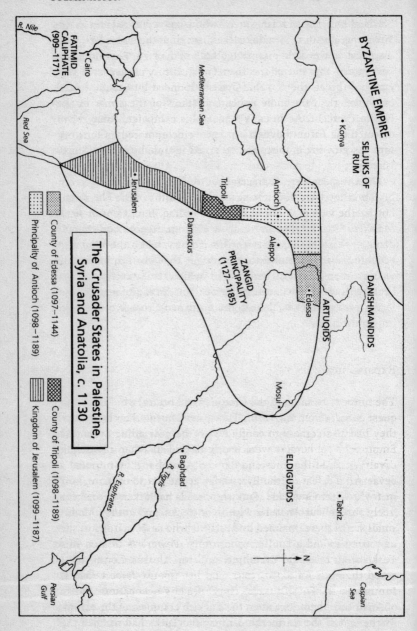

BYZANTINE EMPIRE

FATIMID
CALIPHATE
(909–1171)

SELJUKS OF
RUM

DANISHMANDIDS

• Cairo

• Konya

Mediterranean Sea

R. Nile

Red Sea

• Jerusalem

Tripoli

Antioch

• Damascus

Aleppo

ZANGID
PRINCIPALITY
(1127–1185)

Edessa

ARTUQIDS

Mosul •

ELDIGUZIDS

• Tabriz

• Baghdad

R. Euphrates

R. Tigris

Persian
Gulf

Caspian
Sea

**The Crusader States in Palestine,
Syria and Anatolia, c. 1130**

County of Edessa (1097–1144)

Principality of Antioch (1098–1189)

County of Tripoli (1098–1189)

Kingdom of Jerusalem (1099–1187)

N

Salah ad-Din, the Kurdish general who is known as Saladin in the West, was able in 1187 to take Jerusalem from the Crusaders, who managed, however, to retain a foothold in the Near East along the coast until the end of the thirteenth century. Because of this external threat, the Ayyubid dynasty founded by Saladin lasted far longer than the more ephemeral states of the *amirs* in the Fertile Crescent. At an early stage of his campaign, Saladin had defeated the Fatimid dynasty in Egypt, incorporated its territory into his growing empire, and returned its inhabitants to Sunni Islam.

The Crusades were disgraceful but formative events in Western history; they were devastating for the Muslims of the Near East, but for the vast majority of Muslims in Iraq, Iran, Central Asia, Malaysia, Afghanistan and India, they were remote border incidents. It was only in the twentieth century, when the West had become more powerful and threatening, that Muslim historians would become preoccupied by the medieval Crusades, looking back with nostalgia to the victorious Saladin, and longing for a leader who would be able to contain the neo-Crusade of Western imperialism.

Expansion

The immediate cause of the Crusades had been the Seljuks' conquest of Syria from the Fatimids in 1070. During their campaign, they had also come into conflict with the now ailing Byzantine Empire, whose borders were poorly defended. When the Seljuk cavalry crossed the lines and entered Anatolia, they inflicted a devastating defeat on the Byzantines at the Battle of Manzikurt in 1071. Within a decade, Turkish nomads had taken to roaming freely throughout Anatolia with their flocks, and *amirs* founded small states there, manned by Muslims who saw Anatolia as the new frontier and a land of opportunity. Powerless to stop this Turkish advance, the Byzantine emperor Alexius Comnenus I asked the Pope for aid in 1091, and in response Pope Urban II summoned the First Crusade. The Crusaders' occupation of parts of Anatolia did not long stem the Turkish conquest of the region. By the end of the thirteenth century the Turks had reached the

Mediterranean; during the fourteenth century they crossed the Aegean, settled in the Balkans, and reached the Danube. Never before had any Muslim ruler been able to inflict such a defeat upon Byzantium, which had behind it the prestige of the ancient Roman Empire. It was with pride, therefore, that the Turks called their new state in Anatolia 'Rum' or Rome. Despite the decline of the caliphate, Muslims had now expanded into two areas that had never before been part of the Dar al-Islam – eastern Europe and a portion of north-west India – and which would become highly creative regions in the near future.

Caliph al-Nasir (1180–1225) tried to restore the caliphate in Baghdad and its environs. Seeing the power of the religious revival, he tried to draw upon Islam. Originally, the Shariah had been developed in protest against caliphal rule, but now al-Nasir studied to become an *alim* in all four of the Sunni law schools. He was also initiated into one of the *futuwwah* clubs, with the aim of making himself the Grand Master of all the *futuwwahs* in Baghdad. After al-Nasir's death, his successors continued these policies. But it was too late. The Islamic world was shortly engulfed in a catastrophe which would finally bring the Abbasid caliphate to a violent and tragic end.

The Mongols (1220–1500)

In the Far East, the Mongol chieftain Genghis Khan was building a world empire, and a clash with Islamdom was inevitable. Unlike the Seljuks, he was able to control and discipline his nomadic hordes, and made them into a fighting machine with a destructive power that the world had never seen before. Any ruler who failed to submit immediately to the Mongol chieftains could expect to see his major cities entirely laid waste and their populations massacred. The Mongols' ferocity was a deliberate technique but it also expressed the nomads' pent-up resentment of urban culture. When Muhammad, Shah of the Khwarazmian Turks (1200–1220), attempted to build a Muslim caliphate of his own in Iran and the Oxus region, the Mongol general Hulegu regarded it as an act of insolent hubris. From 1219 to 1229 the Mongol armies pursued Muhammad and his son Jalal al-Din across Iran, through Azerbaijan and into Syria, leaving a trail of death and devastation behind them. In 1231, a new series of raids began. One great Muslim city after another was demolished. Bukhara was reduced to rubble, Baghdad fell after a single battle, and took the moribund caliphate with it: corpses filled the streets, and refugees fled to Syria, Egypt or India. The Ismailis of Alamut were massacred, and though the new Seljuk dynasty of Rum submitted to the Mongols at once, it never fully recovered. The first Muslim ruler who was able to stop the Mongols in their tracks was Baibars, the sultan of the new Egyptian state ruled by a Turkish slave-corps. The Mamluks (slaves) had dominated the army of the Ayyubid Empire founded by Saladin; in 1250 the Mamluk *amirs* had led a successful coup against the Ayyubid state, and founded their own empire in the Near East. In 1260 Baibars inflicted a defeat on the Mongol army at Ain Jalut in northern Palestine. After their sortie into India had been deflected by the new sultanate based in Delhi, the Mongols settled down to enjoy the fruits of victory, creating empires in the heartlands of Islamdom that owed allegiance to Kublai, the Mongol Khan in China.

The Mongols created four large states. The descendants of Hulegu, who were known as Il-Khans (representatives of the Supreme Khan) at first refused to accept that their defeat was final, and destroyed Damascus before they eventually acquiesced and retired to their empire in the Tigris-Euphrates valley and the mountainous regions of Iran. The Chaghatay Mongols established a state in the Syr-Oxus basin, while the White Horde was established in the Irtysh region, and the Golden Horde around the River Volga. It was the greatest political upheaval in the Middle East since the Arab invasions of the seventh century, but unlike the Arab Muslims the Mongols brought no spirituality with them. They were, however, tolerant of all religions, though they tended towards Buddhism. Their law code, the Yasa, which was attributed to Genghis Khan himself, was a narrowly military system, which did not affect civilians. It was Mongol policy to build on local traditions once they had subjugated an area, and so by the end of the thirteenth and the beginning of the fourteenth centuries all four of the Mongol empires had converted to Islam.

The Mongols therefore became the chief Muslim power in the central Islamic heartlands. But whatever their official allegiance

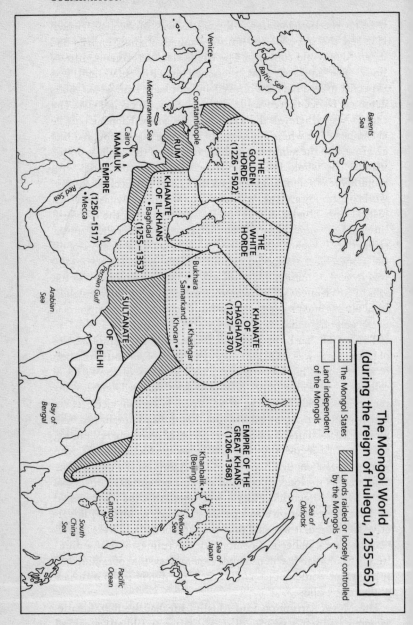

The Mongol World (during the reign of Hulegu, 1255–65)

The Mongol States

Lands raided or loosely controlled by the Mongols

Land independent of the Mongols

Barents Sea

Baltic Sea

Mediterranean Sea

Venice

Constantinople

RUM

THE GOLDEN HORDE (1226–1502)

THE WHITE HORDE

KHANATE OF IL-KHANS (1255–1353)

Baghdad

Cairo

MAMLUK EMPIRE (1250–1517)

Mecca

Red Sea

Persian Gulf

Arabian Sea

Bukhara

Samarkand

Khorasan

KHANATE OF CHAGHATAY (1227–1370)

Khashgar

SULTANATE OF DELHI

Bay of Bengal

EMPIRE OF THE GREAT KHANS (1206–1368)

Khanbalik (Beijing)

Canton

Yellow Sea

Sea of Japan

Sea of Okhotsk

South China Sea

Pacific Ocean

84

to Islam, the main ideology of their states was 'Mongolism', which glorified the imperial and military might of the Mongols and dreamed of world conquest. The whole state was run on military lines. The monarch was the commander-in-chief, and was expected to lead his men himself and not leave campaigns to his deputies. Hence there was, in the early days, no capital city. The capital was wherever the khan and his army happened to be encamped. The whole apparatus of the state was conducted like an army, and the administration accompanied the soldiers on the march. The whole intricate camp-culture was conducted with remarkable efficiency. There were two chief political objectives: world hegemony and the perpetuation of the ruling dynasty, which justified any cruelty. It was an ideology similar to the old absolutist polity, which had believed that the greater the ruler's power, the better the peace and security of the state. The decrees of all the monarchs of a dynasty remained in force as long as the family was in power, marginalizing all other legal systems. All the top jobs in government were given to members of the family and their local clients and *protégés*, who were all drawn into the entourage of the great nomadic army at the core of the state.

There could hardly be a greater contrast with the egalitarianism of Islam, but it was, in a sense, a continuation of the militarization of society that had occurred in the final years of the Abbasid caliphate, where the *amirs* had ruled from the garrisons, leaving the civilians and the *ulama* to their own Islamic devices. There had always been the possibility that the military might interfere more in civil affairs, if an *amir* had achieved anything resembling stability. To a degree, this happened under the Mongol rulers, who were powerful enough to put new constraints on the *ulama*. The Shariah was no longer permitted to be a potentially subversive code. By the fifteenth century it was agreed that the *ulama* could no longer use their own independent judgement (*ijtihad*) in creative legislation; it was said that 'the gates of *ijtihad*' were closed. Muslims were obliged to conform to the rulings of past authorities. The Shariah had in principle become a system of established rules, which could not jeopardize the more dynamic dynastic law of the ruling house.

The Mongol irruption into Muslim life had been traumatic. Mongols had left a swathe of ruined cities and libraries behind them, as well as economic recession. But once they had achieved victory, the Mongols rebuilt the cities they had devastated on a magnificent scale. They also established brilliant courts, which promoted science, art, history and mysticism. Appalling as the Mongol scourge had been, the Mongol rulers were fascinating to their Muslim subjects. Their political structures remained subtly enduring and, as we shall see, influenced later Muslim empires. The Mongols' power had suggested new horizons. They had seemed about to conquer the world, and had been a portent of a new kind of imperialism, which linked the possibility of universal rule with mass destruction. The splendour of their states dazzled, at the same time as they undermined Muslim preconceptions. Muslims were not stunned into passivity by the horrors they had lived through, nor by the political defeat that these Mongol states represented. Islam is a resilient faith. Frequently in their history Muslims had responded positively to disaster, and used it constructively to gain fresh religious insights. So too after the Mongol invasions, when people clearly felt that the world as they had known it was coming to an end, but also that an entirely new global order was possible.

This was clearly evident in the vision of the Sufi mystic Jalal al-Din Rumi (1207–73), who was himself a victim of the Mongols but whose teachings expressed the sense of boundless possibility that they had brought with them. Rumi had been born in Khurasan; his father was an *alim* and a Sufi master, and Rumi himself was learned in *fiqh*, theology, and Arabic and Persian literature. But to escape the approaching Mongol hordes, the family was forced to flee. They came as refugees to Konya, the capital of the Sultanate of Rum, in Anatolia. Rumi's spirituality is suffused by a sense of cosmic homelessness and separation from God, the divine source. The greatest misfortune that could befall any human being, Rumi insisted, was not to feel the pain of severance, which goads a man or woman to the religious quest. We must realize our inadequacy and that our sense of selfhood is illusory. Our ego veils the reality from us, and by divesting ourselves of egotism and selfishness we will find that God is all that remains.

Rumi was a 'drunken Sufi'. His spiritual and personal life veered from one emotional extreme to another; he sought ecstasy in dancing, singing, poetry and music, and the members of the order that he founded are often called the Whirling Dervishes because of their stately, spinning dance, which induces a tranced state of transcendence. Despite his obvious instability, Rumi was known in his lifetime as Mawlanah (our Lord) by his disciples, and his Mawlanah Order has had great influence in Turkey right up to the present day. The *Mathnawi*, his magnum opus, is known as the Sufi scripture. Where Ibn al-Arabi had written for the intellectual, Rumi was summoning all human beings to live beyond themselves, and to transcend the routines of daily life. The *Mathnawi* celebrated the Sufi lifestyle which can make everyone an indomitable hero of a battle waged perpetually in the cosmos and within the soul. The Mongol invasions had led to a mystical movement, which helped people come to terms with the catastrophe they had experienced at the deeper levels of the psyche, and Rumi was its greatest luminary and exemplar. The new Sufi *tariqahs* founded at this time stressed the unlimited potential of human life. Sufis could experience on the spiritual plane what the Mongols had so nearly achieved in terrestrial politics.

Others responded to the upheavals of the period very differently. The destruction of the invasions, when so much had been lost, led to an intensification of the conservatism that always characterized agrarian society. When resources were limited, it was impossible to encourage inventiveness and originality in the way that we do today in the modern West, where we expect to know more than our parents' generation and that our children will experience still greater advance. No society before our own could afford the constant retraining of personnel and replacement of the infrastructure that innovation on this scale demands. Consequently, in all pre-modern societies, including that of agrarian Europe, education was designed to preserve what had already been achieved and to put a brake on the ingenuity and curiosity of the individual, which could undermine the stability of a community that had no means of integrating or exploiting fresh insights. In the *madrasahs*, for example, pupils learned old texts and commentaries by heart, and the teaching consisted of a word-by-word explication of a standard textbook. Public disputations between scholars took it for granted that one of the debaters was right and the other wrong. There was no idea, in the question-and-answer style of study, of allowing the clash of two opposing positions to build a new synthesis. Thus the *madrasahs* promoted an acceptance of those notions that could unite Muslims throughout the world, and stamped down on heterodox ideas that would cause dissension and tempt people to leave the straight path and go their own way.

By the fourteenth century, the study and observance of the Shariah was the only type of piety to be accepted by all Muslims, Sunni and Shii, Sufi and Faylasuf alike. By this time, the *ulama* liked to believe that these laws had been in place from the very beginning of Islamic history. Thus while some Sufis, such as Rumi, were beginning to glimpse new horizons, many of the *ulama* believed that nothing ever changed. Hence they were content that the 'gates of *ijtihad*' were closed. After the loss of so much of the learning of the past, the destruction of manuscripts, and the slaughter of scholars, it was more important to recover what had been lost than to inaugurate more change. Because the Mongol military code made no provision for civil society, the *ulama* continued to govern the lives of the faithful, and their influence tended to be conservative. Where Sufis like Rumi believed that all religions were valid, by the fourteenth century the *ulama* had transformed the pluralism of the Quran into a hard communalism, which saw other traditions as irrelevant relics of the past. Non-Muslims were forbidden now to visit the holy cities of Mecca and Medina, and it became a capital offence to make insulting remarks about the Prophet Muhammad. The trauma of the invasions had, not surprisingly, made Muslims feel insecure. Foreigners were not only suspect; they could be as lethal as the Mongols.

But there were *ulama* who refused to accept the closing of the 'gates of *ijtihad*'. Throughout Islamic history, at times of great political crisis – especially during a period of foreign encroachment – a reformer (*mujdadid*) would often renew the faith so that it could meet the new conditions. These reforms usually followed a similar pattern. They were conservative, since they attempted to go back to basics rather than create an entirely new solution. But in this desire to return to the pristine Islam of the Quran and *sunnah*, the reformers were often iconoclastic in sweeping away later medieval developments that had come to be considered sacred. They were also suspicious of foreign influence, and alien accretions, which had corrupted what they saw as the purity of the faith. This type of reformer would become a feature of Muslim society. Many of the people who are called 'Muslim fundamentalists' in our own day correspond exactly to the old pattern set by the *mujdadids*.

In the post-Mongol world, the great reformer of the day was Ahmad ibn Taymiyyah (1263–1328), an *alim* of Damascus, which had suffered so terribly at the hands of the Mongols. Ibn Taymiyyah came from an old family of *ulama* who belonged to the Hanbali *madhhab*, and wanted to reinforce the values of the Shariah. He declared that even though the Mongols had converted to Islam, they were in fact infidels and apostates, because they had promulgated the Yasa instead of the Shariah. Like a true reformer, he attacked Islamic developments that had occurred after the Prophet and the *rashidun* as inauthentic: Shiism, Sufism and Falsafah. But he also had a positive programme. In these changed times, the Shariah had to be brought up to date to fit the actual circumstances of Muslims, even if this meant getting rid of much of the *fiqh* that had developed over the centuries. It was essential, therefore, that jurists use *ijtihad* to find a legal solution that was true to the spirit of the Shariah, even if it infringed the letter of the law as this had been understood in recent times. Ibn Taymiyyah was a worrying figure to the establishment. His return to the fundamentals of the Quran and *sunnah* and his denial of much of the rich spirituality and philosophy of Islam may have been reactionary, but it was also revolutionary. He outraged the conservative *ulama*, who clung to the textbook answers, and criticized the Mamluk government of Syria for practices which contravened Islamic law as he understood it. Ibn Taymiyyah was imprisoned, and was said to have died of sorrow, since his gaolers would not permit him to write. But the ordinary people of Damascus loved him, because they could see that his Shariah reforms had been liberal, and that he had had their interests at heart. His funeral became a massive demonstration of popular acclaim.

Change could be exciting but it was also disturbing. In Tunis, Abd al-Rahman ibn Khaldun (1332–1406) watched one dynasty after another fail in the Maghrib, the western region of the Islamic world. Plague destroyed whole communities. Nomadic tribes had migrated from Egypt into North Africa, causing massive devastation and a corresponding decline in traditional Berber society. Ibn-Khaldun had himself emigrated to Tunisia from Spain, where the Christians had conducted a successful *reconquista* of Muslim territory, taking Cordova in 1236 and Seville in 1248. All that was left of the thriving Muslim kingdom of al-Andalus was the city-state of Granada, which would be defeated by the Christians in 1492 but not before building the magnificent Alhambra palace there in the mid fourteenth century. Islam was clearly in crisis. 'When there is an entire alteration of conditions,' Ibn-Khaldun reflected, 'it is as if the whole creation had changed and all the world had been transformed, as if there were a new creation, a rebirth, a world brought into existence anew.'[3]

Ibn-Khaldun wanted to discover the underlying causes of this change. He was probably the last great Spanish Faylasuf; his great innovation was to apply the principles of philosophic rationalism to the study of history, hitherto considered to be beneath the notice of a philosopher, because it dealt only with transient, fleeting events instead of eternal truths. But Ibn-Khaldun believed that, beneath the flux of historical incidents, universal laws governed the fortunes of society. He decided that it was a strong sense of group solidarity (*asibiyyah*) that enabled a people to survive and, if conditions were right, to subjugate others. This conquest meant that the dominant group could absorb the resources of the subject peoples, develop a culture and a complex urban life. But as the ruling class became accustomed to a luxurious lifestyle, complacency set in and they began to lose their vigour. They no longer took sufficient heed of their subjects, there was jealousy and infighting, and the economy would begin to decline. Thus the state became vulnerable to a new tribal or nomadic group, which was in the first flush of its own *asibiyyah*, and the whole cycle began again. Ibn-Khaldun's masterpiece *Al-Maqaddimah: An Introduction to History* applied this theory to the history of Islam, and would be read closely by Muslim empire-builders in coming years, as well as by Western historians in the nineteenth century, who saw Ibn-Khaldun as a pioneer of their scientific study of history.

Ibn-Khaldun was able to watch the decline of the Mongol states during the second half of the fourteenth century, which clearly confirmed his theory. Their original *asibiyyah* had peaked, complacency had set in, and the stage was now set for other dominant groups to take control. It seemed likely that the new leaders would come not from the Islamic heartlands, but from the fringes of the Muslim world, which had not been subject to Mongol rule. By this time, the Mamluk Empire in Egypt and Syria had also started its decline. At its height, the Mamluks had created a vibrant society, with a strong *esprit de corps*, and a flourishing culture. But by the fifteenth century the empire had outrun its resources, and, like any agrarian state, had begun to fall apart.

The ruler who most fully expressed the spirit of the age was a Turk from the Syr Valley, who had grown up in the Mongol Chaghaytay state in Samarkand, and was passionate about the Mongol ideal. Timur (1336–1405), known as Timur Lane (Timur the Lame) because of a pronounced limp, and Tamburlaine in the West, seized power in the declining Chaghaytay Empire, claimed Mongol descent, and began to reconquer the old Mongol territory with the savagery that had characterized the original invasions. Timur combined his thirst for achievement and love of destruction with a passion for Islam, and because he so perfectly enshrined the enthusiasms of his day, he became a folk hero. He erected magnificent buildings in Samarkand, where he presided over a splendid court. His version of Islam – bigoted, cruel and violent – bore little relation to the conservative piety of the *ulama* or the Sufi doctrine of love. He saw himself as the scourge of Allah, sent to punish the Muslim *amirs* for their unjust practices. His chief concern was to establish order and punish corruption, and even though his subjects feared Timur's brutality, they appreciated his strong government after the disintegration of recent years. Like the Mongols before him, Timur seemed unstoppable, and for a time it looked as though he would achieve world conquest. By 1387 he had subjugated all the Iranian highlands and the plains of Mesopotamia. In 1395 he conquered the old Golden Horde in Russia, and in 1398 he descended upon India, where he massacred thousands of Hindu prisoners and devastated Delhi. Two years later he had conquered Anatolia, sacked Damascus, and perpetrated a massacre in Baghdad. Finally, in 1404, he set off for China, where he was killed the following year.

No one was able to keep Timur's empire intact. World conquest was clearly still an impossible dream, but the discovery of gunpowder weapons during the fifteenth century would enable new Muslim rulers to establish substantial but more manageable empires in the late fifteenth and early sixteenth centuries, which also attempted to wed the Mongol idea with Islam. These new empires would take root in India, Azerbaijan and Anatolia.

The Sultanate of Delhi had been established during the thirteenth century, and by the early fourteenth century Islam was soundly established in the Ganges basin as far as Bengal. In the mountainous regions, a few Hindu Rajputs, the Indian ruling class, held aloof, but most Hindus accepted Muslim supremacy. This was not as surprising as it might appear. The caste system confined the exercise of political authority to a limited number of families, and when these had been exhausted, Hindus were willing to accept anybody in their place, provided that they did not infringe the caste regulations. As outsiders, Muslims were not bound by these strictures, and they had the strength of a powerful international society behind them. Muslims remained a minority in India. Some lower castes and trades, including some of the 'untouchables', converted to Islam, often as a result of the preaching of Sufi *pirs*. But the majority retained their Hindu, Buddhist or Jain allegiance. It is not true, as often averred, that Muslims destroyed Buddhism in India. There is evidence for only one attack on one monastery, and no concrete data to support widespread slaughter. By 1330 the greater part of the subcontinent acknowledged the authority of the Sultanate of Delhi, but unwise government on the part of the sultans led to rebellions among the Muslim *amirs*, and it became evident that the sultanate was too big for one person to govern. In the usual way, the central power disintegrated and the *amirs* ruled their own states, with the help of the *ulama*. Until the advent of gunpowder, the Delhi sultanate remained one power among many in Muslim India.

On the fringes of the Mongol states, the *ghazi* warriors had been left to run their own amirates, acknowledging the Mongol rulers as their overlords. These *ghazi* states were usually religious with a strong tendency towards Sufism. In Azerbaijan and Anatolia, *tariqahs* were formed which adapted some of the wilder forms of Sufism to the revolutionary ethos of the old Shiah. They revived the *ghuluww* 'extremist' theology that had inspired the very early Shiis, revering Ali as an incarnation of the divine, believing that their dead *amirs* had gone into 'occultation', and often revering their leader as the Mahdi, who had returned to inaugurate a new age of justice. The Bekhtashi dervishes in Anatolia had a broad popular following, and preached the imminent advent of a new order that would sweep away the old religious norms. Similarly iconoclastic was the Safaviyyah order in Azerbaijan, which began as a Sunni *tariqah* but which by the fifteenth century had been attracted by the *ghuluww* ideas, and called themselves Twelver Shiis. They believed that their leader was a descendant of the Seventh Imam, and was thus the only legitimate leader of the Muslim *ummah*. By the early sixteenth century, Ismail, the *pir* of the Order, who may also have believed himself to be a reincarnation of the Hidden Imam, would found a Shii empire in Iran.

When the Mongol states collapsed, the whole of Anatolia was divided into small independent *ghazi* states, which, since the late thirteenth century, had started to wrest towns and villages from the declining Byzantine Empire. One of the smallest of these states was ruled by the Osmanli family, which became increasingly powerful during the early years of the fourteenth century. In 1326 the Osmanlis or Ottomans had conquered Bursa, which became their capital; in 1329 they had taken Iznik, and by 1372 they had seized the greater part of the territory of Byzantium. They established a new capital at Edirne (Adrianople), and had reduced the Byzantine emperor to a dependent ally. The secret of Ottoman success was the discipline of its trained infantry, known as the 'new troop' (*yeni-cheri* or Janissary), a slave corps. Murad I (1360–89) had become the most powerful of the western Muslim rulers, and by 1372 was ready to advance into the Balkans, attacking the independent kingdoms of Bulgar and Serbia, the most important power in the Balkan peninsula. In 1389 the Ottomans defeated the Serbian army at Kossovo Field in central Serbia. Murad was killed, but the Serbian Prince Hrelbeljanovic Lazar was captured and executed. It marked the end of Serbian independence and, to this day, Serbians revere Prince Lazar as a martyr and national hero, and have nurtured a profound hatred of Islam. But the Ottoman advance continued, and was by no means unpopular with the majority of Byzantine subjects. The old empire had been in disarray, the Ottomans brought order and a revived economy, and many of the populace were attracted to Islam. The Ottomans suffered a major setback in 1402, when Timur had defeated their army at Angora, but they were able to reconsolidate their power after Timur's death, and in 1453 Mehmed II (1451–81) was able to conquer Constantinople itself, using the new gunpowder weapons.

For centuries, the Byzantine Empire, which the Muslims had called 'Rum' (Rome), had held Islam at bay. One caliph after another had been forced to concede defeat. Now Mehmed 'the Conqueror' had fulfilled the old dream. The Muslims were on the brink of a new age. They had survived the Mongol trauma and found a new strength. By the end of the fifteenth century Islamdom was the greatest power bloc in the world. It had advanced into eastern Europe, into the Eurasian steppes, and into sub-Saharan Africa in the wake of Muslim traders. In the thirteenth century Muslim merchants had also established themselves along the coast of the southern seas in East Africa, southern Arabia, and the western coast of the Indian subcontinent. Muslim merchants, every one a missionary for the faith, had settled in Malaysia at a time when Buddhist trade had collapsed there, and soon enjoyed immense prestige. Sufi preachers followed the businessmen, and by the fourteenth and fifteenth centuries Malaysia was predominantly Muslim. The whole world seemed to be becoming Islamic: even those who did not live under Muslim rule discovered that the Muslims controlled the high seas, and that when they left their own lands they had to confront Islamdom. Even when the European navigators made their astonishing discoveries in the late fifteenth and early sixteenth centuries, they could not dislodge the Muslims from the seaways. Islam seemed invincible, and now Muslims were ready to establish new empires, which would become the most powerful and up-to-date in the world.

4 ISLAM TRIUMPHANT

Imperial Islam (1500–1700)

The discovery and exploitation of gunpowder led to the development of a military technology that gave rulers more power over their subjects than before. They could control greater areas more effectively, provided that they also developed an efficient, rationalized administration. The military state, which had been a feature of Islamic politics since the decline of Abbasid power, could now come into its own. In Europe also, monarchs were beginning to build large centralized states and absolute monarchies, with a more streamlined government machinery. Three major Islamic empires were created in the late fifteenth and early sixteenth centuries: the Safavid Empire in Iran, the Moghul Empire in India, and the Ottoman Empire in Anatolia, Syria, North Africa and Arabia. Other impressive polities also appeared. A large Muslim state was formed in Uzbekhistan in the Syr-Oxus basin; another state with Shii tendencies was established in Morocco, and even though Muslims were at this time in competition with Chinese, Japanese, Hindu and Buddhist traders for the control of the Malaysian archipelago, the Muslims came out on top in the sixteenth century.

It was, therefore, a period of triumph. The three major empires all seemed to turn their backs on the egalitarian traditions of Islam, and set up absolute monarchies, however. Almost every facet of public life was run with systematic and bureaucratic precision and the empires developed a sophisticated administration. They were all influenced by the Mongol idea of the army state, but involved civilians in their imperial policies, so that the dynasties won more grass-roots support. But these empires were very different from the old Abbasid state in one important respect. The Abbasid caliphs and their court had never been truly Islamic institutions; they had not been subject to the laws of the Shariah and had evolved their own worldly ethos. The new empires, however, all had a strongly Islamic orientation, promoted by the rulers themselves. In Safavid Iran, Shiism became the state religion; Falsafah and Sufism were dominant influences on Moghul policy; while the Ottoman Empire was run entirely on Shariah lines.

But the old problems remained. However pious an absolute monarch might seem to be, such autocracy was fundamentally opposed to the spirit of the Quran. Most of the people still lived in poverty, and suffered the injustices that were endemic to agrarian society. There were also new difficulties. Moghul India and Anatolia, the heartland of the Ottoman Empire, were both places where Muslims were relative newcomers. Both would have to learn to relate to their non-Muslim subjects, who formed the majority of the population. The establishment of a Shii Empire caused a new and decisive rift between Sunnis and Shiis, leading to an intolerance and an aggressive sectarianism that was unprecedented in the Islamic world but which was similar to the bitter conflict between Catholics and Protestants that erupted at the same time in Europe. There was also the challenge of Europe itself, which had hitherto been a backward region and of little interest to Muslims. Europe, however, was just beginning to evolve an entirely new kind of civilization, free of the constraints of agrarian society, which would eventually enable the West not only to overtake but to subjugate the Islamic world. The new Europe was beginning to flex its muscles, but in the sixteenth century it was still no real threat. When the Russians invaded Muslim Kazan and Astrakhan (1552–56), and imposed Christianity there, Muslims profited from this defeat by opening new lines of trade with northern Europe. The Iberian navigators who had discovered the Americas in 1492 and opened new sea-routes around the globe had given Portuguese merchants added mobility. In the second half of the sixteenth century they tried to ruin Muslim trade in the South Seas by conducting a neo-Crusade in the Red Sea. These exploits of the Portuguese were of great importance to the West, but made little impact on the Islamic world. Muslims were far more interested in the establishment of a Shii Empire in Iran; the spectacular successes of the early Safavids were a severe blow to Sunni expectations. For the first time for centuries, a stable, powerful and enduring Shii state had been planted right in the heart of Islamdom.

The Safavid Empire

The Safavid Sufi order in Azerbaijan, which had converted to Twelver Shiism, had for some time been conducting *ghazu* raids against the Christians of Georgia and the Caucasus, but it had also incurred the wrath of the *amirs* of Mesopotamia and western Iran. In 1500, sixteen-year-old Ismail succeeded to the *pir*-ship of the order, and set out to avenge his father, who had died at the hands of the *amirs*. In 1501 Ismail conquered Tabriz in the course of his campaign, and then went on to subjugate the rest of Iran during the next decade. He declared that Twelver Shiism would be the official religion of his new empire.

This was a startling development. Until this date, most Shiis had been Arabs. There were Shii centres in Iran: in Rayy, Kashan and Khurasan, as well as the old garrison town of Qum, but most Iranians were Sunnis. Ismail therefore set about eliminating Sunnism in Iran: the Sufi *tariqahs* were suppressed, and the *ulama* either executed or deported. Members of the administration were required to curse the first three *rashidun*, who had 'usurped' power that should by rights have been given to Ali. No Shii rulers had ever attempted anything on this scale before; modern weaponry was giving the religious establishment a new coercive power. During the last two hundred years there had been a detente between Shiis and Sunnis. For centuries, Twelver Shiism had been an esoteric, mystical sect, which had withdrawn from politics, believing that no government could be legitimate in the absence of the Hidden Imam. How could there be a 'state Shiism'? Shah Ismail was not moved by this reasoning. He probably knew very little about Twelver orthodoxy, since he subscribed to the folk extremist *ghuluww* Shiism of the new *tariqahs*, which believed that the messianic utopia was at hand. He may even have told his followers that he was the Hidden Imam, and had returned to fight the battles of the Last Days. His *jihad* against Sunni Islam did not end in Iran. In 1510 he ousted the Sunni Uzbeks from Khurasan and pushed them north of the Oxus; he also attacked the Sunni

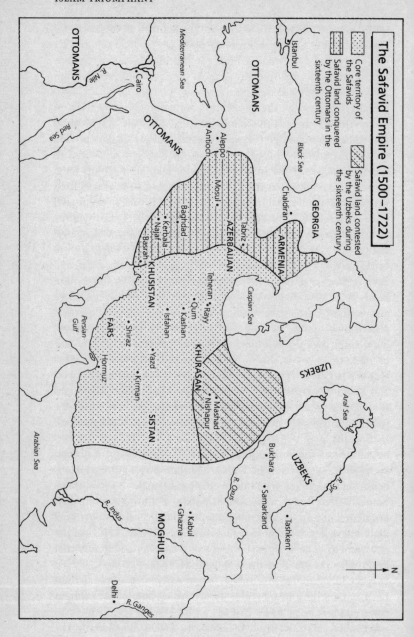

The Safavid Empire (1500–1722)

Core territory of the Safavids

Safavid land conquered by the Ottomans in the sixteenth century

Safavid land contested by the Uzbeks during the sixteenth century

Ottomans, but was defeated by Sultan Selim I at the Battle of Chaldiran in 1514. His attempt to quash the Sunnah outside his domains failed, but Ismail's offensive within Iran was successful. By the late seventeenth century most Iranians were solidly Shii, and have remained so to the present day.

Shah Ismail established a military state, but relied heavily on the civilians, who ran the administration. Like the old Sassanid and Abbasid monarchs, the shah was called the 'Shadow of God on earth', but Safavid legitimacy was based on Ismail's claim to be a descendant of the *Imams*. It did not take the Safavids long, however, to realize that their extremist ideology, which had fired their revolutionary zeal in opposition, would not serve them well once they had become the establishment. Shah Abbas I (1588–1629) rid his bureaucracy of those who held *ghuluww* views, imported Arab Shii *ulama* from abroad to teach the people a more orthodox form of Twelver Shiism, built *madrasahs* for them, and gave them generous financial support. Under Abbas, the empire reached its zenith. He achieved important territorial victories against the Ottomans, and his capital at Isfahan enjoyed a cultural renaissance, which, like the recent Italian renaissance in Europe, drew inspiration from the pagan past of the region; in the case of Iran, this meant the old pre-Islamic Persian culture. This was the period of such great Safavid painters as Bihzad (d. 1535) and Riza-i Abbari (d. 1635), who produced luminous and dream-like miniatures. Isfahan became a magnificent city of parks, palaces, and huge open squares, with imposing mosques and *madrasahs*.

The new *ulama* immigrants were in a strange position, however. As a private group, they had never had their own Shii *madrasahs* before but had met for study and discussion in one another's homes. They had always, on principle, held aloof from government, but now they were required to take over the educational and legal system of Iran, as well as the more religious tasks of the government. The shah gave them generous gifts and grants that eventually made them financially independent. They felt that they could not refuse this unique opportunity of propagating their faith, but were still wary of the state, refusing official government posts and preferring to be ranked as subjects. Their position was potentially very powerful. According to Twelver orthodoxy, the *ulama* and not the shahs were the only legitimate representatives of the Hidden Imam. But as yet, the Safavids were able to keep the *ulama* in line; they would not be able to exploit their position fully until the Iranian people as a whole had converted to the Shiah. But their new power meant that some of the more attractive traits of Twelver Shiism became submerged. Instead of pursuing their profound mystical exegesis, some of them became rather literal-minded. Muhammad Baqir Majlisi (d. 1700) became one of the most influential *ulama* of all time, but he displayed a new Shii bigotry. He tried to suppress the teaching of Falsafah and mysticism (*irfan*) in Isfahan, and mercilessly persecuted the remaining Sufis. Henceforth, he was able to insist, the *ulama* should concentrate on *fiqh*. Majlisi introduced into Iranian Shiism a distrust of mysticism and philosophy that is still prevalent today.

To replace the old Sufi devotions, such as the communal *dhikr* and the cult of Sufi saints, Majlisi promoted the mourning rituals in honour of Husain, the martyr of Kerbala, to teach the populace the values and piety of the Shiah. There were elaborate processions, and highly emotional dirges were sung, while the people wailed and cried aloud. These rites became a major Iranian institution. During the eighteenth century the *taziyeh*, a passion play depicting the Kerbala tragedy, was developed, in which the people were not passive spectators, but provided the emotional response, weeping and beating their breasts, and joining their own sorrows to the suffering of Imam Husain. The rituals provided an important safety-valve. As they moaned, slapped their foreheads, and wept uncontrollably, the audience aroused in themselves that yearning for justice which is at the heart of Shii piety, asking themselves *why* the good always seemed to suffer and evil nearly always prevailed. But Majlisi and the shahs were careful to suppress the revolutionary potential of these rites. Instead of protesting against tyranny at home, the people were taught to inveigh against Sunni Islam. Instead of vowing to follow Husain in the struggle against injustice, the people were told to see him as a patron, who could secure their admission to paradise. The rite was thus neutralized and made to serve the *status quo*, urged the populace to curry favour with the powerful and look only to their own interests. It was not until the Iranian Revolution of 1978–9 that the cult would once again become a means for the oppressed to articulate their grievances against corrupt government.

But some of the *ulama* remained true to the older Shii traditions, and their ideas would inspire reformers and revolutionaries right up to the present day, not just in Iran but throughout the Muslim world. Mir Dimad (d. 1631) and his pupil Mulla Sadra (d. 1640) founded a school of mystical philosophy at Isfahan, which Majlisi did his best to suppress. They continued the tradition of Suhrawardi, linking philosophy and spirituality, and training their disciples in mystical disciplines which enabled them to acquire a sense of the *alam al-mithal* and the spiritual world. Both insisted that a philosopher must be as rational and scientific as Aristotle, but that he must also cultivate the imaginative, intuitive approach to truth. Both were utterly opposed to the new intolerance of some of the *ulama*, which they regarded as a perversion of religion. Truth could not be imposed by force and intellectual conformism was incompatible with true faith. Mulla Sadra also saw political reform as inseparable from spirituality. In his masterpiece *Al-Afsan al-Arbaah (The Fourfold Journey)*, he described the mystical training that a leader must undergo before he could start to transform the mundane world. He must first divest himself of ego, and receive divine illumination and mystical apprehension of God. It was a path that could bring him to the same kind of spiritual insight as the Shii Imams, though not, of course, on the same level as they. Ayatollah Khomeini was profoundly influenced by the teachings of Mulla Sadra, and in his last address to the Iranian people before his death he begged them to continue the study and practice of *irfan*, since there could be no truly Islamic revolution unless there was also a spiritual reformation.

Mulla Sadra was deeply disturbed by a wholly new idea that was gradually gaining ground among the *ulama* of Iran, and which would also have fateful political consequences in our own day. A group who called themselves Usulis believed that ordinary Muslims were incapable of interpreting the basic principles (*usul*) of the faith for themselves. They should, therefore, seek out one of the learned *ulama* and follow his legal rulings, since they alone had the authority of the Hidden Imam. The Shii *ulama* had never agreed to close 'the gates of *ijtihad*' like the Sunnis. Indeed, they called a leading jurist a *mujtahid*, one who had earned the right to exercise 'independent reasoning' when formulating Islamic legislation. The Usulis taught that even the shah should obey the *fatwahs* of the *mujtahid* whom he had chosen for his mentor, since he needed his legal expertise. During the seventeenth century the Usulis did not win widespread support, but by the end of the century, when it was clear that the Safavid Empire was in decline, their position became popular. It had become crucial to establish a strong legal authority that could compensate for the weakness of the state.

By this time, the empire had succumbed to the fate of any agrarian economy, and could no longer keep pace with its responsibilities. Trade had deteriorated, there was economic insecurity, and the later shahs were incompetent. When Afghan tribes attacked Isfahan in 1722, the city surrendered ignominiously. One of the Safavid princes escaped the massacre, and with the help of the brilliant but ruthless commander Nadir Khan, managed to drive out the invaders. For over twenty years Nadir Khan, who got rid of his Safavid colleague and made himself shah, pulled Iran together and achieved notable military victories. But he was a cruel, brutal man and was assassinated in 1748. During this period, two crucial developments gave the *ulama* of Iran a power unparalleled anywhere else in the Muslim world. First, when Nadir Khan had tried, unsuccessfully, to re-establish Sunni Islam in Iran, the leading *ulama* had left the empire and taken up residence in the holy Shii cities of Najaf and Kerbala (dedicated respectively to Ali and Husain). This seemed a disaster at first, but in Najaf and Kerbala, which were in Ottoman Iraq, they had a base from which they could instruct the people which was out of reach of the temporal rulers of Iran. Second, during the dark interregnum that followed Nadir Khan's death, when there was no central authority in Iran until Aqa Muhammad of the Turcoman Qajar tribe managed to seize control in 1779 and founded the Qajar dynasty, the *ulama* stepped into the power vacuum. The Usuli position became mandatory, and events would show that the *ulama* could command the devotion and obedience of the Iranian people far more effectively than any shah.

The Moghul Empire

The turmoil occasioned by Shah Ismail's Shii *jihad* against Sunni Islam was, in part, responsible for the establishment of the new Muslim Empire in India. Its founder, Babur (d. 1530), had been an ally of Ismail, and had fled as a refugee to Kabul in the Afghan mountains during the war between the Safavids and the Uzbeks, where he had seized control of the remnants of the state established there by Timur Lane. Thence he managed briefly to establish a power base in north India, which he intended to run on the Mongol lines favoured by Timur. His state did not last, and there was factional strife among the Afghan *amirs* until 1555, when Humayun, the ablest of Babur's descendants, secured the throne and, though he died almost immediately, a dependable regent held the 'Mongol' (or 'Moghul') power intact until Humayun's son Akbar (1542–1605) attained his majority in 1560. Akbar was able to establish an integrated state in north India, where he was acknowledged as the undisputed ruler. He retained the old Mongol habit of running the central government as an army under the direct command of the sultan. He set up an efficient bureaucracy and, with the aid of his firearms, the Moghul Empire began to expand at the expense of the other Muslim rulers, until he controlled Hindustan, the Punjab, Malva and the Deccan.

Unlike Ismail, however, Akbar did not oppress or persecute his subjects, nor did he attempt to convert them to his own faith. Had he done so, his empire would not have survived. The Muslims were a small ruling minority in a country that had never attempted to impose religious conformity. Each Hindu caste had its own religious practices, and Buddhists, Jacobites, Jews, Jains, Christians, Zoroastrians, Sunni Muslims and Ismailis had all been allowed to worship without hindrance. During the fourteenth and fifteenth centuries, Hindus of all castes and even a few Muslims had joined forces in establishing a spiritualized, contemplative form of monotheism, which forswore sectarian intolerance. The Sikh religion, founded by Guru Nanak (d. 1539) had grown from these circles, insisting on the unity and compatibility of Hinduism and Islam. There was, however, always a possibility of aggressive confrontation. Universalism was firmly established in India, and an intolerant polity would run against the grain of Indic culture.

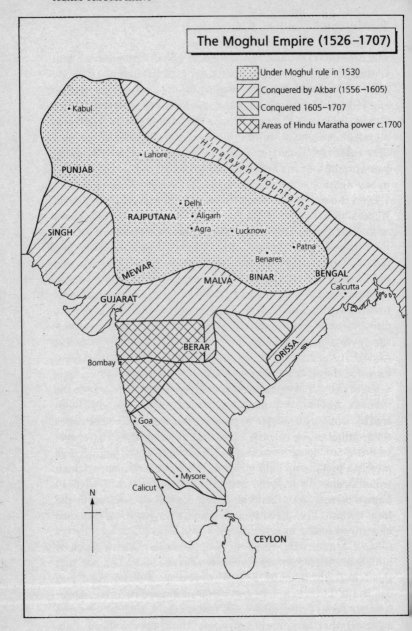

The Moghul Empire (1526–1707)

- ⠿ Under Moghul rule in 1530
- ⫽ Conquered by Akbar (1556–1605)
- ⧵ Conquered 1605–1707
- ⊠ Areas of Hindu Maratha power c.1700

Kabul

Lahore

Himalayan Mountains

PUNJAB

Delhi
Aligarh
RAJPUTANA
Agra
Lucknow

SINGH

Patna

Benares

MEWAR
MALVA
BINAR
BENGAL

GUJARAT
Calcutta

BERAR

Bombay

ORISSA

Goa

Mysore

Calicut

N

CEYLON

Muslim rulers had long been aware of this and had employed Hindus in their armies and administration. Akbar accentuated this tradition. He abolished the *jizyah* tax that the Shariah prescribed for *dhimmis*, became a vegetarian, so as not to offend Hindu sensibilities, and gave up hunting (a sport he greatly enjoyed). Akbar was respectful of all faiths. He built temples for Hindus, and in 1575 set up a 'house of worship' where scholars of all religions could meet for discussion. He also founded his own Sufi order, dedicated to 'divine monotheism' (*tawhid-e ilahi*), based on the Quranic belief that the one God could reveal himself in any rightly guided religion.

Even though it was certainly true to the spirit of the Quran, Akbar's pluralism was very different from the hardline communalism that had been developing in some Shariah circles, and it was light years from the bigotry of the recent Sunni/Shii conflict. But any other policy would have been politically disastrous in India. Akbar had courted the *ulama* at the beginning of his reign, but he was never very interested in the Shariah. His own bent was towards Sufism and Falsafah, both of which inclined towards a universalist vision. Akbar wanted to build the model society that the Faylasufs had described. His biographer, the Sufi historian Abdulfazl Allami (1551–1602), saw Akbar as the ideal philosopher-king. He also believed that he was the Perfect Man, whom Sufis thought to exist in each generation to give divine guidance to the *ummah*. Akbar was establishing a civilization, which, Allami argued, would help people to cultivate a spirit of such generosity that conflict would become impossible. It was a polity that expressed the Sufi ideal of *sulh-e kull* (universal peace), which was merely a prelude to *mahabbat-e kull*, the 'universal love' which would positively seek the material and spiritual welfare of all human beings. From this perspective, bigotry was non-sense; the ideal Faylasuf king, like Akbar, was above the parochial prejudice of narrow sectarianism.

Some Muslims, however, were offended by Akbar's religious pluralism. Ahmad Sirhindi (d. 1625), who was also a Sufi, felt that this universalism (which he laid at the door of Ibn al-Arabi) was dangerous. Sirhindi proclaimed that he himself rather than Akbar was the Perfect Man of the age. Unity with God could only be achieved when Muslims piously observed the laws of the Shariah, which by this time was becoming more sectarian in its outlook. In the early part of the seventeenth century, however, few Muslims in India subscribed to Sirhindi's views. Shah Jihan, Akbar's grandson, who reigned from 1627 to 1658, kept in the main to Akbar's policies. His Taj Mahal continued his grand-father's tradition of blending Muslim with Hindu styles of archi-tecture. At his court, he patronized Hindu poets and Muslim scientific works were translated into Sanskrit. But Shah Jihan tended to be hostile to Sufism and his piety was based more strictly on the Shariah than Akbar's had been.

He proved to be a transitional figure. By the end of the century, it was clear that the Moghul Empire had begun its decline. The army and the court had both become too expensive, the emperors still invested in cultural activities, but neglected agriculture on which their wealth depended. The economic crisis came to a head during the reign of Aurengzebe (1658–1707), who believed that the answer lay in greater discipline in Muslim society. His inse-curity was expressed in murderous hatred of Muslim 'heretics' as well as adherents of other faiths. He was supported in his sectarian policies by those Muslims who, like Sirhindi, had been unhappy with the old pluralism. Shii celebrations in honour of Husain were suppressed in India, wine was prohibited by law (which made socializing with Hindus difficult), and the number of Hindu fes-tivals attended by the emperor was drastically reduced. The *jizyah* was reimposed, and the taxes of Hindu merchants were doubled. Worst of all, Hindu temples were destroyed all over the empire. The response showed how wise the previous tolerance had been. There were serious revolts, led by Hindu chieftains and Sikhs, who started to campaign for a state of their own in the Punjab. When Aurengzebe died, the empire was in a parlous state and never fully recovered. His successors abandoned his communalist policies, but the damage was done. Even Muslims were dis-affected: there had been nothing authentically Islamic about Aur-engzebe's zeal for the Shariah, which preaches justice for all, including the *dhimmis*. The empire began to disintegrate, and local Muslim officials tended to control their regions as autono-mous units.

The Moghuls managed to remain in power however, until 1739, and there was a rapprochement during the eighteenth century between Hindus and Muslims in the court; they learned to speak one another's languages and to read and translate books from Europe together. But Sikhs and the Hindu chieftains from the mountainous regions still fought the regime, and in the north-west the Afghan tribes which had brought down the Safavid Empire in Iran made an unsuccessful bid to establish a new Muslim empire in India. Indian Muslims began to feel uneasy about their position, and their problems foreshadowed many of the difficulties and debates that would continue to exercise Muslims during the modern period. They now felt that they were a beleaguered minority in an area which was not, like the Anatolian heartlands of the Ottoman Empire, a peripheral region, but one of the core cultures of the civilized world. Not only were they contending with Hindus and Sikhs, but the British were also establishing a strong trading presence in the subcontinent, which was becoming increasingly political. For the first time, Muslims faced the prospect of being governed by infidels, and, given the importance of the *ummah* in Islamic piety, this was profoundly disturbing. It was not simply a matter of politics, but touched the deepest recesses of their beings. A new insecurity would continue to characterize Muslim life in India. Was Islam to become simply another Hindu caste? Would Muslims lose their cultural and religious identity, and be swamped by foreign traditions that were different from those of the Middle East, in which Islam had come to birth? Had they lost touch with their roots?

The Sufi thinker Shah Valli-Ullah (1703–62) believed that the answer lay in Sirhindi's position, and his views would continue to influence the Muslims of India well into the twentieth century. He expressed the new embattled vision, and as Muslims felt their power slipping away in other parts of the world and experienced similar fears about the survival of Islam, other philosophers and reformers would reach similar conclusions. First, Muslims must unite, bury their sectarian differences with one another, and present a united front against their enemies. The Shariah must be adapted to meet the special conditions of the subcontinent, and become a means of resisting Hinduization. It was essential that Muslims retain the upper hand militarily and politically. So concerned was he, that Shah Valli-Ullah even supported the disastrous Afghan attempt to revive Muslim power. A defensive strain had entered Muslim thinking, and this would continue to characterize Islamic piety in the modern period.

The Ottoman Empire

When the Ottomans had conquered Constantinople (which now became known as Istanbul) in 1453, they were in a position to establish an empire, which, because it had been able to evolve so gradually, was more firmly grounded than the other empires, and would become the most successful and enduring. The early Ottoman chieftains had been typical *ghazi* rulers, but in Istanbul the sultans established an absolute monarchy, on the Byzantine model, with an elaborate court ritual. The state was chiefly based on the old Mongol idea, however, seeing the central power as a huge army at the personal disposal of the sultan. Mehmed the Conqueror's power was based on the support of the Balkan nobility, many of whom were now converting to Islam, and the infantry – the 'new troop' (*yani-cheri*) – which had become more important since the advent of gunpowder. The Janissaries, who, as converted slaves, were outsiders with no landed interests, became an independent force, solidly behind the sultans. The Ottomans also retained the ethos of their old ideal, seeing themselves as manning a frontier state, dedicated to a *jihad* against the enemies of Islam. To the west they faced Christendom, and to the east were the Shii Safavids. The Ottomans became as murderously sectarian as the Safavids, and there were massacres of Shiis living in Ottoman domains.

The *jihad* was phenomenally successful. The campaign of Selim I (1467–1520) against the Safavids, which had stopped the Iranian advance, developed into a victorious war of conquest which brought the whole of Syria and Egypt under Ottoman rule. North Africa and Arabia were also incorporated into the empire. To the west, the Ottoman armies continued their conquest of Europe and reached the gates of Vienna in the 1530s. The sultans now ruled a massive empire, with superb bureaucratic efficiency, unrivalled by any other state at this time. The sultan did not impose uniformity on his subjects nor did he try to force the disparate elements of his empire into one huge party. The

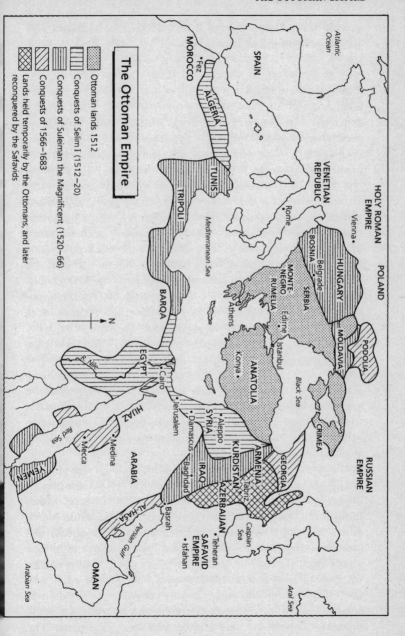

The Ottoman Empire

Ottoman lands 1512

Conquests of Selim I (1512–20)

Conquests of Suleiman the Magnificent (1520–66)

Conquests of 1566–1683

Lands held temporarily by the Ottomans, and later reconquered by the Safavids

government merely provided a framework which enabled the different groups – Christians, Jews, Arabs, Turks, Berbers, merchants, *ulama*, *tariqahs* and trade guilds – to live together peacefully, each making its own contribution, and following its own beliefs and customs. The empire was thus a collection of communities, each of which claimed the immediate loyalty of its members. The empire was divided into provinces, ruled by a governor (*pasha*) who was directly responsible to Istanbul.

The empire reached its apogee under Suleiman al-Qanuni ('the Lawgiver') (1520–66), who was known as Suleiman the Magnificent in the West. Under his rule, the empire reached the limits of its expansion, and Istanbul enjoyed a cultural renaissance, which was chiefly characterized by superb architecture, notably that of the court architect Sinan Pasha (d. 1578). The Ottoman mosques that appeared all over the empire shared a distinctive style: they were spacious, filled with light, had low domes and high minarets. The court also patronized painting, history and medicine to a high level, built an observatory in 1579, and was intrigued by the new European discoveries in navigation and geography. There was an eager interchange of information with the West during these expansive years when, despite Europe's achievements, the Ottoman state was the most powerful in the world.

Like the other two empires, the Ottomans also gave their state a special Islamic orientation. Under Suleiman, the Shariah received a more exalted status than in any previous Muslim state. It became the official law of the land for all Muslims, and the Ottomans were the first to give regular form to the Shariah courts. Legal experts – the *qadis*, who dispensed justice in the courts, their consultants (*muftis*) who interpreted the law, and the teachers in the *madrasahs* – became an official government corps, creating a moral and religious link between the sultan and his subjects. This was especially valuable in the Arab provinces, where the partnership between the state and the *ulama* helped people to accept Turkish rule. Not only did the *ulama* have the backing of the sacred law and so gave legitimacy to the regime, but it was often the case that the *ulama*, who were native to a particular province, acted as essential intermediaries between the indigenous population and the Turkish governor.

Ottoman subjects were, in the main, proud of belonging to the Shariah state. The Quran had taught that an *ummah* which lived according to God's law would prosper, because it was in harmony with the fundamental principles of existence. The spectacular successes of the early Ottomans, whose legitimacy was largely based on their devotion to God's revealed law, seemed to endorse this belief. The *ulama* could also feel that the empire was *their* state and that the Ottomans had achieved a rare integration of public policy and Muslim conscience. But this partnership – fruitful as it was – had a negative side, since instead of empowering the *ulama*, it would eventually muzzle and even discredit them. The Shariah had begun as a protest movement, and much of its dynamism derived from its oppositional stance. Under the Ottoman system, this was inevitably lost. The *ulama* became dependent upon the state. As government officials, the sultan and his *pashas* could – and did – control them by threatening to withdraw their subsidies. Abu al-Suud Khola Chelebi (1490–1574), who worked out the principles of the Ottoman–*ulama* alliance, made it clear that the *qadis* derived their authority from the sultan, the guardian of the Shariah, and were therefore bound to apply the law according to his directives. Thus the Shariah was made to endorse the system of absolute monarchy (now more powerful than ever before) which it had been originally designed to oppose.

The Shii *ulama* of Iran had broken free of the state, and had won the support of the people. Many of the Iranian *ulama* would become committed reformers and were able to provide the people with effective leadership against despotic shahs. A significant number would be open to the democratic and liberal ideas of the modern period. But in the Ottoman Empire the *ulama* would become emasculated; deprived of their political edge, they became conservative and opposed any change. After Suleiman's reign, the curriculum of the *madrasahs* became narrower: the study of Falsafah was dropped in favour of a greater concentration on *fiqh*. The Islamic stance of the Ottoman Empire, a huge *ghazi* state, was communalist and sectarian. Muslims felt that they were the champions of orthodoxy against infidels who pressed on all sides. The *ulama* and even the Sufis imbibed this ethos, and when the empire began to show the first signs of weakness, this tendency became even more marked. Where the court was still open to the new ideas coming from Europe, the *madrasahs* became centres of opposition to any experimentation that derived from the European infidels. The *ulama* opposed the use of printing for Islamic books, for example. They turned away from the Christian communities in the empire, many of whom were looking eagerly towards the new West. The *ulama's* influence with the people coloured major sectors of Ottoman society, making them resistant to the idea of change at a time when change was inevitable. Left behind in the old ethos, the *ulama* would become unable to help the people when Western modernity hit the Muslim world, and they would have to look elsewhere for guidance.

Even the mighty Ottoman Empire was not proof against the limitations of agrarian society, which could not keep pace with its expansion. Military discipline weakened, so that the sultans found that they could no longer wield absolute power. The foundering of the economy led to corruption and tax abuse. The upper classes lived in opulence, while revenues decreased; trade declined as a result of more effective European competition, and local governors tended to line their own pockets. Nevertheless, the empire did not collapse, but retained a vigorous cultural life throughout the seventeenth century. By the eighteenth century, however, the decline was evident, especially in the peripheral regions. There local reformers tried to restore order by means of religious reform.

In the Arabian peninsula, Muhammad ibn Abd al-Wahhab (1703–92) managed to break away from Istanbul and establish a state in central Arabia and the Persian Gulf. He was a typical reformer, in the tradition of Ibn Taymiyyah. He believed that the current crisis was best met by a fundamentalist return to the Quran and *sunnah*, and by a militant rejection of all later accretions, which included medieval *fiqh*, mysticism and Falsafah, which most Muslims now regarded as normative. Because the Ottoman sultans did not conform to his vision of true Islam, Abd al-Wahhab declared that they were apostates and worthy of death. Instead, he tried to create an enclave of pure faith, based on his view of the first *ummah* of the seventh century. His aggressive techniques would be used by some fundamentalists in the twentieth century, a period of even greater change and unrest. Wahhabism is the form of Islam that is still practised today in Saudi Arabia, a puritan religion based on a strictly literal interpretation of scripture and early Islamic tradition.

In Morocco, the Sufi reformer Ahmad ibn Idris (1760–1836) approached the problem differently. His solution was to educate the people and make them better Muslims. He travelled extensively in North Africa and the Yemen, instructing the ordinary people in their own dialect, and teaching them how to perform such basic rituals as the *salat* prayer correctly. In his view, the *ulama* had failed in their duty, had locked themselves away in their *madrasahs*, interested only in the minutiae of *fiqh*, and had left the people to their own devices. Other Neo-Sufis, as these reformers are called, performed similar missions in Algeria and Medina. Muhammad ibn Ali al-Sanusi (d. 1832) founded the Sanusiayyah movement, which is still the predominant form of Islam in Libya. The Neo-Sufis had no interest in and no knowledge of the new West, but they evolved ideas similar to those espoused by the European Enlightenment by means of their own mystical traditions. They insisted that the people rely on their own insights, instead of relying on the *ulama*. Ibn Idris went so far as to reject the authority of every single Muslim thinker, except the Prophet. He thus encouraged Muslims to cast off habits of deference and to value what was new, instead of clinging to past tradition. His mysticism was based on the figure of the Prophet, and taught the people to model themselves on an ideal human being rather than yearn for a distant God, in a sort of devotional humanism.

There was, therefore, no intrinsic reason why Muslims should reject the ethos of the new Europe. Over the centuries they had cultivated virtues that would also be crucial to the modern West: a passion for social justice, an egalitarian polity, freedom of speech, and, despite the ideal of *tawhid*, a *de facto* or (in the case of Shiism) a principled separation of religion and politics. But by the end of the eighteenth century the most alert Muslims had been forced to recognize that Europe had overtaken them. The Ottomans had inflicted stunning defeats on the European powers in the early days, but by the eighteenth century they could no longer hold their own against them, nor deal with them as equals. In the sixteenth century Suleiman had granted European traders diplomatic immunity. The treaties known as the Capitulations (because they were formulated under *capita*: headings) meant that European traders living in Ottoman territory were not required to observe the law of the land; their offences were tried according to their own laws in their own courts, which were presided over by their own consul. Suleiman had negotiated these treaties with the nations of Europe as an equal. But by the eighteenth century it was clear that these Capitulations were weakening Ottoman sovereignty, especially when they were extended in 1740 to the Christian *millets* in the empire, who were now 'protected' like the European expatriates, and no longer subject to government control.

By the late eighteenth century the Ottoman Empire was in a critical state. Trade had declined still further; the Bedouin tribes were out of control in the Arab provinces, and the local *pashas* were no longer adequately managed by Istanbul, were often corrupt, and exploited the population. The West, however, was going from one triumph to another. But the Ottomans were not unduly worried. Sultan Selim III tried to take a leaf out of Europe's book, assuming that an army reform along Western lines would restore the balance of power. In 1789 he opened a number of military schools with French instructors, where students learned European languages and studied the new Western sciences along-side modern martial arts. But this would not be sufficient to contain the Western threat. Muslims had not yet realized that Europe had evolved a wholly different type of society since the Ottoman Empire had been established, that they had now pulled irrevocably ahead of Islamdom, and would shortly achieve world power.

The three great empires were all in decline by the end of the eighteenth century. This was not due to the essential incompetence or fatalism of Islam, as Europeans often arrogantly assumed. Any agrarian polity had a limited lifespan, and these Muslim states, which represented the last flowering of the agrarian ideal, had simply come to a natural and inevitable end. In the pre-modern period, Western and Christian empires had also experienced decline and fall. Islamic states had collapsed before; on each occasion, Muslims had been able to rise phoenix-like from the ruins and had gone on to still greater achievements. But this time, it was different. The Muslim weakness at the end of the eighteenth century coincided with the rise of an entirely different type of civilization in the West, and this time the Muslim world would find it far more difficult to meet the challenge.

5   ISLAM AGONISTES

The Arrival of the West (1750–2000)

The rise of the West is unparalleled in world history. The countries north of the Alps had for centuries been regarded as a backward region, which had attached itself to the Greco-Roman culture of the south and had, gradually, developed its own distinctive version of Christianity and its own form of agrarian culture. Western Europe lagged far behind the Christian empire of Byzantium, where the Roman Empire had not collapsed as it had in Europe. By the twelfth and thirteenth centuries these western European countries had just about caught up with the other core cultures, and by the sixteenth century had begun a process of major transformation that would enable the West to dominate the rest of the world. The achievement of such ascendancy by an outgroup is unique. It is similar to the emergence of the Arab Muslims as a major world power in the seventh and eighth centuries, but the Muslims had not achieved world hegemony, and had not developed a new kind of civilization, as Europe had begun to do in the sixteenth century. When the Ottomans had tried to reorganize their army along Western lines in the hope of containing the threat from Europe, their efforts were doomed because they were too superficial. To beat Europe at its own game, a conventional agrarian society would have to transform itself from top to bottom, and recreate its entire social, economic, educational, religious, spiritual, political and intellectual structures. And they would have to do this very quickly, an impossible task, since it had taken the West almost three hundred years to achieve this development.

The new society of Europe and its American colonies had a different economic basis. Instead of relying upon a surplus of agricultural produce, it was founded on a technology and an investment of capital that enabled the West to reproduce its resources indefinitely, so that Western society was no longer subject to the same constraints as an agrarian culture. This major revolution in reality constituted a second Axial Age, which demanded a revolution of the established mores on several fronts at the same time: political, social and intellectual. It had not been planned or thought out in advance, but had been the result of a complex process which had led to the creation of democratic, secular social structures. By the sixteenth century Europeans had achieved a scientific revolution that gave them greater control over the environment than anybody had achieved before. There were new inventions in medicine, navigation, agriculture and industry. None of these was in itself decisive, but their cumulative effect was radical. By 1600 innovations were occurring on such a scale that progress seemed irreversible: a discovery in one field would often lead to fresh insights in another. Instead of seeing the world as governed by immutable laws, Europeans had found that they could alter the course of nature. Where the conservative society created by agrarian culture had not been able to afford such change, people in Europe and America were becoming more confident. They were now prepared to invest and reinvest capital in the firm expectation of continuing progress and the continuous improvement of trade. By the time this technicalization of society had resulted in the industrial revolution of the nineteenth century, Westerners felt such assurance that they no longer looked back to the past for inspiration, as in the agrarian cultures and religions, but looked forward to the future.

The modernization of society involved social and intellectual change. The watchword was efficiency: an invention or a polity had to be seen to work effectively. An increasing number of people were needed to take part in the various scientific and industrial projects at quite humble levels – as printers, clerks, factory workers – and in order to acquire a modicum of the new standards, they had to receive some kind of education. More people were needed to buy the mass-produced goods, so that to keep the economy going an increasing number of people had to live above subsistence level. As more of the workers became literate, they demanded a greater share in the decisions of government. If a nation wanted to use all its human resources to enhance its productivity, it had to bring groups who had hitherto been segregated and marginalized, such as the Jews, into mainstream culture. Religious differences and spiritual ideals must not be allowed to impede the progress of society, and scientists, monarchs and government officials insisted that they be free of ecclesiastical control. Thus the ideals of democracy, pluralism, toleration, human rights and secularism were not simply beautiful ideals dreamed up by political scientists, but were, at least in part, dictated by the needs of the modern state. It was found that in order to be efficient and productive, a modern nation had to be organized on a secular, democratic basis. But it was also found that if societies did organize all their institutions according to the new rational and scientific norms, they became indomitable and that the conventional agrarian states were no match for them.

This had fateful consequences for the Islamic world. The progressive nature of modern society and an industrialized economy meant that it had continuously to expand. New markets were needed, and, once the home countries had been saturated, they had to be sought abroad. The Western states therefore began, in various ways, to colonize the agrarian countries outside modern Europe in order to draw them into their commercial network. This too was a complex process. The colonized country provided raw materials for export, which were fed into European industry. In return, it received cheap manufactured Western goods, which meant that local industry was usually ruined. The colony also had to be transformed and modernized along European lines, its financial and commercial life rationalized and brought into the Western system, and at least some of the 'natives' had to acquire some familiarity with the modern ideas and ethos.

This colonization was experienced by the agrarian colonies as invasive, disturbing and alien. Modernization was inevitably superficial, since a process that had taken Europe three centuries had to be achieved at top speed. Where modern ideas had time to filter down gradually to all classes of society in Europe, in the colonies only a small number of people, who were members of the upper classes and – significantly – the military, could receive a Western education and appreciate the dynamic of modernity. The vast majority of the population were left perforce to rot in the old agrarian ethos. Society was divided, therefore, and increasingly neither side could understand the other. Those who had been left outside the modernizing process had the disturbing experience of watching their country become utterly strange, like a friend disfigured by disease and become unrecognizable. They were ruled by secular foreign law-codes which they could not understand. Their cities were transformed, as Western buildings 'modernized' the towns, often leaving the 'old city' as a museum piece, a tourist trap, and a relic of a superseded age. Western tourists have often felt disoriented and lost in the winding alleys and apparent chaos of an oriental city: they do not always appreciate that for many of the indigenous population, their modernized capitals are equally alien. People felt lost in their own countries. Above all, local people of all classes of society resented the fact that they were no longer in control of their own destiny. They felt that they had severed all connection with their roots, and experienced a sinking loss of identity.

Where Europeans and Americans had been allowed to modernize at their own pace, and to set their own agendas, the inhabitants of the colonized countries had to modernize far too rapidly and were forced to comply with somebody else's programme. But even Western people had found the transformation of their society painful. They had experienced almost four hundred years of political and often bloody revolutions, reigns of terror, ethnic cleansing, violent wars of religion, the despoliation of the countryside, vast social upheavals, exploitation in the factories, spiritual malaise and profound anomie in the new megacities. Today we are seeing similar violence, cruelty, revolution and disorientation in the developing countries, which are making an even more difficult rite of passage to modernity. It is also true that the modern spirit that developed in the West is fundamentally different. In Europe and America it had two main characteristics: innovation and autonomy (the modernizing process was punctuated in Europe and America by declarations of independence on the political, intellectual, religious and social fronts). But in the developing world, modernity has been accompanied not by autonomy but by a loss of independence and national autonomy. Instead of innovation, the developing countries can only modernize by imitating the West, which is so far advanced that they have no hope of catching up. Since the modernizing process has not been the same, it is unlikely that the end product will conform to what the West regards as the desirable norm. If the correct ingredients of a cake are not available – if rice is used instead of flour, dried eggs instead of fresh, and spices instead of sugar – the result will be different from the cake described in the cookbook. Very different ingredients have gone into the modern cake of the colonized countries, and democracy, secularism, pluralism and the rest are not likely to emerge from the process in the way that they did in the West.

The Islamic world has been convulsed by the modernization process. Instead of being one of the leaders of world civilization, Islamdom was quickly and permanently reduced to a dependent bloc by the European powers. Muslims were exposed to the contempt of the colonialists, who were so thoroughly imbued with the modern ethos that they were often appalled by what they could only see as the backwardness, inefficiency, fatalism and corruption of Muslim society. They assumed that European culture had always been progressive, and lacked the historical perspective to see that they were simply seeing a pre-modern agrarian society, and that a few centuries earlier Europe had been just as 'backward'. They often took it for granted that Westerners were inherently and racially superior to 'orientals' and expressed their contempt in myriad ways. All this not unnaturally had a corrosive effect. Western people are often bewildered by the hostility and rage that Muslims often feel for their culture, which, because of their very different experience, they have found to be liberating and empowering. But the Muslim response is not bizarre and eccentric; because the Islamic world was so widespread and strategically placed, it was the first to be subjected in a concerted, systematic manner to the colonization process in the Middle East, India, Arabia, Malaysia and a significant part of Africa. Muslims in all these places very early felt the brunt of this modernizing assault. Their response has not been simply *a* reaction to the new West, but *the* paradigmatic reaction. They would not be able to come to modernity as successfully or as smoothly as, for example, Japan, which had never been colonized, whose economy and institutions had remained intact, and which had not been forced into a debilitating dependency on the West.

The European invasion of the Islamic world was not uniform, but it was thorough and effective. It began in Moghul India. During the latter half of the eighteenth century, British traders had established themselves in Bengal, and at this time, when modernization was still in its infancy, the British lived on a par with the Hindu and Muslim merchants. But this phase of British activity is known as the 'plundering of Bengal', because it permanently damaged the local industry, and changed its agriculture so that Bengalis no longer grew crops for themselves but produced raw materials for the industrialized Western markets. Bengal had been reduced to second-class status in the world economy. Gradually as the British became more 'modern' and efficient themselves, their attitude became more superior, and they were determined to 'civilize' the Indians, backed up by the Protestant missionaries who started to arrive in 1793. But the Bengalis were not encouraged to evolve a fully industrialized society of their own; the British administrators introduced only those aspects of modern technology that would reinforce their supremacy and keep Bengal in a complementary role. The Bengalis did benefit from British efficiency, which kept such disasters as disease, famine and war at bay, and the population increased as a result; but this created new problems of overcrowding and poverty, since there was no option of migration to the towns, as in the West, and the people all had to stay on the land.

The plundering of Bengal economically led to political domination. Between 1798 and 1818, by treaty or by military conquest, British rule was established throughout India, except in the Indus Valley, which was subdued between 1843 and 1849. In the meantime, the French had tried to set up an empire of their own. In 1798 Napoleon Bonaparte occupied Egypt, hoping to establish a base in Suez that would cut the British sea-routes to India. He brought with him a corps of scholars, a library of modern European literature, a scientific laboratory and a printing press with Arabic type. From the start, the advanced culture of Europe, coming as it did with a superbly efficient modern army, was experienced in the Muslim Middle East as an assault. Napoleon's expedition to Egypt and Syria failed. He had intended to attack British India from the north, with the help of Russia. This gave Iran a wholly new strategic importance, and for the next century Britain established a base in the south of the country, while the Russians tried to get control of the north. Neither wanted to make Iran a full colony or protectorate (until oil was discovered there in the early twentieth century), but both powers dominated the new Qajar dynasty, so that the shahs did not dare to make a move without the support of at least one of them. As in Bengal, both Britain and Russia promoted only the technology that furthered their own interests and blocked such inventions as the railway, which might have benefited the Iranian people, in case it endangered their own strategic position.

The European powers colonized one Islamic country after another. France occupied Algeria in 1830, and Britain Aden nine years later. Tunisia was occupied in 1881, Egypt in 1882, the Sudan in 1889, and Libya and Morocco in 1912. In 1915 the Sykes-Picot agreement divided the territories of the moribund Ottoman Empire (which had sided with Germany during the First World War) between Britain and France in anticipation of victory. After the war, Britain and France duly set up protectorates and mandates in Syria, Lebanon, Palestine, Iraq and Transjordan. This was experienced as an outrage, since the European powers had promised the Arab provinces of the Ottoman Empire independence. In the Ottoman heartlands, Mustafa Kemal, known as Atatürk (1881–1938), was able to keep the Europeans at bay and set up the independent state of Turkey. Muslims in the Balkans, Russia and Central Asia became subject to the new Soviet Union. Even after some of these countries had been allowed to become independent, the West often continued to control the economy, the oil or such resources as the Suez Canal. European occupation often left a legacy of bitter conflict. When the British withdrew from India in 1947, the Indian subcontinent was partitioned between Hindu India and Muslim Pakistan, which are to this day in a state of deadly hostility, with nuclear weapons aimed at each other's capitals. In 1948 the Arabs of Palestine lost their homeland to the Zionists, who set up the Jewish secular state of Israel there, with the support of the United Nations and the international community. The loss of Palestine became a potent symbol of the humiliation of the Muslim world at the hands of the Western powers, who seemed to feel no qualms about the dispossession and permanent exile of hundreds of thousands of Palestinians.

Nevertheless, in the very early days, some Muslims were in love with the West. The Iranian intellectuals Mulkum Khan (1833–1908) and Aqa Khan Kirmani (1853–96) urged Iranians to acquire a Western education and replace the Shariah with a modern secular legal code, seeing this as the only route to progress. Secularists from these circles joined the more liberal *ulama* in the Constitutional Revolution of 1906, and forced the Qajars to set up a modern constitution, to limit the powers of the monarchy and give Iranians parliamentary representation. Most of the leading *mujtahids* in Najaf supported the constitution. Sheikh Muhammad Husain Naini expressed their view most cogently in his *Admonition to the Nation* (1909), which argued that limiting tyranny in this way was clearly an act worthy of the Shiah, and that constitutional government, Western-style, was the next best thing to the return of the Hidden Imam. The Egyptian writer Rifah al-Tahtawi (1801–73) was enthralled by the ideas of the European Enlightenment whose vision reminded him of Falsafah. He loved the way everything worked properly in Paris, was impressed by the rational precision of French culture, by the literacy of even the common people, and intrigued by the passion for innovation. He longed to help Egypt enter this brave new world. In India, Sayyid Ahmad Khan (1817–98) tried to adapt Islam to modern Western liberalism, claiming that the Quran was quite in accordance with the natural laws that were being discovered by modern science. He founded a college at Aligharh where Muslims could study science and English alongside the conventional Islamic subjects. He wanted to help Muslims to live in a modernized society without becoming carbon-copies of the British, retaining a sense of their own cultural identity.

Before colonization had got under way in their areas, some Muslim rulers had tried to modernize on their own initiative. The Ottoman Sultan Mahmud II had inaugurated the Tanzimat (Regulations) in 1826, which abolished the Janissaries, modernized the army, and introduced some of the new technology. In 1839 Sultan Abdulhamid issued the Gülhane decree, which made his rule dependent upon a contractual relationship with his subjects, and looked forward to major reform of the empire's institutions. More dramatic, however, was the modernization programme of the Albanian *pasha* of Egypt Muhammad Ali (1769–1848), who made Egypt virtually independent of Istanbul, and almost single-handedly dragged this backward province into the modern world. But the brutality of his methods showed how difficult it was to modernize at such breakneck speed. He massacred the political opposition; twenty-three thousand peasants are said to have died in the conscripted labour bands that improved Egypt's irrigation and water-communications; other peasants so feared conscription into Muhammad Ali's modernized army that they frequently resorted to self-mutilation, cutting off their own fingers and even blinding themselves. To secularize the country, Muhammad Ali simply confiscated much religiously endowed property, systematically marginalized the *ulama*, and divested them of any shred of power. As a result, the *ulama*, who had experienced modernity as a shocking assault, became even more insular, and closed their minds against the new world that was coming into being in their country. Muhammad Ali's grandson, Ismail Pasha (1803–95) was even more successful: he paid for the construction of the Suez Canal, built nine hundred miles of railways, irrigated some 1,373,000 acres of hitherto uncultivable land, set up modern schools for boys and girls, and transformed Cairo into a modern city. Unfortunately, the cost of this ambitious programme made Egypt bankrupt, forced the country into debt, and gave Britain a pretext for establishing its military occupation in 1882 to safeguard the interests of the European shareholders. Muhammad Ali and Ismail had wanted to make Egypt a modern independent state; instead, as a result of modernization, it simply became a virtual British colony.

None of these early reformers fully appreciated the ideas behind the transformation of Europe. Their reforms were, therefore, superficial. But later reformers up to and including Saddam Hussein have also simply tried to acquire the military technology and outer trappings of the modern West, without bothering overmuch about its effects upon the rest of society. From an early date, however, some reformers were acutely aware of these dangers. One of the first to sound the alarm was the Iranian activist Jamal al-Din (1839–97), who styled himself 'al-Afghani' ('the Afghan'), probably hoping that he would attract a wider audience in the Muslim world as an Afghan Sunni than as an Iranian Shii. He had been in India at the time of the great mutiny of Hindus and Muslims against British rule in 1857; wherever he travelled in Arabia, Egypt, Turkey, Russia or Europe he was aware of the ubiquitous power of the West, and was convinced that it would soon dominate and crush the Muslim world. He could see dangers of a shallow imitation of Western life, and asked the people of the Islamic world to join forces against the European threat; they must come to the scientific culture of the new world on their own terms. They must, therefore, cultivate their own cultural traditions, and that meant Islam. But Islam itself must respond to the changed conditions and become more rational and modern. Muslims must rebel against the long closing of the 'gates of *ijtihad*' and use their own unfettered reason, as both the Prophet and the Quran had insisted.

The Western encroachment had made politics central to the Islamic experience once more. From the time of the Prophet Muhammad, Muslims had seen current events as theophanies; they had encountered a God who was present in history, and had issued a constant challenge to build a better world. Muslims had sought a divine meaning in political events, and even their setbacks and tragedies had led to major developments in theology and spirituality. When Muslims had achieved a type of polity that was more in accordance with the spirit of the Quran after the decline of the Abbasid caliphate, they had agonized less about the political health of the *ummah*, and felt free to develop a more interior piety. But the intrusion of the West into their lives raised major religious questions. The humiliation of the *ummah* was not merely a political catastrophe, but touched a Muslim's very soul. This new weakness was a sign that something had gone gravely awry in Islamic history. The Quran had promised that a society which surrendered to God's revealed will could not fail. Muslim history had proved this. Time and again, when disaster had struck, the most devout Muslims had turned to religion, made it speak to their new circumstances, and the *ummah* had not only revived but had usually gone on to greater achievements. How could Islamdom be falling more and more under the domination of the secular, Godless West? From this point, a growing number of Muslims would wrestle with these questions, and their attempts to put Muslim history back on the straight path would sometimes appear desperate and even despairing. The suicide bomber – an almost unparalleled phenomenon in Islamic history – shows that some Muslims are convinced that they are pitted against hopeless odds.

Al-Afghani's political campaigns, which were often either bizarre or downright immoral, smacked of this new desperation. In 1896, for example, one of his disciples assassinated the Shah of Iran. But his friend and colleague, the Egyptian scholar Muhammad Abdu (1849–1905), was a deeper and more measured thinker. He believed that education and not revolution was the answer. Abdu had been devastated by the British occupation of Egypt, but he loved Europe, felt quite at ease with Europeans, and was widely read in Western science and philosophy. He greatly respected the political, legal and educational institutions of the modern West, but did not believe that they could be transplanted wholesale in a deeply religious country, such as Egypt, where modernization had been too rapid and had perforce excluded the vast mass of the people. It was essential to graft modern legal and constitutional innovations on to traditional Islamic ideas that the people could understand; a society in which people cannot understand the law becomes in effect a country without law. The Islamic principle of *shurah* (consultation), for example, could help Muslims to understand the meaning of democracy. Education also needed reform. *Madrasah* students should study modern science, so that they could help Muslims to enter the new world in an Islamic context that would make it meaningful to them. But the Shariah would need to be brought up to date, and both Abdu and his younger contemporary, the journalist Rashid Rida (1865–1935), knew that this would be a long and complex process. Rida was alarmed by the growing secularism of Arab intellectuals and pundits, who sometimes poured scorn upon Islam in the belief that it was holding their people back. This, Rida believed, could only weaken the *ummah* and make it even more prey to Western imperialism. Rida was one of the first Muslims to advocate the establishment of a fully modernized but fully Islamic state, based on the reformed Shariah. He wanted to establish a college where students could be introduced to the study of international law, sociology, world history, the scientific study of religion, and modern science, at the same time as they studied *fiqh*. This would ensure that Islamic jurisprudence would develop in a truly modern context that would wed the traditions of East and West, and make the Shariah, an agrarian law code, compatible with the new type of society that the West had evolved.

The reformers constantly felt that they had to answer the European criticisms of Islam. In religious as in political affairs, the West was now setting the Muslim agenda. In India, the poet and philosopher Muhammad Iqbal (1876–1938) insisted that Islam was just as rational as any Western system. Indeed, it was the most rational and advanced of all the confessional faiths. Its strict monotheism had liberated humanity from mythology, and the Quran had urged Muslims to observe nature closely, reflect upon their observations, and subject their actions to constant scrutiny. Thus the empirical spirit that had given birth to modernity had in fact originated in Islam. This was a partial and inaccurate interpretation of history, but no more biased than the Western tendency at this time to see Christianity as the superior faith and Europe as always having been in the vanguard of progress. Iqbal's emphasis on the rational spirit of Islam led him to denigrate Sufism. He represented the new trend away from mysticism that would become increasingly prevalent in the Muslim world, as modern rationalism came to seem the only way forward. Iqbal had been deeply influenced by Western thought and had received a PhD in London. Yet he believed that the West had elevated progress at the expense of continuity; its secular individualism separated the notion of personality from God and made it idolatrous and potentially demonic. As a result, the West would eventually destroy itself, a position that was easy to understand after the First World War, which could be seen as the collective suicide of Europe. Muslims therefore had a vital mission to witness to the divine dimension of life, not by retiring from the world to engage in contemplation, but by an activism that implemented the social ideals of the Shariah.

The reformers we have considered so far were intellectuals, who spoke chiefly to the educated elite. In Egypt, the young schoolteacher Hasan al-Banna (1906–49) founded an organization that brought their ideas to the masses. The Society of Muslim Brothers became a mass movement throughout the Middle East, and was the only ideology at this time that was able to appeal to all sectors of society. Al-Banna knew that Muslims needed Western science and technology, and that they must reform their political and social institutions. But he was also convinced, like the reformers, that this must go hand in hand with a spiritual reformation.

When al-Banna saw the British living in luxury in the Suez Canal Zone, he was moved to tears by the contrast with the miserable hovels of the Egyptian workers. He saw this as a religious problem that needed an Islamic solution. Where Christians would often respond to the challenge of modernity by a reassertion of doctrine, Muslims have responded by making a social or political effort (*jihad*). Al-Banna insisted that Islam was a total way of life; religion could not be confined to the private sphere, as the West contended. His society tried to interpret the Quran to meet the spirit of the new age, but also to unify the Islamic nations, raise the standard of living, achieve a higher level of social justice, fight against illiteracy and poverty, and liberate Muslim lands from foreign domination. Under the colonialists, Muslims had been cut off from their roots. As long as they copied other peoples, they would remain cultural mongrels. Besides training the Brothers and Sisters in the rituals of prayer and Quranic living, al-Banna built schools, founded a modern scout movement, ran night schools for workers and tutorial colleges to prepare for the civil service examinations. The Brothers founded clinics and hospitals in the rural areas, built factories, where Muslims got better pay, health insurance and holidays than in the state sector, and taught Muslims modern labour laws so that they could defend their rights.

The society had its faults. A small minority engaged in terrorism and this brought about its dissolution (though it has since revived, under different auspices). But most of the members – who numbered millions of Muslims by 1948 – knew nothing about these fringe activities and saw their welfare and religious mission as crucial. The instant success of the society, which had become the most powerful political institution in Egypt by the Second World War, showed that the vast mass of the people wanted to be modern *and* religious, whatever the intellectuals or the secularist government maintained. This type of social work has continued to characterize many of the modern Islamic movements, notably the Mujamah (Islamic Congress) founded by Sheikh Ahmed Yasin in Gaza, which built a similar welfare empire to bring the benefits of modernity to Palestinians in the territories occupied by Israel after the June War of 1967, but in an Islamic context.

What is a Modern Muslim State?

The colonial experience and the collision with Europe had dislocated Islamic society. The world had irrevocably changed. It was hard for Muslims to know how to respond to the West, because the challenge was unprecedented. If they were to participate as full partners in the modern world, Muslims had to incorporate these changes. In particular, the West had found it necessary to separate religion and politics in order to free government, science and technology from the constraints of conservative religion. In Europe, nationalism had replaced the allegiance of faith, which had formerly enabled its societies to cohere. But this nineteenth-century experiment proved problematic. The nation states of Europe embarked on an arms race in 1870, which led ultimately to two world wars. Secular ideologies proved to be just as murderous as the old religious bigotry, as became clear in the Nazi Holocaust and the Soviet Gulag. The Enlightenment *philosophes* had believed that the more educated people became, the more rational and tolerant they would be. This hope proved to be as utopian as any of the old messianic fantasies. Finally, modern society was committed to democracy, and this had, in general, made life more just and equitable for more people in Europe and America. But the people of the West had had centuries to prepare for the democratic experiment. It would be a very different matter when modern parliamentary systems would be imposed upon societies that were still predominantly agrarian or imperfectly modernized, and where the vast majority of the population found modern political discourse incomprehensible.

Politics has never been central to the Christian religious experience. Jesus had, after all, said that his Kingdom was not of this world. For centuries, the Jews of Europe had refrained from political involvement as a matter of principle. But politics was no secondary issue for Muslims. We have seen that it had been the theatre of their religious quest. Salvation did not mean redemption from sin, but the creation of a just society in which the individual could more easily make that existential surrender of his or her whole being that would bring them fulfilment. The polity was therefore a matter of supreme importance, and throughout the twentieth century there has been one attempt after another to create a truly Islamic state. This has always been difficult. It was an aspiration that required a *jihad*, a struggle that could find no simple outcome.

The ideal of *tawhid* would seem to preclude the ideal of secularism, but in the past both Shiis and Sunnis had accepted a separation of religion and politics. Pragmatic politics is messy and often cruel; the ideal Muslim state is not a 'given' that is simply applied, but it takes creative ingenuity and discipline to implement the egalitarian ideal of the Quran in the grim realities of political life. It is not true that Islam makes it impossible for Muslims to create a modern secular society, as Westerners sometimes imagine. But it is true that secularization has been very different in the Muslim world. In the West, it has usually been experienced as benign. In the early days, it was conceived by such philosophers as John Locke (1632–1704) as a new and better way of being religious, since it freed religion from coercive state control and enabled it to be more true to its spiritual ideals. But in the Muslim world, secularism has often consisted of a brutal attack upon religion and the religious.

Atatürk, for example, closed down all the *madrasahs*, suppressed the Sufi orders, and forced men and women to wear modern Western dress. Such coercion is always counterproductive. Islam in Turkey did not disappear, it simply went underground. Muhammad Ali had also despoiled the Egyptian *ulama*, appropriated their endowments, and deprived them of influence. Later Jamal Abd al-Nasser (1918–70) became for a time quite militantly anti-Islamic, and suppressed the Muslim Brotherhood. One of the Brothers, who belonged to the secret terrorist wing of the society, had made an attempt on al-Nasser's life, but the majority of the thousands of Brothers who languished for years in al-Nasser's concentration camps had done nothing more inflammatory than hand out leaflets or attend a meeting. In Iran, the Pahlavi monarchs were also ruthless in their secularism. Reza Shah Pahlavi (1878–41) deprived the *ulama* of their endowments, and replaced the Shariah with a civil system; he suppressed the Ashura celebrations in honour of Husain, and forbade Iranians to go on the *hajj*. Islamic dress was prohibited, and Reza's soldiers used to tear off women's veils with their bayonets and rip them to pieces in the street. In 1935, when protestors peacefully demonstrated against the Dress Laws in the shrine of the Eighth Imam at Mashhad, the soldiers fired on the unarmed crowd and there were hundreds of casualties. The *ulama*, who had enjoyed unrivalled power in Iran, had to watch their influence crumble. But Ayatollah Muddaris, the cleric who attacked Reza in the parliamentary Assembly, was murdered by the regime in 1937 and the *ulama* became too frightened to make any further protest. Reza's son and successor, Muhammad Reza Shah (1919–80) proved to be just as hostile and contemptuous of Islam. Hundreds of *madrasah* students who dared to protest against the regime were shot in the streets, *madrasahs* were closed, and leading *ulama* were tortured to death, imprisoned and exiled. There was nothing democratic about this secular regime. SAVAK, the shah's secret police, imprisoned Iranians without trial, subjected them to torture and intimidation, and there was no possibility of truly representative government.

Nationalism, from which Europeans themselves had begun to retreat in the latter part of the twentieth century, was also problematic. The unity of the *ummah* had long been a treasured ideal; now the Muslim world was split into kingdoms and republics, whose borders were arbitrarily drawn up by the Western powers. It was not easy to build a national spirit, when Muslims had been accustomed to think of themselves as Ottoman citizens and members of the Dar al-Islam. Sometimes what passed as nationalism took a purely negative stance and became identified with the desire to get rid of the West. Some of the new nations had been so constructed that there was bound to be tension among their citizens. The southern part of the Sudan, for example, was largely Christian, while the north was Muslim. For a people who were accustomed to defining their identity in religious terms, it would be hard to establish a common 'Sudanese' nationalism. The problem was even more acute in Lebanon, where the population was equally divided between at least three religious communities – Sunni, Shii and Maronite Christian – which had always been autonomous before. Power-sharing proved to be an impossibility. The demographic time-bomb led to the civil war (1975–90), which tragically tore the country apart. In other countries, such as Syria, Egypt, or Iraq, nationalism would be adopted by an elite, but not by the more conservative masses. In Iran, the nationalism of the Pahlavis was directly hostile to Islam, since it tried to sever the country's connection with Shiism and based itself on the ancient Persian culture of the pre-Islamic period.

Democracy also posed problems. The reformers who wanted to graft modernity on to an Islamic substructure pointed out that in itself the ideal of democracy was not inimical to Islam. Islamic law promoted the principles of *shurah* (consultation), and *ijmah*, where a law had to be endorsed by the 'consensus' of a representative portion of the *ummah*. The *rashidun* had been elected by a majority vote. All this was quite compatible with the democratic ideal. Part of the difficulty lay in the way that the West formulated democracy as 'government of the people, by the people, and for the people'. In Islam, it is God and not the people who gives a government legitimacy. This elevation of humanity could seem like idolatry (*shirk*), since it was a usurpation of God's sovereignty. But it was not impossible for the Muslim countries to introduce representative forms of government without complying with the Western slogan. But the democratic ideal had often been tainted in practice. When the Iranians set up their Majlis (Assembly) after the Constitutional Revolution of 1906, the Russians helped the shah to close it down. Later, when the British were trying to make Iran a protectorate during the 1920s, the Americans noted that they often rigged the elections to secure a result favourable to themselves. Later American support for the unpopular Muhammad Reza Shah, who not only closed down the Majlis to effect his modernization programme, but systematically denied Iranians fundamental human rights that democracy was supposed to guarantee, made it seem that there was a double standard. The West proudly proclaimed democracy for its own people, but Muslims were expected to submit to cruel dictatorships. In Egypt there were seventeen general elections between 1923 and 1952, all of which were won by the popular Wafd party, but the Wafd were only permitted to rule five times. They were usually forced to stand down by either the British or by the King of Egypt.

It was, therefore, difficult for Muslims to set up a modern democratic nation state, in which religion was relegated to the private sphere. Other solutions seemed little better. The Kingdom of Saudi Arabia, founded in 1932, was based on the Wahhabi ideal.

The official view was that a constitution was unnecessary, since the government was based on a literal reading of the Quran. But the Quran contains very little legislation and it had always been found necessary in practice to supplement it with more complex jurisprudence. The Saudis proclaimed that they were the heirs of the pristine Islam of the Arabian peninsula, and the *ulama* granted the state legitimacy; in return the kings enforced conservative religious values. Women are shrouded from view and secluded (even though this had not been the case in the Prophet's time), gambling and alcohol are forbidden, and traditional punishments, such as the mutilation of thieves, are enshrined in the legal system. Most Muslim states and organizations do not consider that fidelity to the Quran requires these pre-modern penal practices. The Muslim Brotherhood, for example, from a very early date condemned the Saudis' use of Islamic punishments as inappropriate and archaic, especially when the lavish wealth of the ruling elite and the unequal distribution of wealth offended far more crucial Quranic values.

Pakistan was another modern Islamic experiment. Muhammad Ali Jinnah (1876–1948), the founder of the state, was imbued with the modern secular ideal. Ever since the time of Aurengzebe, Muslims had felt unhappy and insecure in India: they had feared for their identity and felt anxious about the power of the Hindu majority. This naturally became more acute after the partition of the subcontinent by the British in 1947, when communal violence exploded on both sides and thousands of people lost their lives. Jinnah had wanted to create a political arena in which Muslims were not defined or limited by their religious identity. But what did it mean for a Muslim state which made great use of Islamic symbols to be 'secular'? The Jamaat-i Islami, founded by Abul Ala Mawdudi (1903–79) pressed for a more strict application of Shariah norms, and in 1956 the constitution formally defined Pakistan as an Islamic Republic. This represented an aspiration, which now had to be incarnated in the political institutions of the country. The government of General Muhammad Ayub Khan (1958–69) was a typical example of the aggressive secularism that we have already considered. He nationalized the religious endowments (*awqaf*), placed restrictions on *madrasah* education, and promoted a purely secular legal system. His aim was to make Islam a civil religion, amenable to state control, but this led inevitably to tension with the Islamists and eventually to Khan's downfall.

During the 1970s, the Islamist forces became the main focus of opposition to the government, and the leftist, secularist Prime Minister Zulfaqir Ali Bhutto (1928–79) tried to mollify them by banning alcohol and gambling, but this was not sufficient and in July 1977 the devout Muslim Muhammad Zia al-Haqq led a successful coup, and established an ostensibly more Islamic regime. He reinstated traditional Muslim dress, and restored Islamic penal and commercial law. But even President Zia kept Islam at bay in political and economic matters, where his policy was avowedly secularist. Since his death in a plane crash in 1988, Pakistani politics has been dominated by ethnic tension, rivalries and corruption scandals among members of the elite classes, and the Islamists have been less influential. Islam remains important to Pakistan's identity and is ubiquitous in public life, but it still does not affect *realpolitik*. The compromise is reminiscent of the solutions of the Abbasids and Mongols, which saw a similar separation of powers. The state seems to have forced the Islamic parties into line, but this state of affairs is far from ideal. As in India, disproportionate sums are spent on nuclear weapons, while at least a third of the population languish in hopeless poverty, a situation which is abhorrent to a truly Muslim sensibility. Muslim activists who feel coerced by the state look towards the fundamentalist government of the Taliban in neighbouring Afghanistan.

The fact that Muslims have not yet found an ideal polity for the twentieth century does not mean that Islam is incompatible with modernity. The struggle to enshrine the Islamic ideal in state structures and to find the right leader has preoccupied Muslims throughout their history. Because, like any religious value, the notion of the true Islamic state is transcendent, it can never be perfectly expressed in human form and always eludes the grasp of frail and flawed human beings. Religious life is difficult, and the secular rationalism of our modern culture poses special problems for people in all the major traditions. Christians, who are more preoccupied by doctrine than by politics, are currently wrestling with dogmatic questions in their effort to make their faith speak to the modern sensibility. They are debating their belief in the

divinity of Christ, for example, some clinging to the older for-
mulations of the dogma, others finding more radical solutions.
Sometimes these discussions become anguished and even acri-
monious, because the issues touch the nub of religiosity that lies
at the heart of the Christian vision. The struggle for a modern
Islamic state is the Muslim equivalent of this dilemma. All religious people in any age have to make their traditions address the
challenge of their particular modernity, and the quest for an ideal
form of Muslim government should not be viewed as aberrant but
as an essentially and typically religious activity.

Fundamentalism

The Western media often give the impression that the embattled
and occasionally violent form of religiosity known as 'fundamentalism' is a purely Islamic phenomenon. This is not the
case. Fundamentalism is a global fact and has surfaced in every
major faith in response to the problems of our modernity. There
is fundamentalist Judaism, fundamentalist Christianity, fundamentalist Hinduism, fundamentalist Buddhism, fundamentalist Sikhism, and even fundamentalist Confucianism.
This type of faith surfaced first in the Christian world in the
United States at the beginning of the twentieth century. This was
not accidental. Fundamentalism is not a monolithic movement;
each form of fundamentalism, even within the same tradition,
develops independently and has its own symbols and enthusiasms,
but its different manifestations all bear a family resemblance. It
has been noted that a fundamentalist movement does not arise
immediately, as a knee-jerk response to the advent of Western
modernity, but only takes shape when the modernization process
is quite far advanced. At first religious people try to reform their
traditions and effect a marriage between them and modern
culture, as we have seen the Muslim reformers do. But when these
moderate measures are found to be of no avail, some people resort
to more extreme methods, and a fundamentalist movement is
born. With hindsight, we can see that it was only to be expected
that fundamentalism should first make itself known in the United
States, the showcase of modernity, and only appear in other parts

of the world at a later date. Of the three monotheistic religions, Islam was in fact the last to develop a fundamentalist strain, when modern culture began to take root in the Muslim world in the late 1960s and 1970s. By this date, fundamentalism was quite well established among Christians and Jews, who had had a longer exposure to the modern experience.

Fundamentalist movements in all faiths share certain characteristics. They reveal a deep disappointment and disenchantment with the modern experiment, which has not fulfilled all that it promised. They also express real fear. Every single fundamentalist movement that I have studied is convinced that the secular establishment is determined to wipe religion out. This is not always a paranoid reaction. We have seen that secularism has often been imposed very aggressively in the Muslim world. Fundamentalists look back to a 'golden age' before the irruption of modernity for inspiration, but they are not atavistically returning to the Middle Ages. All are intrinsically modern movements and could have appeared at no time other than our own. All are innovative and often radical in their reinterpretation of religion. As such, fundamentalism is an essential part of the modern scene. Wherever modernity takes root, a fundamentalist movement is likely to rise up alongside it in conscious reaction. Fundamentalists will often express their discontent with a modern development by overstressing those elements in their tradition that militate against it. They are all – even in the United States – highly critical of democracy and secularism. Because the emancipation of women has been one of the hallmarks of modern culture, fundamentalists tend to emphasise conventional, agrarian gender roles, putting women back into veils and into the home. The fundamentalist community can thus be seen as the shadow-side of modernity; it can also highlight some of the darker sides of the modern experiment.

Fundamentalism, therefore, exists in a symbiotic relationship with a coercive secularism. Fundamentalists nearly always feel assaulted by the liberal or modernizing establishment, and their views and behaviour become more extreme as a result. After the famous Scopes Trial (1925) in Tennessee, when Protestant fundamentalists tried to prevent the teaching of evolution in the public schools, they were so ridiculed by the secularist press that their theology became more reactionary and excessively literal, and they turned from the left to the extreme right of the political spectrum. When the secularist attack has been more violent, the fundamentalist reaction is likely to be even greater. Fundamentalism therefore reveals a fissure in society, which is polarized between those who enjoy secular culture, and those who regard it with dread. As time passes, the two camps become increasingly unable to understand one another. Fundamentalism thus begins as an internal dispute, with liberalizers or secularists within one's *own* culture or nation. In the first instance, for example, Muslim fundamentalists will often oppose their fellow-countrymen or fellow-Muslims who take a more positive view of modernity, rather than such external foes as the West or Israel. Very often, fundamentalists begin by withdrawing from mainstream culture to create an enclave of pure faith (as, for example, within the ultra-Orthodox Jewish communities in Jerusalem or New York). Thence they will sometimes conduct an offensive which can take many forms, designed to bring the mainstream back to the right path and resacralize the world. All fundamentalists feel that they are fighting for survival, and because their backs are to the wall, they can believe that they have to fight their way out of the impasse. In this frame of mind, on rare occasions, some resort to terrorism. The vast majority, however, do not commit acts of violence, but simply try to revive their faith in a more conventional, lawful way.

Fundamentalists have been successful in so far as they have pushed religion from the sidelines and back to centre stage, so that it now plays a major part in international affairs once again, a development that would have seemed inconceivable in the mid-twentieth century when secularism seemed in the ascendant. This has certainly been the case in the Islamic world since the 1970s. But fundamentalism is not simply a way of 'using' religion for a political end. These are essentially rebellions against the secularist exclusion of the divine from public life, and a frequently desperate attempt to make spiritual values prevail in the modern world. But the desperation and fear that fuel fundamentalists also tend to distort the religious tradition, and accentuate its more aggressive aspects at the expense of those that preach toleration and reconciliation.

Muslim fundamentalism corresponds very closely to these general characteristics. It is not correct, therefore, to imagine that Islam has within it a militant, fanatic strain that impels Muslims into a crazed and violent rejection of modernity. Muslims are in tune with fundamentalists in other faiths all over the world, who share their profound misgivings about modern secular culture. It should also be said that Muslims object to the use of the term 'fundamentalism', pointing out quite correctly that it was coined by American Protestants as a badge of pride, and cannot be usefully translated into Arabic. *Usul*, as we have seen, refers to the fundamental principles of Islamic jurisprudence, and as all Muslims agree on these, all Muslims could be said to subscribe to *usuliyyah* (fundamentalism). Nevertheless, for all its shortcomings, 'fundamentalism' is the only term we have to describe this family of embattled religious movements, and it is difficult to come up with a more satisfactory substitute.

One of the early fundamentalist idealogues was Mawdudi, the founder of the Jamaat-i Islami in Pakistan. He saw the mighty power of the West as gathering its forces to crush Islam. Muslims, he argued, must band together to fight this encroaching secularism, if they wanted their religion and their culture to survive. Muslims had encountered hostile societies before and had experienced disasters but, starting with Afghani, a new note had crept into Islamic discourse. The Western threat had made Muslims defensive for the first time. Mawdudi defied the whole secularist ethos: he was proposing an Islamic liberation theology. Because God alone was sovereign, nobody was obliged to take orders from any other human being. Revolution against the colonial powers was not just a right but a duty. Mawdudi called for a universal *jihad*. Just as the Prophet had fought the *jahiliyyah* (the 'ignorance' and barbarism of the pre-Islamic period), Muslims must use all means in their power to resist the modern *jahiliyyah* of the West. Mawdudi argued that *jihad* was the central tenet of Islam. This was an innovation. Nobody had ever claimed before that *jihad* was equivalent to the five Pillars of Islam, but Mawdudi felt that the innovation was justified by the present emergency. The stress and fear of cultural and religious annihilation had led to the development of a more extreme and potentially violent distortion of the faith.

But the real founder of Islamic fundamentalism in the Sunni world was Sayyid Qutb (1906–66), who was greatly influenced by Mawdudi. Yet he had not originally been an extremist but had been filled with enthusiasm for Western culture and secular politics. Even after he joined the Muslim Brotherhood in 1953 he had been a reformer, hoping to give Western democracy an Islamic dimension that would avoid the excesses of a wholly secularist ideology. However, in 1956 he was imprisoned by al-Nasser for membership of the Brotherhood, and in the concentration camp he became convinced that religious people and secularists could not live in peace in the same society. As he witnessed the torture and execution of the Brothers, and reflected upon al-Nasser's avowed determination to cast religion into a marginal role in Egypt, he could see all the characteristics of *jahiliyyah*, which he defined as the barbarism that was for ever and for all time the enemy of faith, and which Muslims, following the example of the Prophet Muhammad, were bound to fight to the death. Qutb went further than Mawdudi, who had only seen non-Muslim societies as *jahili*. Qutb applied the term *jahiliyyah*, which in conventional Muslim historiography had been used simply to describe the pre-Islamic period in Arabia, to contemporary Muslim society. Even though a ruler such as al-Nasser outwardly professed Islam, his words and actions proved him to be an apostate and Muslims were duty-bound to overthrow such a government, just as Muhammad had forced the pagan establishment of Mecca (the *jahiliyyah* of his day) into submission.

The violent secularism of al-Nasser had led Qutb to espouse a form of Islam that distorted both the message of the Quran and the Prophet's life. Qutb told Muslims to model themselves on Muhammad: to separate themselves from mainstream society (as Muhammad had made the *hijrah* from Mecca to Medina), and then engage in a violent *jihad*. But Muhammad had in fact finally achieved victory by an ingenious policy of non-violence; the Quran adamantly opposed force and coercion in religious matters, and its vision – far from preaching exclusion and separation – was tolerant and inclusive. Qutb insisted that the Quranic injunction to toleration could only occur *after* the political victory of Islam and the establishment of a true Muslim state. The new intransigence sprang from the profound fear that is at the core of fundamentalist religion. Qutb did not survive. At al-Nasser's personal insistence, he was executed in 1966.

Every Sunni fundamentalist movement has been influenced by Qutb. Most spectacularly it has inspired Muslims to assassinate such leaders as Anwar al-Sadat, denounced as a *jahili* ruler because of his oppressive policies towards his own people. The Taliban, who came to power in Afghanistan in 1994, are also affected by his ideology. They are determined to return to what they see as the original vision of Islam. The *ulama* are the leaders of the government, women are veiled and not permitted to take part in professional life. Only religious broadcasting is permitted and the Islamic punishments of stoning and mutilation have been reintroduced. In some circles of the West, the Taliban are seen as quintessential Muslims, but their regime violates crucial Islamic precepts. Most of the Taliban ('students' of the *madrasahs*) belong to the Pakhtum tribe, and they tend to target non-Pakhtums, who fight the regime from the north of the country. Such ethnic chauvinism was forbidden by the Prophet and by the Quran. Their harsh treatment of minority groups is also opposed to clear Quranic requirements. The Taliban's discrimination against women is completely opposed to the practice of the Prophet and the conduct of the first *ummah*. The Taliban are typically fundamentalist, however, in their highly selective vision of religion (which reflects their narrow education in some of the *madrasahs* of Pakistan), which perverts the faith and turns it in the opposite direction of what was intended. Like all the major faiths, Muslim fundamentalists, in their struggle to survive, make religion a tool of oppression and even of violence.

But most Sunni fundamentalists have not resorted to such an extreme. The fundamentalist movements that sprang up during the 1970s and 1980s all tried to change the world about them in less drastic but telling ways. After the humiliating defeat of the Arab armies in the Six-Day War against Israel in 1967, there was a swing towards religion throughout the Middle East. The old secularist policies of such leaders as al-Nasser seemed discredited. People felt that the Muslims had failed because they had not been true to their religion. They could see that while secularism and democracy worked very well in the West, they did not benefit ordinary Muslims but only an elite in the Islamic world. Fundamentalism can be seen as a 'post-modern' movement, which rejects some of the tenets and enthusiasms of modernity, such as colonialism. Throughout the Islamic world, students and factory workers started to change their immediate environment. They created mosques in their universities and factories, where they could make *salat*, set up Banna-style welfare societies with an Islamic orientation, demonstrating that Islam worked for the people better than the secularist governments. When students declared a shady patch of lawn – or even a noticeboard – to be an Islamic zone, they felt that they had made a small but significant attempt to push Islam from the marginal realm to which it had been relegated in secularist society, and reclaimed a part of the world – however tiny – for Islam. They were pushing forward the frontiers of the sacred, in rather the same way as the Jewish fundamentalists in Israel who made settlements in the occupied West Bank, reclaiming Arab land and bringing it under the aegis of Judaism.

The same principle underlines the return to Islamic dress. When this is forced upon people against their will (as by the Taliban) it is coercive and as likely to create a backlash as the aggressive techniques of Reza Shah Pahlavi. But many Muslim women feel that veiling is a symbolic return to the pre-colonial period, before their society was disrupted and deflected from its true course. Yet they have not simply turned the clock back. Surveys show that a large proportion of veiled women hold progressive views on such matters as gender. For some women, who have come from rural areas to the university and are the first members of their family to advance beyond basic literacy, the assumption of Islamic dress provides continuity and makes their rite of passage to modernity less traumatic than it might otherwise have been. They are coming to join the modern world but on their own terms and in an Islamic context that gives it sacred meaning. Veiling can also be seen as a tacit critique of some of the less positive aspects of modernity. It defies the strange Western compulsion to 'reveal all' in sexual matters. In the West, people often flaunt their tanned, well-honed bodies as a sign of privilege; they try to counteract the signs of ageing and hold on to this life. The shrouded Islamic body declares that it is oriented to transcendence, and the uniformity of dress abolishes class difference and stresses the importance of community over Western individualism.

People have often used religion as a way of making modern ideas and enthusiasms comprehensible. Not all the American Calvinists at the time of the 1776 American Revolution shared or even understood the secularist ethos of the Founding Fathers, for example. They gave the struggle a Christian colouration so that they were able to fight alongside the secularists in the creation of a new world. Some Sunni and Shii fundamentalists are also using religion to make the alien tenor of modern culture familiar, giving it a context of meaning and spirituality that makes it more accessible. Again, they are tacitly asserting that it is possible to be modern on other cultural terms than those laid down by the West. The Iranian Revolution of 1978–9 can be seen in this light. During the 1960s Ayatollah Ruhollah Khomeini (1902–89) brought the people of Iran out on to the streets to protest against the cruel and unconstitutional policies of Muhammad Reza Shah, whom he identified with Yazid, the Umayyad caliph who had been responsible for the death of Husain at Kerbala, the type of the unjust ruler in Shii Islam. Muslims had a duty to fight such tyranny, and the mass of the people, who would have been quite unmoved by a socialist call to revolution, could respond to Khomeini's summons, which resonated with their deepest traditions. Khomeini provided a Shii alternative to the secular nationalism of the shah. He came to seem more and more like one of the Imams: like all the Imams, he had been attacked, imprisoned, and almost killed by an unjust ruler; like some of the Imams, he was forced into exile and deprived of what was his own; like Ali and Husain, he had bravely opposed injustice and stood up for true Islamic values; like all the Imams, he was known to be a practising mystic; like Husain, whose son was killed at Kerbala, Khomeini's son Mustafa was killed by the shah's agents.

When the revolution broke in 1978, after a slanderous attack on Khomeini in the semi-official newspaper *Ettelaat*, and the shocking massacre of young *madrasah* students who came out on to the streets in protest, Khomeini seemed to be directing operations from afar (from Najaf, his place of exile) rather like the Hidden Imam. Secularists and intellectuals were willing to join forces with the *ulama* because they knew that only Khomeini could command the grass-roots support of the people. The Islamic Revolution was the only revolution inspired by a twentieth-century ideology (the Russian and Chinese revolutions both owed their inspiration to the nineteenth-century vision of Karl Marx). Khomeini had evolved a radically new interpretation of Shiism: in the absence of the Hidden Imam, only the mystically inspired jurist, who knew the sacred law, could validly govern the nation. For centuries, Twelver Shiis had prohibited clerics from participating in government, but the revolutionaries (if not many of the *ulama*) were willing to subscribe to this theory of Velayat-i Faqih (the Mandate of the Jurist).[1] Throughout the revolution, the symbolism of Kerbala was predominant. Traditional religious ceremonies to mourn the dead and the Ashura celebrations in honour of Husain became demonstrations against the regime. The Kerbala myth inspired ordinary Shiis to brave the shah's guns and die in their thousands, some donning the white shroud of martyrdom. Religion was proved to be so powerful a force that it brought down the Pahlavi state, which had seemed the most stable and powerful in the Middle East.

But, like all fundamentalists, Khomeini's vision was also distorting. The taking of the American hostages in Tehran (and, later, by Shii radicals in Lebanon, who were inspired by the Iranian example) violates clear Quranic commands about the treatment of prisoners, who must be handled with dignity and respect, and freed as soon as possible. The captor is even obliged to contribute to the ransom from his own resources. Indeed, the Quran expressly forbids the taking of prisoners except during a conventional war, which obviously rules out hostage-taking when hostilities are not in progress.[2] After the revolution, Khomeini insisted on what he called 'unity of expression', suppressing any dissentient voice. Not only had the demand for free speech been one of the chief concerns of the revolution, but Islam had never insisted on ideological conformity, only upon a uniformity of practice. Coercion in religious matters is forbidden in the Quran, and was abhorred by Mulla Sadra, Khomeini's spiritual mentor. When Khomeini issued his *fatwah* against novelist Salman Rushdie for his allegedly blasphemous portrait of Muhammad in *The Satanic Verses* on 14 February 1989, he also contravened Sadra's impassioned defence of freedom of thought. The *fatwah* was declared un-Islamic by the *ulama* of al-Azhar and Saudi Arabia, and was condemned by forty-eight out of the forty-nine member states of the Islamic Conference the following month.

But it appears that the Islamic revolution may have helped the Iranian people to come to modernity on their own terms. Shortly before his death, Khomeini tried to pass more power to the parliament, and, with his apparent blessing, Hashami Rafsanjani, the Speaker of the Majlis, gave a democratic interpretation of Velayat-i Faqih. The needs of the modern state had convinced Shiis of the necessity of democracy, but this time it came in an Islamic package that made it acceptable to the majority of the people. This seemed confirmed on 23 May 1997, when Hojjat ol-Islam Seyyid Khatami was elected to the presidency in a landslide victory. He immediately made it clear that he wanted to build a more positive relationship with the West, and in September 1998 he dissociated his government from the *fatwah* against Rushdie, a move which was later endorsed by Ayatollah Khameini, the Supreme Faqih of Iran. Khatemi's election signalled the strong desire of a large segment of the population for greater pluralism, a gentler interpretation of Islamic law, more democracy, and a more progressive policy for women. The battle is still not won. The conservative clerics who opposed Khomeini and for whom he had little time are still able to block many of Khatemi's reforms, but the struggle to create a viable Islamic state, true to the spirit of the Quran and yet responsive to current conditions, is still a major preoccupation of the Iranian people.

Muslims in a Minority

The spectre of Islamic fundamentalism sends a shiver through Western society, which seems not nearly so threatened by the equally prevalent and violent fundamentalism of other faiths. This has certainly affected the attitude of Western people towards the Muslims living in their own countries. Five to six million Muslims reside in Europe, and seven to eight million in the United States. There are now about a thousand mosques each in Germany and France, and five hundred in the United Kingdom. About half the Muslims in the West today have been born there to parents who immigrated in the 1950s and 1960s. They rejected their parents' meeker stance, are better educated, and seek greater visibility and acceptance. Sometimes their efforts are ill-advised, as, for example, Dr Kalim Siddiqui's call for a Muslim parliament in the United Kingdom in the early 1990s, a project which received very little support from most British Muslims but which made people fear that Muslims were not willing to integrate into mainstream society. There was immense hostility towards the Muslim community during the crisis over *The Satanic Verses*, when Muslims in Bradford publicly burned the book. Most British Muslims may have disapproved of the novel, but had no desire to see Rushdie killed. Europeans seem to find it difficult to relate to their Muslim fellow-countrymen in a natural balanced manner. Turkish migrant workers have been murdered in race riots in Germany, girls who choose to wear a *hijab* to school have received extremely hostile coverage in the French press. In Britain, there is often outrage when Muslims request separate schools for their children, even though people do not voice the same objections about special schools for Jews, Roman Catholics or Quakers. It is as though Muslims are viewed as a Fifth Column, plotting to undermine British society.

Muslims have fared better in the United States. The Muslim immigrants there are better educated and middle class. They work as doctors, academics and engineers, whereas in Europe the Muslim community is still predominantly working class. American Muslims feel that they are in the United States by choice. They want to become Americans, and in the land of the melting-pot integration is more of a possibility than in Europe. Some Muslims, such as Malcolm X (1925–65), the charismatic leader of the black separatist group called the Nation of Islam, gained widespread respect at the time of the Civil Rights movement, and became an emblem of Black and Muslim power. The Nation of Islam, however, was a heterodox party. Founded in 1930 by Wali Fard Muhammad Fard, a pedlar of Detroit, and, after the mysterious disappearance of Fard in 1934, led by Elijah Muhammad (1897–1975), it claimed that God had been incarnated in Fard, that white people are inherently evil, and that there was no life after death – all views that are heretical from an Islamic perspective. The Nation of Islam demanded a separate state for

African Americans to compensate them for the years of slavery, and is adamantly hostile to the West. Malcolm X became disillusioned with the Nation of Islam, however, when he discovered the moral laxity of Elijah Muhammad, and took his followers into Sunni Islam: two years later, he was assassinated for this apostasy. But the Nation of Islam still gains far more media coverage than the much larger American Muslim Mission, founded by Malcolm X, which is now wholly orthodox, sends its members to study at al-Azhar, and explores the possibility of working alongside white Americans for a more just society. The bizarre and rejectionist stance of the Nation may seem closer to the Western stereotype of Islam as an inherently intolerant and fanatical faith.

In India, those Muslims who did not emigrate to Pakistan in 1947 and their descendants now number 115 million. But despite their large numbers, many feel even more beleaguered and endangered than their brothers and sisters in the West. The Hindus and Muslims of India are all still haunted by the tragic violence of the partition of the subcontinent in 1947, and though many Hindus stand up for Muslim rights in India, Muslims tend to get a bad press. They are accused of a ghetto mentality, of being loyal at heart to Pakistan or Kashmir; they are blamed for having too many children, and for being backward. Indian Muslims are being squeezed out of the villages, cannot easily get good jobs, and are often refused decent accommodation. The only signs of the glorious Moghul past are the great buildings: the Taj Mahal, the Red Fort and the Juneh Mosque, which have also become a rallying point for the Hindu fundamentalist group, the Bharatiya Janarta Party (BJP), which claims that they were really built by Hindus, that the Muslims destroyed the temples of India, and erected mosques in their place. The BJP's chief target was the Mosque of Babur, the founder of the Moghul dynasty, at Ayodhya, which the BJP dismantled in ten hours in December 1992, while the press and army stood by and watched. The impact on the Muslims of India has been devastating. They fear that this symbolic destruction was only the beginning of further troubles, and that soon they and their memory will be erased in India. This dread of annihilation lay behind their frantic opposition to *The Satanic Verses*, which seemed yet another threat to the faith. Yet the communalism and intolerance is against the most tolerant and civilized traditions of Indian Islam. Yet again, fear and oppression have distorted the faith.

The Way Forward

On the eve of the second Christian millennium, the Crusaders massacred some thirty thousand Jews and Muslims in Jerusalem, turning the thriving Islamic holy city into a stinking charnel house. For at least five months the valleys and ditches around the city were filled with putrefying corpses, which were too numerous for the small number of Crusaders who remained behind after the expedition to clear away, and a stench hung over Jerusalem, where the three religions of Abraham had been able to coexist in relative harmony under Islamic rule for nearly five hundred years. This was the Muslims' first experience of the Christian West, as it pulled itself out of the dark age that had descended after the collapse of the Roman Empire in the fifth century, and fought its way back on to the international scene. The Muslims suffered from the Crusaders, but were not long incommoded by their presence. In 1187 Saladin was able to recapture Jerusalem for Islam and though the Crusaders hung on in the Near East for another century, they seemed an unimportant passing episode in the long Islamic history of the region. Most of the inhabitants of Islamdon were entirely unaffected by the Crusades and remained uninterested in western Europe, which, despite its dramatic cultural advance during the crusading period, still lagged behind the Muslim world.

Europeans did not forget the Crusades, however, nor could they ignore the Dar al-Islam, which, as the years went by, seemed to rule the entire globe. Ever since the Crusades, the people of Western Christendom developed a stereotypical and distorted image of Islam, which they regarded as the enemy of decent civilization. The prejudice became entwined with European fantasies about Jews, the other victims of the Crusaders, and often reflected buried worry about the conduct of Christians. It was, for example, during the Crusades, when it was Christians who had instigated a series of brutal holy wars against the Muslim world, that Islam was described by the learned scholar-monks of Europe as an inherently violent and intolerant faith, which had only been able to establish itself by the sword. The myth of the supposed fanatical intolerance of Islam has become one of the received ideas of the West.

As the millennium drew to a close, however, some Muslims seemed to live up to this Western perception, and, for the first time, have made sacred violence a cardinal Islamic duty. These fundamentalists often call Western colonialism and post-colonial Western imperialism *al-Salibiyyah*: the Crusade. The colonial crusade has been less violent but its impact has been more devastating than the medieval holy wars. The powerful Muslim world has been reduced to a dependent bloc, and Muslim society has been gravely dislocated in the course of an accelerated modernization programme. All over the world, as we have seen, people in all the major faiths have reeled under the impact of Western modernity, and have produced the embattled and frequently intolerant religiosity that we call fundamentalism. As they struggle to rectify what they see as the damaging effects of modern secular culture, fundamentalists fight back and, in the process, they depart from the core values of compassion, justice and benevolence that characterize all the world faiths, including Islam. Religion, like any other human activity, is often abused, but at its best it helps human beings to cultivate a sense of the sacred inviolability of each individual, and thus to mitigate the murderous violence to which our species is tragically prone. Religion has committed atrocities in the past, but in its brief history secularism has proved that it can be just as violent. As we have seen, secular aggression and persecution have often led to a heightening of religious intolerance and hatred.

This became tragically clear in Algeria in 1992. During the religious revival of the 1970s, the Islamic Salvation Front (FIS) challenged the hegemony of the secular nationalist party, the National Liberation Front (FLN), which had led the revolution against French colonial rule in 1954, and had established a socialist government in the country in 1962. The Algerian revolution against France had been an inspiration to Arabs and Muslims who were also struggling to gain independence from Europe. The FLN was similar to the other secular and socialist governments in the Middle East at this time, which had relegated Islam to the private sphere, on the Western pattern. By the 1970s, however, people all over the Muslim world were becoming dissatisfied with these secularist ideologies which had not delivered what they had promised. Abbas Madani, one of the founding members of FIS, wanted to create an Islamic political ideology for the modern world; Ali ibn Hajj, the *imam* of a mosque in a poor neighbourhood in Algiers, led a more radical wing of FIS. Slowly, FIS began to build its own mosques, without getting permission from the government; it took root in the Muslim community in France, where workers demanded places of prayer in the factories and offices, incurring the wrath of the right-wing party led by Jean-Marie Le Pen.

By the 1980s, Algeria was in the grip of an economic crisis. FLN had set the country on the path to democracy and statehood, but over the years it had become corrupt. The old *garde* were reluctant to attempt more democratic reforms. There had been a population explosion in Algeria; most of its thirty million inhabitants were under thirty, many were unemployed, and there was an acute housing shortage. There were riots. Frustrated with the stagnation and ineptitude of the FLN, the young wanted something new and turned to the Islamic parties. In June 1990 the FIS scored major victories in the local elections, especially in the urban areas. FIS activists were mostly young, idealistic and well-educated; they were known to be honest and efficient in government, though they were dogmatic and conservative in some areas, such as their insistence upon traditional Islamic dress for women. But the FIS was not anti-Western. Leaders spoke of encouraging links with the European Union and fresh Western investment. After the electoral victories at the local level, they seemed certain to succeed in the legislative elections that were scheduled for 1992.

There was to be no Islamic government in Algeria, however. The military staged a coup, ousted the liberal FLN President Benjedid (who had promised democratic reforms), suppressed FIS, and threw its leaders into prison. Had elections been prevented in such a violent and unconstitutional manner in Iran and Pakistan, there would have been an outcry in the West. Such a coup would have been seen as an example of Islam's supposedly endemic aversion to democracy, and its basic incompatibility with the modern world. But because it was an Islamic government that had been thwarted by the coup, there was jubilation in the Western press. Algeria had been saved from the Islamic menace; the bars, casinos, and discotheques of Algiers had been spared; and in some mysterious way, this undemocratic action had made Algeria safe for democracy. The French government threw its support behind the new hardline FLN of President Liamine Zeroual and strengthened his resolve to hold no further dialogue with FIS. Not surprisingly, the Muslim world was shocked by this fresh instance of Western double standards.

The result was tragically predictable. Pushed outside the due processes of law, outraged, and despairing of justice, the more radical members of FIS broke away to form a guerrilla organization, the Armed Islamic Group (GIA), and began a terror campaign in the mountainous regions south of Algiers. There were massacres, in which the population of entire villages were killed. Journalists and intellectuals, secular and religious, were also targeted. It was generally assumed that the Islamists were wholly responsible for these atrocities, but gradually questions were asked which pointed to the fact that some elements in the Algerian military forces not only acquiesced but also participated in the killing to discredit the GIA. There was now a ghastly stalemate. Both FLN and FIS were torn apart by an internal feud between the pragmatists who wanted a solution, and the hardliners who refused to negotiate. The violence of the initial coup to stop the elections had led to an outright war between the religious and secularists. In January 1995 the Roman Catholic Church helped to organize a meeting in Rome to bring the two sides together, but Zeroual's government refused to participate. A golden opportunity had been lost. There was more Islamic terror, and a constitutional referendum banned all religious political parties.

The tragic case of Algeria must not become a paradigm for the future. Suppression and coercion had helped to push a disgruntled Muslim minority into a violence that offends every central tenet of Islam. An aggressive secularism had resulted in a religiosity that was a travesty of true faith. The incident further tarnished the notion of democracy, which the West is so anxious to promote, but which, it appeared, had limits, if the democratic process might lead to the establishment of an elected Islamic government. The people of Europe and the United States were shown to be ignorant about the various parties and groups within the Islamic world. The moderate FIS was equated with the most violent fundamentalist groups and was associated in the Western mind with the violence, illegality and anti-democratic behaviour that had this time been displayed by the secularists in the FLN.

But whether the West likes it or not, the initial success of the FIS in the local elections showed that the people wanted some form of Islamic government. It passed a clear message to Egypt, Morocco and Tunisia, where secularist governments had long been aware of the growing religiosity of their countries. In the middle of the twentieth century, secularism had been dominant, and Islam was thought to be irredeemably *passé*. Now any secularist government in the Middle East was uncomfortably aware that if there were truly democratic elections, an Islamic government might well come to power. In Egypt, for example, Islam is as popular as Nasserism was in the 1950s. Islamic dress is ubiquitous and, since Mubarak's government is secularist, is clearly voluntarily assumed. Even in secularist Turkey, recent polls showed that some seventy per cent of the population claimed to be devout, and that twenty per cent prayed five times a day. People are turning to the Muslim Brotherhood in Jordan, and Palestinians are looking to Mujamah, while the PLO, which in the 1960s carried all before it, often appears cumbersome, corrupt and out of date. In the republics of Central Asia, Muslims are rediscovering their religion after decades of Soviet oppression. People have tried the secularist ideologies, which have worked so successfully in Western countries where they are on home ground. Increasingly, Muslims want their governments to conform more closely to the Islamic norm.

The precise form that this will take is not yet clear. In Egypt it seems that a majority of Muslims would like to see the Shariah as the law of the land, whereas in Turkey only three per cent want this. Even in Egypt, however, some of the *ulama* are aware that the problems of transforming the Shariah, an agrarian law code, to the very different conditions of modernity will be extreme. Rashid Rida had been aware of this as early as the 1930s. But that is not to say that it cannot be done.

It is not true that Muslims are now uniformly filled with hatred of the West. In the early stages of modernization, many leading thinkers were infatuated with European culture, and by the end of the twentieth century some of the most eminent and influential Muslim thinkers were now reaching out to the West again. President Khatemi of Iran is only one example of this trend. So is the Iranian intellectual Abdolkarim Sorush, who held important posts in Khomeini's government, and though he is often harried by the more conservative *mujtahids*, he strongly influences those in power. Sorush admires Khomeini, but has moved beyond him. He maintains that Iranians now have three identities: pre-Islamic, Islamic and Western, which they must try to reconcile. Sorush rejects the secularism of the West, believes that human beings will always need spirituality, but advises Iranians to study the modern sciences, while holding on to Shii tradition. Islam must develop its *fiqh*, so as to accommodate the modern industrial world, and evolve a philosophy of civil rights and an economic theory capable of holding its own in the twenty-first century.

Sunni thinkers have come to similar conclusions. Western hostility towards Islam springs from ignorance, Rashid al-Ghannouchi, the leader of the exiled Renaissance Party in Tunisia, believes. It also springs from a bad experience of Christianity, which did stifle thought and creativity. He describes himself as a 'democratic Islamist' and sees no incompatibility between Islam and democracy, but he rejects the secularism of the West, because the human being cannot be so divided and fragmented. The Muslim ideal of *tawhid* rejects the duality of body and spirit, intellect and spirituality, men and women, morality and the economy, East and West. Muslims want modernity, but not one that has been imposed upon them by America, Britain or France. Muslims admire the efficiency and beautiful technology of the West; they are fascinated by the way a regime can be changed in the West without bloodshed. But when Muslims look at Western society, they see no light, no heart, and no spirituality. They want to hold on to their own religious and moral traditions and, at the same time, to try to incorporate some of the best aspects of Western civilization. Yusuf Abdallah al-Qaradawi, a graduate of al-Azhar, and a Muslim Brother, who is currently the director of the Centre for Sunnah and Sirah at the University of Qatar, takes a similar line. He believes in moderation, and is convinced that the bigotry that has recently appeared in the Muslim world will impoverish people by depriving them of the insights and visions of other human beings. The Prophet Muhammad said that he had come to bring a 'Middle Way' of religious life that shunned extremes, and Qaradawi thinks that the current extremism in some quarters of the Islamic world is alien to the Muslim spirit and will not last. Islam is a religion of peace, as the Prophet had shown when he made an unpopular treaty with the Quraysh at Hudaybiyyah, a feat which the Quran calls 'a great victory'.[3] The West, he insists, must learn to recognize the Muslims' right to live their religion and, if they choose, to incorporate the Islamic ideal in their polity. They have to appreciate that there is more than one way of life. Variety benefits the whole world. God gave human beings the right and ability to choose, and some may opt for a religious way of life – including an Islamic state – while others prefer the secular ideal.

'It is better for the West that Muslims should be religious,' Qaradawi argues, 'hold to their religion, and try to be moral.'[4] He raises an important point. Many Western people are also becoming uncomfortable about the absence of spirituality in their lives. They do not necessarily want to return to pre-modern religious lifestyles or to conventionally institutional faith. But there is a growing appreciation that, at its best, religion has helped human beings to cultivate decent values. Islam kept the notions of social justice, equality, tolerance and practical compassion in the forefront of the Muslim conscience for centuries. Muslims did not always live up to these ideals and frequently found difficulty in incarnating them in their social and political institutions. But the struggle to achieve this was for centuries the mainspring of Islamic spirituality. Western people must become aware that it is in their interests too that Islam remains healthy and strong. The West has not been wholly responsible for the extreme forms of Islam, which have cultivated a violence that violates the most sacred canons of religion. But the West has certainly contributed to this development and, to assuage the fear and despair that lies at the root of all fundamentalist vision, should cultivate a more accurate appreciation of Islam in the third Christian millennium.

Postscript

On September 11th 2001, nineteen Muslim extremists hijacked four passenger jets and drove them into the World Trade Center in New York City and the Pentagon in Washington DC, killing over three thousand people. The fourth plane crashed in Pennsylvania. The hijackers were disciples of Osama bin Laden, whose militant brand of Islam was deeply influenced by Sayyid Qutb.

The ferocity of this attack against the United States took the fundamentalist war against modernity into a new phase. When this book was first published in 2000, I had predicted that, if Muslims continued to feel that their religion was under attack, fundamentalist violence was likely to become more extreme and to take new forms. The hijackers, some of whom drank alcohol, forbidden in Islam, before boarding the doomed planes, and were frequenters of night clubs, were quite unlike normal Muslim fundamentalists, who live strictly orthodox lives and regard night clubs as a symbol of the *jahiliyyah* that is forever and for all time the enemy of true faith.

The vast majority of Muslims recoiled in horror from this September Apocalypse, and pointed out that such an atrocity contravened the most sacred tenets of Islam. The Quran condemns all aggressive warfare and teaches that the only just war is a war of self-defense. But Osama bin Laden and his disciples claimed that Muslims *were* under attack. He pointed to the presence of American troops on the sacred soil of Arabia, to the continued bombing of Iraq by American and British fighter planes, to the American-led sanctions against Iraq, as a result of which thousands of civilians and children had died, to the deaths of hundreds of Palestinians at the hands of Israel, America's chief ally in the Middle East, and the support that the United States gives to governments which Bin Laden regards as corrupt and oppressive, such as the Royal Family of Saudi Arabia. However we view American foreign policy, none of this can justify such a murderous attack, which has no sanction in either the Quran or the Shariah. Islamic law forbids Muslims to declare war against a country in which Muslims are allowed to practice their religion freely, and strongly prohibits the killing of innocent civilians. The fear and rage that lies at the heart of all fundamentalist vision nearly always tends to distort the tradition that fundamentalists are trying to defend, and this has never been more evident than on September 11th. There has seldom been a more flagrant and wicked abuse of religion.

Immediately after the attack, there was a backlash against Muslims in Western countries. Muslims were attacked in the streets and people of oriental appearance were forbidden to board aircraft; women felt afraid to leave their houses wearing the *hijab*, and graffiti appeared on public buildings urging 'sand niggers' to go home. It was widely assumed that there was something in the religion of Islam that impelled Muslims to cruelty and violence, and the media all too frequently encouraged this assumption. Recognizing the danger of such an approach, President George W. Bush quickly proclaimed that Islam was a great and peaceful religion, and that Bin Laden and the hijackers should not be regarded as typical representatives of the faith. He was careful to have a Muslim standing beside him at the ceremony of mourning in Washington National Cathedral, and visited mosques to show his support for American Muslims. This was a wholly new and extremely welcome development. Nothing similar had happened at the time of the Salman Rushdie crisis or during the Desert Storm campaign against Saddam Hussein. It was also heartening to see Americans descending upon the bookstores, reading everything they could find about Islam, and struggling to understand the Muslim faith, even though they were reeling in horror from this terrorist attack.

It has never been more important for Western people to acquire a just appreciation and understanding of Islam. The world changed on September 11th. We now realize that we in the privileged Western countries can no longer assume that events in the rest of the world do not concern us. What happens in Gaza, Iraq, or Afghanistan today, is likely to have repercussions in New York, Washington or London tomorrow, and small groups will soon have the capacity to commit acts of mass-destruction that were previously only possible for powerful nation states. In the campaign against terror on which the United States has now embarked, accurate intelligence and information are vital. To cultivate a distorted image of Islam, to see it as inherently the enemy of democracy and decent values, and to revert to the bigoted views of the medieval Crusaders would be a catastrophe. Not only will such an approach antagonize the 1.2 billion Muslims with whom we share the world, but it will also violate the disinterested love of truth and the respect for the sacred rights of others that characterize both Islam and Western society at their best.

Key Figures in the History of Islam

Abbas I, Shah (1588–1629): presided over the zenith of the Safavid Empire in Iran, building a magnificent court at Isfahan and importing Shii *ulama* from abroad to instruct Iranians in Twelver Orthodoxy.

Abd al-Malik: Umayyad caliph (685–705) who restored Umayyad power after a period of civil war; the Dome of the Rock was completed under his auspices in 691.

Abd al-Wahhab, Muhammad ibn (1703–92): a Sunni reformer who tried to effect a radical return to the fundamentals of Islam. Wahhabism is the form of Islam practised today in Saudi Arabia.

Abdu, Muhammad (1849–1905): an Egyptian reformer who sought to modernize Islamic institutions to enable Muslims to make sense of the new Western ideals and reunify the country.

Abdulfazl Allami (1551–1602): Sufi historian and biographer of the Moghul emperor Akbar.

Abdulhamid: Ottoman sultan (1839–61), who issued the Gülhane decrees which modified absolute rule and made the government dependent upon a contractual agreement with Ottoman subjects.

Abu Bakr: one of the first converts to Islam; a close friend of the Prophet Muhammad, he became the first caliph (632–4) after Muhammad's death.

Abu al-Hakam (also known in the Quran as **Abu Jahl**: Father of Lies): he led the opposition against Muhammad in Mecca.

Abu Hanifah (699–767): a pioneer of *fiqh* and the founder of the Hanafi school of jurisprudence.

Abu al-Qasim Muhammad: also known as the **Hidden Imam**. He was the Twelfth Imam of the Shiah, who was said to have gone into hiding in 874 to save his life; in 934 his 'Occultation' was declared: God, it was said, had miraculously concealed the imam and he could make no further direct contact with Shiis. Shortly before the Last Judgement, he would return as the Mahdi to inaugurate a golden age of justice and peace, having destroyed the enemies of God.

Abu Sufyan: led the opposition against the Prophet Muhammad after the death of Abu al-Hakam (q.v.), but eventually, when he realized that

Muhammad was invincible, he converted to Islam. He belonged to the Umayyad family in Mecca, and his son Muawiyyah (q.v.) became the first Umayyad caliph.

Ahmad ibn Hanbal (780–855): *hadith*-collector, legist and leading figure of the *ahl al-hadith*. His spirit is enshrined in the Hanbali school of Islamic jurisprudence.

Ahmad ibn Idris (1760–1836): the Neo-Sufi reformer, active in Morocco, North Africa and the Yemen, who bypassed the *ulama* and tried to bring a more vibrant form of Islam directly to the people.

Ahmad Khan, Sir Sayyid (1817–98): an Indian reformer, who tried to adapt Islam to modern Western liberalism, and who urged Indians to collaborate with the Europeans and accept their institutions.

Ahmad Sirhindi (d. 1625): Sufi reformer who opposed the pluralism of the Moghul emperor Akbar (q.v.).

Aisha: the favourite wife of the Prophet Muhammad, who died in her arms. She was the daughter of Abu Bakr (q.v.) and led the Medinan opposition to Ali ibn Abi Talib (q.v.) during the first *fitnah*.

Akbar: Moghul emperor of India (1560–1605). He established a tolerant policy of cooperation with the Hindu population, and his reign saw the zenith of Moghul power.

Ali ibn Abi Talib: the cousin, ward, and son-in-law of the Prophet Muhammad and his closest surviving male relative. He became the fourth caliph in 656, but was murdered by a Kharajite extremist in 661. Shiis believe that he should have succeeded the Prophet Muhammad, and they revere him as the First Imam of the Islamic community. His shrine is at Najaf in Iraq, and is a major place of Shii pilgrimage.

Ali al-Hadi: the Tenth Shii Imam. In 848 he was summoned to Samarra by Caliph al-Mutawakkil and placed under house arrest there. He died in the Askari fortress in 868.

Ali al-Rida: the Eighth Shii Imam. Caliph al-Mamun appointed him as his successor in 817 in an attempt to court the malcontent Shiis in his empire, but it was an unpopular move, and al-Rida died – possibly murdered – the following year.

Ali Zayn al-Abidin (d. 714): the Fourth Shii Imam, a mystic, who lived in retirement in Medina and took no active role in politics.

Aqa, Muhammad Khan (d. 1797): the founder of the Qajar dynasty in Iran.

Aurengzebe: Moghul emperor (1658–1707), who reversed the tolerant policies of Akbar, and inspired Hindu and Sikh rebellions.

Baibars, Rukn ad-Din (d. 1277): Mamluk sultan, who defeated the Mongol hordes at Ain Jalut in northern Palestine, and eliminated most of the last Crusader strongholds on the Syrian coast.

Banna, Hasan al- (1906–49): an Egyptian reformer and founder of the Society of Muslim Brothers. He was assassinated by the secularist government of Egypt in 1949.

Bhutto, Zulfaqir Ali: Prime Minister of Pakistan (1971–7), who made concessions to the Islamists but was overthrown by the more devout Zia al-Haqq.

Bistami, Abu Yazid al- (d. 874): one of the earliest of the 'drunken Sufis', who preached the doctrine of *fanah* (annihilation) in God, and discovered the divine in the deepest recesses of his being after prolonged mystical exercises.

Bukhari, al- (d. 870): the author of an authoritative collection of *ahadith*.

Chelebi, Abu al-Sund Khola (1490–1574): worked out the legal principles of the Ottoman Shariah state.

Farabi, Abu Nasr al- (d. 950): the most rationalistic of all the Faylasufs, who was also a practising Sufi and who worked as the court musician in the Hamdanid court in Aleppo.

Ghannouchi, Rashid al- (1941–): Tunisian leader of the exiled Renaissance Party, who describes himself as a 'democratic Islamist'.

Ghazzali, Abu Hamid Muhammad (d. 1111): the Baghdad theologian who gave definitive expression to Sunni Islam, and brought Sufism into the mainstream of piety.

Hagar: in the Bible, she is the wife of Abraham and the mother of Abraham's son Ishmael (in Arabic Ismail, q.v.), who became the father of the Arab peoples. Hence Hagar is revered as one of the matriarchs of Islam and remembered with especial reverence in the ceremonies of the *hajj* pilgrimage to Mecca.

Haqq Zia al-: Prime Minister of Pakistan (1977–88), who pursued a more avowedly Islamic government, which still separated religion from political and economic policy.

Hasan ibn Ali (d. 669): the son of Ali ibn Abi Talib (q.v.) and the grandson of the Prophet Muhammad. He is revered by Shiis as the Second Shii Imam. After the murder of his father, Shiis acclaimed him as caliph, but Hasan agreed to retire from politics and lived a quiet and somewhat luxurious life in Medina.

Hasan al-Ashari (d. 935): the philosopher who reconciled the Mutazilah and the *ahl al-hadith*; his atomistic philosophy becomes one of the chief expressions of the spirituality of Sunni Islam.

Hasan al-Askari (d. 874): the Eleventh Shii Imam, who lived and died in the Askari fortress in Samarra, as the prisoner of the Abbasid caliphs. Like most of the Imams, he is believed to have been poisoned by the Abbasid authorities.

Hasan al-Basri (d. 728): preacher in Basrah and leader of a religious reform; he was the outspoken critic of the Umayyad caliphs.

Hidden Imam: see **Abu al-Qasim Muhammad**.

Husain ibn Ali: the second son of Ali ibn Abi Talib (q.v.) and the grandson of the Prophet Muhammad. He is revered by Shiis as the Third Imam and his death at the hands of Caliph Yazid (q.v.) is mourned annually during the month of Muharram.

Ibn al-Arabi, Muid ad-Din (d. 1240): a Spanish mystic and philosopher, who travelled extensively in the Muslim empire. A prolific and highly influential writer, he preached a unitive and pluralistic theological vision, in which spirituality is fused indissolubly with his philosophy.

Ibn Hazam (994–1064): a Spanish poet and religious thinker of the court of Cordova.

Ibn Ishaq, Muhammad (d. 767): author of the first major biography of the Prophet Muhammad, which is based on carefully sifted *hadith* reports.

Ibn Khaldun, Abd al-Rahman (1332–1406): author of *al-Maqaddimah, An Introduction to History*. A Faylasuf, he applied the principles of philosophy to the study of history and sought the universal laws operating behind the flux of events.

Ibn Rushd, Abu al-Walid Ahmad (1126–98): a Faylasuf and Qadi of Cordova, Spain, known in the West as Averroes, where his rationalistic philosophy was more influential than it was in the Muslim world.

Ibn Sina, Abu Ali (980–1037): known in the West as Avicenna, he represents the apogee of Falsafah, which he linked to religious and mystical experience.

Ibn Taymiyyah (1263–1328): a reformer who tried to counter the influence of Sufism and to return to the fundamental principles of the Quran and the *sunnah*. He died in prison in Damascus.

Ibn al-Zubayr, Abdallah (d. 692): one of the chief opponents of the Umayyads during the second *fitnah*.

Iqbal, Muhammad (1876–1938): Indian poet and philosopher, who emphasized the rationality of Islam to prove that it was quite compatible with Western modernity.

Ismail: the prophet who is known as Ishmael in the Bible, the eldest son of Abraham, who was cast out into the wilderness at God's command with his mother Hagar but saved by God. Muslim tradition has it that

Hagar and Ismail lived in Mecca, that Abraham came to visit them there, and that Abraham and Ismail rebuilt the Kabah (which had been originally constructed by Adam, the first prophet and father of mankind).

Ismail ibn Jafar: he was appointed the Seventh Imam of the Shiah by his father Jafar as-Sadiq (q.v.). Some Shiis (known as Ismailis or Seveners) believe that he was the last of the direct descendants of Ali ibn Abi Talib (q.v.) to succeed to the imamate, and do not recognize the imamate of Musa al-Kazim, the younger son of Jafar as-Sadiq, who is revered by Twelver Shiis as the Seventh Imam.

Ismail Pasha: he became the governor of Egypt (1863–79) and was given the title Khedive (great prince). His ambitious modernizing programme bankrupted the country and led ultimately to the British occupation of Egypt.

Ismail, Shah (1487–1524): the first Safavid shah of Iran, who imposed Twelver Shiism on the country.

Jafar as-Sadiq (d. 765): the Sixth Shii Imam, who developed the doctrine of the imamate, and urged his followers to withdraw from politics and concentrate on the mystical contemplation of the Quran.

Jamal al-Din, 'al-Afghani' (1839–97): an Iranian reformer who urged Muslims of all persuasions to band together and modernize Islam to avoid the political and cultural hegemony of Europe.

Jinnah, Muhammad Ali (1876–1948): the leader of the Muslim League in India at the time of the partition of the country, who is therefore hailed as the architect of Pakistan.

Junaid of Baghdad (d. 910): the first of the 'sober Sufis' who insisted that the experience of God lay in enhanced self-possession and that the wild exuberance of the 'drunken Sufis' was merely a stage that the true mystic should transcend.

Khadija: the first wife of the Prophet Muhammad and the mother of all his surviving children. She was also the first convert to Islam and died before the *hijrah* during the persecution of the Muslims by the Quraysh in Mecca (616–19), possibly as a result of the privations she suffered.

Khan, Muhammad Ayub: Prime Minister of Pakistan (1958–69), who followed a strongly secularizing policy, which led eventually to his downfall.

Khatemi, Hojjat ol-Islam Seyyid: President of Iran (1997–). He wants to see a more liberal interpretation of Islamic law in Iran and to foster relations with the West.

Khomeini, Ayatollah Ruhollah (1902–89): the spiritual mentor of the

Islamic Revolution against the Pahlavi regime and the Supreme Faqih of Iran (1979–89).

Kindi, Yaqub ibn Ishaq al- (d. 870): the first major Faylasuf, who worked alongside the Mutazilah in Baghdad but also sought wisdom from Greek sages.

Kirmani, Aqa Khan (1853–96): an Iranian secularist reformer.

Mahdi, Caliph al-: Abbasid caliph (775–85) who recognized the piety of the more religious Muslims, encouraged the study of *fiqh*, and helped the religious to come to terms with his regime.

Mahmud II: Ottoman sultan (1808–39) who introduced the modernizing Tanzimat reforms.

Majlisi, Muhammad Baqir (d. 1700): an *alim* who showed the less attractive form of Twelver Shiism after it had become the establishment faith in Iran, vigorously suppressing the teaching of Falsafah and persecuting the Sufis.

Malcolm X (1925–65): the charismatic leader of the black separatist group Nation of Islam, who achieved a high profile in the United States during the Civil Rights movement. In 1963 he seceded from the heterodox Nation of Islam and took his followers into mainstream Sunni Islam; as a result, he was assassinated two years later.

Malik ibn Anas (d. 795): the founder of the Maliki school of Islamic jurisprudence.

Mamun, Caliph al-: Abbasid caliph (813–33), whose reign marked the beginning of the Abbasid decline.

Mansur, Caliph al-: Abbasid caliph (754–75). Strongly suppressed Shii dissidents and moved the capital of the empire to the new city of Baghdad.

Mansur, Husain al- (also known as **al-Hallaj**: the Wool Carder): one of the most famous of the 'drunken Sufis' who is said in ecstasy to have cried '*Ana al-haqq!*' ('I am the Truth!') so convinced was he of his total union with God. He was executed for heresy in 922.

Mawdudi, Abul Ala (1903–79): a Pakistani fundamentalist ideologue, whose ideas have been very influential in the Sunni world.

Mehmed II: Ottoman sultan (1451–61), who is known as 'The Conqueror' because he achieved the conquest of Byzantine Constantinople in 1453.

Mir Dimad (d. 1631): founder of the school of mystical philosophy at Isfahan and the teacher of Mulla Sadra (q.v.).

Muawiyyah ibn Abi Sufyan: the first of the Umayyad caliphs who ruled from 661 to 680 and brought strong, effective government to the Muslim community after the turmoil of the first *fitnah*.

Muddaris, Ayatollah Hasan (d. 1937): an Iranian cleric who attacked Reza Shah in the Majlis and was murdered by the regime.

Muhammad ibn Abdallah (c.570–632): the prophet who brought the Quran to the Muslims and established the monotheistic faith and a single polity in Arabia.

Muhammad Ali, Pasha (1769–1849): an Albanian officer in the Ottoman army who made Egypt virtually independent of Istanbul and who achieved a major modernization of the country.

Muhammad ibn Ali al-Sanusi (d. 1832): the Neo-Sufi reformer who founded the Sanusiyyah movement, which is still predominant in Libya.

Muhammad al-Baqir (d. 735): the Fifth Shii Imam. He lived in retirement in Medina and is said to have developed the esoteric method of reading the Quran which was characteristic of Twelver Shiism.

Muhammad, Khwarazmshah: ruler of a dynasty (1200–20) in Khwarazm, who tried to establish a strong monarchy in Iran but incurred the wrath of the Mongols and brought about the first Mongol invasions.

Muhammad Reza Pahlavi, Shah: the second Pahlavi shah of Iran (1944–79), whose aggressively modernizing and secularizing policies led to the Islamic revolution.

Mulkum Khan, Mirza (1833–1908): Iranian secularist reformer.

Mulla Sadra (d. 1640): Shii mystical philosopher, whose work was an inspiration to intellectuals, revolutionaries and modernizers, especially in Iran.

Murad I: Ottoman sultan (1360–89), who defeated the Serbians at the Battle of Kossovo Field.

Muslim (d. 878): the collector of an authoritative anthology of *hadith* reports.

Mustafa Kemal also known as **Atatürk** (1881–1938): the founder of modern, secular Turkey.

Mutawakkil, Caliph al-: Abbasid caliph (847–61), who was responsible for imprisoning the Shii imams in the Askari fortress in Samarra.

Nadir Khan (d. 1748): temporarily revived the military power of Shii Iran after the fall of the Safavid dynasty.

Naini, Sheikh Muhammad Husain (1850–1936): an Iranian *mujtahid* whose treatise *Admonition to the Nation* gave a strong Shii endorsement to the notion of constitutional rule.

Nasir, Caliph al-: one of the last of the Abbasid caliphs, who tried to use Islamic institutions to strengthen his rule in Baghdad.

Nasser, Jamal Abd al-: President of Egypt (1952–70), leading a militantly nationalistic, secularist and socialist government.

Nizamulmulk: the brilliant Persian vizier who ruled the Seljuk Empire from 1063 to 1092.

Qutb, Sayyid (1906–66): a Muslim Brother, executed by al-Nasser's regime; his ideology is crucial to all Sunni fundamentalism.

Rashid, Caliph Harun al-: Abbasid caliph (786–809), whose reign coincided with the zenith of caliphal absolute power, and who presided over a magnificent cultural florescence.

Reza Khan: shah of Iran (1921–41) and the founder of the Pahlavi dynasty. His government was aggressively secularist and nationalist.

Rida, Muhammad Rashid (1865–1935): journalist who founded the Salafiyyah movement in Cairo and was the first to advocate a fully modernized Islamic state.

Rumi, Jalal al-Din (1207–75): a highly influential Sufi leader who had a large popular following and founded the Mawlani Order, often known as the Whirling Dervishes.

Salah ad-Din, Yusuf ibn Ayyub (d. 1193): the Kurdish general who became the sultan of an extensive empire in Syria and Egypt, returned Egypt to Sunni Islam after defeating the Fatimid caliphate, and ejected the Crusaders from Jerusalem. Salah ad-Din (known as **Saladin** in the West) was the founder of the Ayyubid dynasty.

Selim I: Ottoman sultan (1512–20), who conquered Syria, Palestine and Egypt from the Mamluks.

Selim III: Ottoman sultan (1789–1807), who attempted a Westernizing reform of the empire.

Shafii, Muhammad Idris al- (d. 820): revolutionized the study of *fiqh* by laying down the principles (*usul*) of Islamic law; founder of the Shafii school of jurisprudence.

Shah Jihan: Moghul emperor (1627–58), whose reign saw the height of Moghul refinement and sophistication; he commissioned the Taj Mahal.

Shah Valli-ullah (1703–62): a Sufi reformer in India who was one of the first Muslim thinkers to see the threat that Western modernity posed to Islam.

Sinan Pasha (d. 1578): architect of the Suleymaniye mosque in Istanbul and the Selimye mosque in Edirne.

Sorush, Abdolkarim (1945–): leading Iranian intellectual, who advocates a more liberal interpretation of Shiism, while still rejecting Western secularism.

Suhrawardi, Yahya (d. 1191): Sufi philosopher, founder of the school of illumination (*ishraq*) based on pre-Islamic Iranian mysticism. He was executed for his allegedly heterodox beliefs by the Ayyubid regime in Aleppo.

Suleiman I: Ottoman sultan (1520–66), known as **al-Qanuni**: the Lawgiver in the Islamic world, and the Magnificent in the West. He crafted the distinctive institutions of the empire, which reached the fullest extent of its power during his reign.

Tabari, Abu Jafar (d. 923): a scholar of Shariah and historian, who produced a universal history, tracing the success and failure of the various communities who had been called to the worship of God, concentrating particularly on the Muslim *ummah*.

Tahtawi, Rifah al (1801–73): an Egyptian *alim* who described his passionate appreciation of European society in his published diary, was responsible for the translation of European books into Arabic, and who promoted the idea of modernization in Egypt.

Umar II: an Umayyad caliph (717–20), who tried to rule according to the principles of the religious movement. He was the first caliph to encourage positively the conversion of the subject people of the empire to Islam.

Umar ibn al-Khattab: one of the Prophet Muhammad's closest companions. He became the second caliph after the Prophet's death (634–44), and masterminded the first Arab wars of conquest and the building of the garrison towns. He was murdered by a Persian prisoner of war.

Uthman ibn Affan: one of Muhammad's first converts and his son-in-law. He became the third caliph (644–56), but was a less able ruler than his predecessors. His policies opened him to the charge of nepotism and inspired a mutiny during which he was himself assassinated in Medina. His murder led to the first *fitnah* wars.

Walid I, Caliph al-: an Umayyad caliph (705–17), who ruled during the peak of Umayyad power and success.

Wasan ibn Ata (d. 748): founder of the Mutazilah school of rational theology.

Yasin, Sheikh Ahmad (1936–): the creator of Mujamah (Islamic Congress), in Israeli-occupied Gaza, a welfare organization. The terrorist group HAMAS was an offshoot from this movement.

Yazid I: Umayyad caliph (680–83), who is chiefly remembered for the murder of Husain ibn Ali (q.v.) at Kerbala.

Zayd ibn Ali (d. 740): the brother of the Fifth Shii Imam; Zayd was a political activist and the Fifth Imam may have developed his quietist philosophy in order to counter his claim to the leadership. Thereafter Shiis who engaged in political activism and eschewed the Twelvers' withdrawal from politics were sometimes known as Zaydites.

Glossary of Arabic Terms

Ahadith (singular, **hadith**): news, reports. Documented traditions of the teachings and actions of the Prophet Muhammad, which were not in the Quran but which were recorded for posterity by his close companions and the members of his family.

Ahl al-hadith: Hadith People. A school of thought which first appeared during the Umayyad period, which would not permit jurists to use **ijtihad** (q.v.) but insisted that all legislation be based upon valid **ahadith** (q.v.).

Ahl al-kitab: People of the Book. The Quranic term for people, such as Jews or Christians who adhered to the earlier scriptures. Since the Prophet and most of the early Muslims were illiterate, and had very few – if any – books, it has been suggested that this term should more accurately be translated: 'followers of an earlier revelation'.

Alam al-mithal: the world of pure images. A realm of the human psyche, which is the source of the visionary experience of Muslim mystics and the seat of the creative imagination.

Alim see **ulama**.

Amir: commander.

Ansar: the Medinese Muslims who became the 'helpers' of the Prophet by giving the first Muslims a home when they were forced to leave Mecca in 622, and assisted them in the project of establishing the first Muslim community.

Batin: the 'hidden' dimension of existence and of scripture, which cannot be perceived by the senses or by rational thought, but which is discerned in the contemplative, intuitive disciplines of mysticism.

Dar al-Islam: the House of Islam. Lands under Muslim rule.

Dhikr: the 'remembrance' of God, especially by means of the chanting of the Names of God as a mantra to induce alternative states of consciousness. A Sufi devotion.

Dhimmi: a 'protected subject' in the Islamic empire, who belonged to the religions tolerated by the Quran, the **ahl al-kitab** (q.v.): they included Jews, Christians, Zoroastrians, Hindus, Buddhists and Sikhs. *Dhimmis* were allowed full religious liberty, were able to organize their community according to their own customal law, but were required to recognize Islamic sovereignty.

Faqih: a jurist; an expert in Islamic law.

Fatwah: a formal legal opinion or decision of a religious scholar on a matter of Islamic law.

Fiqh: Islamic jurisprudence. The study and application of the body of sacred Muslim law.

Fitnah: temptation, trial. Specifically, the term is used to describe the civil wars that rent the Muslim community apart during the time of the *rashidun* (q.v.) and the early Umayyad period.

Futuwwah: a corporate group of young urban men, formed after the twelfth century, with special ceremonies of initiation, rituals and sworn support to a leader that were strongly influenced by **Sufi** (q.v.) ideals and practices.

Ghazu: originally, the 'raids' undertaken by Arabs in the pre-Islamic period for booty. Later a **ghazi** warrior was a fighter in a holy war for Islam; often the term was applied to organized bands of raiders on the frontiers of the **Dar al-Islam** (q.v.).

Ghulat: exaggerators; adjective: **ghuluww**. The extreme speculations adopted by the early **Shii Muslims** (q.v.), which overstressed some aspects of doctrine.

Hadith: see **ahadith**.

Hajj: the pilgrimage to Mecca.

Hijrah: the 'migration' of the Prophet Muhammad and the first Muslim community from Mecca to Medina in 622.

Ijmah: the 'consensus' of the Muslim community that gives legitimacy to a legal decision.

Ijtihad: the 'independent reasoning' used by a jurist to apply the **Shariah** (q.v.) to contemporary circumstances. During the fourteenth century **Sunni Muslims** (q.v.) declared that the 'gates of *ijtihad*' were closed, and that scholars must rely on the legal decisions of past authorities instead of upon their own reasoned insights.

Ilm: a knowledge of what is right and how Muslims should behave.

Imam: the leader of the Muslim community; **Shii Muslims** (q.v.) use the term to denote the descendants of the Prophet, through his daughter Fatimah and her husband Ali ibn Abi Talib, whom Shiis consider to be the true rulers of the Muslim community.

Irfan: the Muslim mystical tradition.

Islam: 'surrender' to the will of God.

Jahiliyyah: the Age of Ignorance. Originally the term was used to describe the pre-Islamic period in Arabia. Today Muslim fundamentalists often apply it to any society, even a nominally Muslim society, which has, in their view, turned its back upon God and refused to submit to God's sovereignty (adjective: **jahili**).

Jihad: struggle, effort. This is the primary meaning of the term as used in the Quran, which refers to an internal effort to reform bad habits in the Islamic community or within the individual Muslim. The term is also used more specifically to denote a war waged in the service of religion.

Jizyah: the poll tax, which the **dhimmis** (q.v.) were required to pay in return for military protection.

Kabah: the cube-shaped shrine in the holy city of Mecca, which Muhammad dedicated to God and made the most sacred place in the Islamic world.

Kalam: a discussion, based on Islamic assumptions, of theological questions. The term is often used to describe the tradition of Muslim scholastic theology.

Khanqah: a building where such **Sufi** (q.v.) activities as **dhikr** (q.v.) take place; where Sufi masters live and instruct their disciples.

Madhhab: ('chosen way'): one of the four legitimate schools of Islamic jurisprudence.

Madrasah: a college of Muslim higher education, where **ulama** (q.v.) study such disciplines as **fiqh** (q.v.), or **kalam** (q.v.).

Mawali: (clients) the name given to the early non-Arab converts to Islam, who had to become nominal clients of one of the tribes when they became Muslims.

Mujtahid: a jurist who has earned the right to exercise **ijtihad** (q.v.), usually in the Shii world.

Mutazilah: (from the Arabic *itazahu*: to withdraw); an eighth century school, which promoted **Kalan** (q.v.)

Pir: a **Sufi** (q.v.) master, who can guide disciples along the mystical path.

Qadi: a judge who administers the **Shariah** (q.v.).

Qiblah: the 'direction' which Muslims face during prayer. In the very early days the *qiblah* was Jerusalem; later Muhammad changed it to Mecca.

Rashidun: the four 'rightly guided' caliphs, who were the companions and the immediate successors of the Prophet Muhammad: Abu Bakr, Umar ibn al-Khattab, Uthman ibn Affan and Ali ibn Abi Talib.

Salat: the ritual prayers which Muslims make five times daily.

Shahadah: the Muslim declaration of faith: 'I proclaim that there is no god but Allah, and that Muhammad is his Prophet.'

Shariah: 'the Path to the Watering Hole'. The body of Islamic sacred laws derived from the Quran, the **sunnah** (q.v.) and the **ahadith** (q.v.).

Shii Muslims: they belong to the Shiah-i Ali, the Party of Ali; they believe that Ali ibn Abi Talib, the Prophet's closest male relative, should have ruled in place of the **rashidun** (q.v.), and revere a number of **imams** (q.v.) who are the direct male descendants of Ali and his wife Fatimah, the Prophet's daughter. Their difference from the Sunni majority is purely political.

Sufi; Sufism: the mystical tradition of **Sunni Islam** (q.v.).

Sunnah: custom. The habits and religious practice of the Prophet Muhammad, which were recorded for posterity by his companions and family and are regarded as the ideal Islamic norm. They have thus been enshrined in Islamic law, so that Muslims can approximate closely to the archetypal figure of the Prophet, in his perfect surrender (*islam*) to God.

Sunni Islam: the term used to describe the Muslim majority, who revere the four **rashidun** (q.v.) and validate the existing political Islamic order.

Tariqah: one of the brotherhoods or orders, who follow the **Sufi** (q.v.) 'way', and have their own special **dhikr** (q.v.) and revered leaders.

Tawhid: making one. The divine unity, which Muslims seek to imitate in their personal and social lives by integrating their institutions and priorities, and by recognizing the overall sovereignty of God.

Ulama (singular, **alim**): learned men, the guardians of the legal and religious traditions of Islam.

Ummah: the Muslim community.

Umrah: the ritual circumambulations around the **Kabah** (q.v.).

Zakat: purity. The term used for a tax of fixed proportion of income and capital (usually 2.5 per cent), which must be paid by all Muslims each year to assist the poor.

Notes

I BEGINNINGS (pages 1 to 32)

1. Jalal al-Din Suyuti, *al-ifqan fi ulum al aqram* in Maxime Rodinson, *Mohammed* (trans. Anne Carter, London, 1971), 74.
2. Muhammad ibn Ishaq, *Sirat Rasul Allah* (trans. and ed. A. Guillaume, *The Life of Muhammad*, London, 1955), 158.
3. Quran 25:3; 29:17; 44:47; 69:44. Quotations from the Quran are all taken from Muhammad Asad (trans.) *The Message of the Qur'an*, Gibraltar, 1980.
4. Quran 80:11.
5. Quran 2:129–32; 61:6.
6. Quran 2:256.
7. Quran 29:46.
8. Quran 25:4–7.
9. Quran 74:1–5, 8–10; 88:21–2.
10. Muhammad's concubine Mariam, who was a Christian and not one of his wives, bore him a son, Ibrahim who, to the Prophet's immense sorrow, died in infancy.
11. Quran 33:28–9.
12. Quran 33:35.
13. Quran 4:3.
14. Genesis 16; 18:18–20.
15. D. Sidersky, *Les Origenes dans legendes musulmans dans le Coran et dans les vies des prophetes* (Paris, 1933).
16. Quran 2:129–32; 3:58–62; 2:39.
17. Quran 6:159, 161–2.
18. Quran 8:16–17.
19. Quran 2:194, 252; 5:65; 22:40–42.

2 DEVELOPMENT (pages 33 to 65)

1. Quran 49:12.
2. Quran 9:106–7.
3. Little is known about the early Shiah. We do not know for certain whether Ali's male descendants really were revered by a group of

mystically inclined Shiis, or whether this history was projected back on to the early imams after the line had become extinct, and when 'Twelver Shiism' received definitive form.

4. Quran 2:234; 8:2; 23:57–61.

5. The origins of 'Sevener' or Ismaili Shiism are obscure. The story of the sect's fidelity to Imam Ismail may have developed after the theology of 'Twelver Shiism' was finally formulated, to give justification for the Ismaili position. Seveners, who were usually politically active, may have originally been 'Zaydis', i.e. Shiis who followed the example of Zayd ibn Ali, the brother of the Fifth Imam, and believed that Muslims had a duty to lead armed revolts against an unjust regime.

3 CULMINATION (pages 69 to 94)

1. The Ismaili dynasty in Cairo is often called the 'Fatimid' dynasty, because, like the Twelvers, Ismailis venerated imams who were direct descendants of Ali and Fatimah, the Prophet's daughter.

2. Quran 2:109.

3. *Al-Muqaddimah*, quoted in Youssef M. Choueiri, *Islamic Fundamentalism* (London, 1990), 18.

5 ISLAM AGONISTES (pages 121 to 158)

1. The theory of Velayat-i Faqih had been discussed by jurists before, but was little known and had always been considered eccentric and even heretical. Khomeini made it central to his political thought and, later, it became the basis of his rule in Iran.

2. Quran 2:178; 8:68; 24:34; 47:5.

3. Quran 48:1.

4. Joyce M. Davis, *Between Jihad and Salaam: Profiles in Islam* (New York, 1997), 231.

Suggestions for Further Reading

The Prophet Muhammad

ANDRAE, Tor, *Muhammad: The Man and His Faith* (trans. Theophil Menzel, London, 1936)

ARMSTRONG, Karen, *Muhammad, A Biography of the Prophet* (London, 1991)

GABRIELI, Francesco, *Muhammad and the Conquests of Islam* (trans. Virginia Luling and Rosamund Linell, London, 1968)

GUIALLAUME, A. (trans. and ed.), *The Life of Muhammad: A Translation of Ishaq's Sirat Rasul Allah* (London, 1955)

LINGS, Martin, *Muhammad, His Life Based on the Earliest Sources* (London, 1983)

NASR, Sayyid Hossein, *Muhammad, the Man of Allah* (London, 1982)

RODINSON, Maxime, *Mohammed* (trans. Anne Carter, London, 1971)

SARDAR, Ziauddin and Zafar Abbas Malik, *Muhammad for Beginners* (Cambridge, 1994)

SCHIMMEL, Annemarmie, *And Muhammad Is His Messenger: The Veneration of the Prophet in Islamic Piety* (Chapel Hill and London, 1985)

WATT, W. Montgomery, *Muhammad at Mecca* (Oxford, 1953)

—— *Muhammad at Medina* (Oxford, 1956)

—— *Muhammad's Mecca: History in the Qur'an* (Edinburgh, 1988)

ZAKARIA, Rafiq, *Muhammad and the Quran* (London, 1991)

Islamic History

AHMED, Akbar, *Living Islam, From Samarkand to Stornoway* (London, 1993)

—— *Islam Today, A Short Introduction to the Muslim World* (London, 1999)

ALGAR, Hamid, *Religion and State in Iran, (1785–1906)* (Berkeley, 1969)

BAYAT, Margol, *Mysticism and Dissent: Socioreligious Thought in Qajar Iran* (Syracuse, NY, 1982)

ESPOSITO, John, *Islam, the Straight Path* (rev. edn, Oxford and New York, 1998)

—— (ed.), *The Oxford History of Islam* (Oxford, 1999)

GABRIELI, Francesco, *Arab Historians of the Crusades* (trans. E. J. Costello, London, 1984)

HODGSON, Marshall G. S., *The Venture of Islam, Conscience and History in a World Civilization*, 3 vols. (Chicago and London, 1974)

HOURANI, Albert, *A History of the Arab Peoples* (London, 1991)

HOURANI, Albert with Philip S. Khoury and Mary C. Wilson (eds.) *The Modern Middle East* (London, 1993)

KEDDIE, Nikki R. (ed.), *Scholars, Saints and Sufis, Muslim Religious Institutions in the Middle East since 1500* (Berkeley, Los Angeles and London, 1972)

—— (ed.), *Religion and Politics in Iran: Shiism from Quietism to Revolution* (New Haven and London, 1983)

LAPIDUS, Ira M., *A History of Islamic Societies* (Cambridge, 1988)

LEWIS, Bernard, *The Arabs in History* (London, 1950)

—— *Islam from the Prophet Muhammad to the Capture of Constantinople*, 2 vols. (New York and London, 1976)

—— *The Jews of Islam* (New York and London, 1982)

—— *The Muslim Discovery of Europe* (New York and London, 1982)

—— *The Middle East, 2000 Years of History from the Rise of Christianity to the Present Day* (London, 1995)

MAALOUF, Amin, *The Crusades Through Arab Eyes* (London, 1984)

MOMEN, Moojan, *An Introduction to Shi'i Islam, The History and Doctrines of Twelver Shiism* (New Haven and London, 1985)

MOTTAHEDEH, Roy, *The Mantle of the Prophet, Religion and Politics in Iran* (London, 1985)

NASR, Seyyid Hosain, *Ideals and Realities of Islam* (London, 1966)

PETERS, F. E., *The Hajj, The Muslim Pilgrimage to Mecca and the Holy Places* (Princeton, 1994)

—— *Mecca, A Literary History of the Muslim Holy Land* (Princeton, 1994)

PETERS, Rudolph, *Jihad in Classical and Medieval Islam* (Princeton, 1996)

RAHMAN, Fazlur, *Islam* (Chicago, 1979)

RUTHVEN, Malise, *Islam in the World* (London, 1984)

SAUNDERS, J. J., *A History of Medieval Islam* (London and Boston, 1965)

SMITH, Wilfred Cantwell, *Islam in Modern History* (Princeton and London, 1957)

VON GRUNEBAUM, G. E., *Classical Islam: A History 600–1258* (trans. Katherine Watson, London, 1970)

WALKER, Benjamin, *Foundations of Islam, the Making of a World Faith* (London, 1998)

WATT, W. Montgomery, *Islam and the Integration of Society* (London, 1961)

—— *The Majesty that was Islam, The Islamic World 660–1100* (London and New York, 1974)

WENSINCK, A. J., *The Muslim Creed: Its Genesis and Historical Development* (Cambridge, 1932)

WHEATCROFT, Andrew, *The Ottomans* (London, 1993)

Islamic Philosophy and Theology

AL-FARABI, *Philosophy of Plato and Aristotle* (trans. Muhsin Mahdi, Glencoe, Ill., 1962)

CORBIN, Henri, *Histoire de la philosophie islamique* (Paris, 1964)

FAKHRY, Majid, *A History of Islamic Philosophy* (New York and London, 1970)

LEAMAN, Oliver, *An Introduction to Medieval Islamic Philosophy* (Cambridge, 1985)

McCARTHIE, Richard, *The Theology of al-Ashari* (Beirut, 1953)

MOREWEDGE, P., *The Metaphysics of Avicenna* (London, 1973)

—— (ed.), *Islamic Philosophical Theology* (New York, 1979)

—— (ed.), *Islamic Philosophy and Mysticism* (New York, 1981)

NETTON, I. R., *Muslim Neoplatonists, An Introduction to the Thought of the Brethren of Purity* (Edinburgh, 1991)

ROSENTHAL, F., *Knowledge Triumphant, The Concept of Knowledge in Medieval Islam* (Leiden, 1970)

SHARIF, M. M., *A History of Muslim Philosophy* (Wiesbaden, 1963)

VON GRUNEBAUM, G. E., *Medieval Islam* (Chicago, 1946)

WATT, W. Montgomery, *Free Will and Predestination in Early Islam* (London, 1948)

—— *Muslim Intellectual: The Struggle and Achievement of Al-Ghazzali* (Edinburgh, 1963)

—— *The Formative Period of Islamic Thought* (Edinburgh, 1973)

Islamic Mysticism and Spirituality

AFFIFI, A. E., *The Mystical Philosophy of Ibnu 'l-Arabi* (Cambridge, 1938)

ARBERRY, A. J., *Sufism: An Account of the Mystics of Islam* (London, 1950)

BAKHTIAR, L., *Sufi Expression of the Mystic Quest* (London, 1979)

CHITTICK, William C., *The Sufi Path of Love: The Spiritual Teachings of Rumi* (Albany, 1983)

—— *The Sufi Path of Knowledge, Ibn al-Arabi's Metaphysics of Imagination* (Albany, 1989)

CORBIN, Henri, *Avicenna and the Visionary Recital* (trans. W. Trask, Princeton, 1960)

—— *Creative Imagination in the Sufism of Ibn Arabi* (trans. W. Trask, London, 1970)

—— *Spiritual Body and Celestial Earth, From Mazdean Iran to Shiite Iran* (trans. Nancy Pearson, London, 1990)

MASSIGNON, Louis, *The Passion of al-Hallaj*, 4 vols. (trans. H. Mason, Princeton, 1982)

NASR, Seyyid Hossein (ed.), *Islamic Spirituality*, 2 vols. (London, 1987)

NICHOLSON, Reynold A., *The Mystics of Islam* (London, 1914)

SCHIMMEL, A. M., *Mystical Dimensions of Islam* (Chapel Hill and London, 1975)

—— *The Triumphant Sun: A Study of Mawlana Rumi's Life and Work* (London and The Hague, 1978)

SMITH, Margaret, *Rabia the Mystic and Her Fellow Saints in Islam* (London, 1928)

VALIUDDIN, Mir, *Contemplative Disciplines in Sufism* (London, 1980)

Islamic Response to the Modern World

AHMED, Akbar S., *Postmodernism and Islam, Predicament and Promise* (London and New York, 1992)

AKHAVI, Shahrough, *Religion and Politics in Contemporary Iran: Clergy–State Relations in the Pahlavi Period* (Albany, 1980)

AL-E AHMAD, Jalal, *Occidentosis: A Plague from the West* (trans. R. Campbell, ed. Hamid Algar, Berkeley, 1984)

DAVIS, Joyce M., *Between Jihad and Salaam: Profiles in Islam* (New York, 1997)

DJAIT, Hichem, *Europe and Islam: Cultures and Modernity* (Berkeley, 1985)

ESPOSITO, John (ed.), *Voices of Resurgent Islam* (New York and Oxford, 1983)

—— *The Islamic Threat: Myth or Reality* (Oxford and New York, 1995)

—— with John L. Donohue (eds.), *Islam in Transition, Muslim Perspectives* (New York and Oxford, 1982)

—— with Yvonne Yazbeck Haddad, *Muslims on the Americanization Path?* (Atlanta, 1998)

GELLNER, Ernest, *Postmodernism, Reason and Religion* (London and New York, 1992)

GILSENAN, Michael, *Recognizing Islam, Religion and Society in the Modern Middle East* (London, 1990)

HALLIDAY, Fred, *Islam and the Myth of Confrontation, Religion and Politics in the Middle East* (London and New York, 1996)

HANNA, Sami and George H. Gardner (eds.), *Arab Socialism: A Documentary Survey* (Leiden, 1969)

HOURANI, Albert, *Arabic Thought in the Liberal Age, 1878–1939* (Oxford, 1962)

IQBAL, Allama Muhammad, *The Reconstruction of Religious Thought in Islam* (Lahore, 1989)

KEDDIE, Nikki R., *Islamic Response to Imperialism: Political and Religious Writings of Sayyid Jamal ad-Din 'al-Afghani'* (Berkeley, 1968)

MATIN-ASGARI, Afshin, 'Abdolkarim Sorush and the Secularization of Islamic Thought in Iran', *Iranian Studies*, 30, 1997

MITCHELL, Richard P., *The Society of the Muslim Brothers* (London, 1969)

RAHMAN, Fazlur, *Islam and Modernity, Transformation of an Intellectual Tradition* (Chicago, 1982)

SHARIATI, Ali, *The Sociology of Islam* (Berkeley, 1979)

—— *What Is To Be Done? The Enlightened Thinkers and an Islamic Renaissance* (n.p., 1986)

—— *Hajj* (Tehran, 1988)

TIBI, Bassam, *The Crisis of Political Islam, A Pre-Industrial Culture in the Scientific-Technological Age* (Salt Lake City, 1988)

VOLL, John, *Islam: Continuity and Change in the Modern World* (Boulder, 1982)

Islamic Fundamentalism

APPLEBY, R. Scott (ed.), *Spokesmen for the Despised, Fundamentalist Leaders of the Middle East* (Chicago, 1997)

ARMSTRONG, Karen, *The Battle for God: Fundamentalism in Judaism, Christianity and Islam* (London and New York, 2000)

CHOUEIRI, Youssef M., *Islamic Fundamentalism* (London, 1990)

FISCHER, Michael J., *Iran: From Religious Dispute to Revolution* (Cambridge, Mass. and London, 1980)

GAFFNEY, Patrick D., *The Prophet's Pulpit: Islamic Preaching in Contemporary Egypt* (Berkeley, Los Angeles and London, 1994)

HAMAS, *The Covenant of the Islamic Resistance Movement* (Jerusalem, 1988)

HEIKAL, Mohamed, *Autumn of Fury, The Assassination of Sadat* (London, 1984)

HUSSAIN, Asaf, *Islamic Iran, Revolution and Counter-Revolution* (London, 1985)

JANSEN, Johannes J. G., *The Neglected Duty, The Creed of Sadat's Assassins and Islamic Resurgence in the Middle East* (New York and London, 1988)

KEPEL, Gilles, *The Prophet and Pharoah, Muslim Extremism in Egypt* (trans. Jon Rothschild, London, 1985)

KHOMEINI, Sayeed Ruhollah, *Islam and Revolution* (trans. Hamid Algar, Berkeley, 1981)

LAWRENCE, *Defenders of God: The Fundamentalist Revolt Against the Modern Age* (London and New York, 1990)

MARTY, Martin E. and R. Scott Appleby (eds.), *Fundamentalisms Observed* (Chicago and London, 1991)

—— *Fundamentalisms and Society* (Chicago and London, 1993)

—— *Fundamentalisms and the State* (Chicago and London, 1993)

—— *Accounting for Fundamentalisms* (Chicago and London, 1994)

—— *Fundamentalisms Comprehended* (Chicago and London, 1995)

MAWDUDI, Abud Ala, *Islamic Law and Constitution* (Lahore, 1967)

—— *Jihad in Islam* (Lahore, 1976)

—— *The Economic Problem of Man and Its Islamic Solution* (Lahore, 1978)

—— *Islamic Way of Life* (Lahore, 1979)

MILTON-EDWARDS, Beverley, *Islamic Politics in Palestine* (London and New York, 1996)

NASR, Seyyed Vali Reza, *The Vanguard of the Islamic Revolution, the Jama'at-i Islami of Pakistan* (London and New York, 1994)

QUTB, *Islam and Universal Peace* (Indianapolis, 1977)

—— *Milestones* (Delhi, 1988)

—— *This Religion of Islam* (Gary, Indiana, n.d.)

RUTHVEN, Malise, *A Satanic Affair: Salman Rushdie and the Rage of Islam* (London, 1990)

SICK, Gary, *All Fall Down; America's Fateful Encounter with Iran* (London, 1985)

SIDHARED, Abdel Salam and Anonshirivan Ehteshani (eds.), *Islamic Fundamentalism* (Boulder, 1996)

Islam and Women

AFSHAR, Haleh, *Islam and Feminisms, An Iranian Case-Study* (London and New York, 1998)

AHMED, Leila, *Women and Gender in Islam: Historical Roots of a Modern Debate* (New Haven and London, 1992)

—— *A Border Passage* (New York, 1999)

GÖLE, Nilufa, *The Forbidden Modern: Civilization and Veiling* (Ann Arbor, 1996)

HADDAD, Yvonne Yazbeck and John L. Esposito (eds.) *Islam, Gender and Social Change* (Oxford and New York, 1998)

KARAM, Azza M., *Women, Islamisms and the State; Contemporary Feminisms in Egypt* (New York, 1998)

KEDDIE, Nikki R. and Beth Baron (eds.), *Women in Middle Eastern History, Shifting Boundaries in Sex and Gender* (New Haven and London, 1991)

MERNISSI, Fatima, *Women and Islam, An Historical and Theological Enquiry* (trans. Mary Jo Lakehead, Oxford, 1991)

—— *The Harem Within, Tales of a Moroccan Girlhood* (London, 1994)

—— *Women's Rebellion and Islamic Memory* (London, 1996)

Western Perceptions of Islam

ARMSTRONG, Karen, *Holy War, The Crusades and their Impact on Today's World* (London, 1988; New York, 1991)

DANIEL, Norman, *Islam and the West: The Making of an Image* (Edinburgh, 1960)

—— *The Arabs and Medieval Europe* (London and Beirut, 1975)

GIBB, H. A. R. and H. Bowen, *Islamic Society and the West* (London, 1957)

HOURANI, Albert, *Islam in European Thought* (Cambridge, 1991)

KABBANI, Rana, *Europe's Myths of Orient* (London, 1986)

—— *Letter to Christendom* (London, 1989)

KEDAR, Benjamin, *Crusade and Mission: European Approaches towards the Muslims* (Princeton, 1984)

RODINSON, Maxime, *Europe and the Mystique of Islam* (London, 1984)

SAID, Edward W., *Orientalism: Western Conceptions of Orient* (New York, 1978)

SOUTHERN, R. W., *Western Views of Islam in the Middle Ages* (Cambridge, Mass., 1962)

Index